Greater Health, Wealth & Love

YOUR EXTRAORDINARY LIFE

A step-by-step guide for creating a life of fulfillment and happiness

BY TOM POLAND

To create a life of greater health, wealth and love,
join us at
www.TheGas.Community and start your free trial
today.

Your Extraordinary Life: A Step-by-Step Guide for Setting and Achieving Goals

Third Edition

Copyright 2005 by Tom Poland

All rights reserved. No part of this book may be reproduced or transmitted in any form or by any means, electronic or mechanical, including photocopying, recording or by any information storage and retrieval system, without written permission from the publisher, except for the inclusion of brief quotations in a review.

ISBN: 9780977503254

This book is dedicated to two Extra-Ordinary beings: John and Tui, my father and mother.

Thank you.

Contents

Preface   9

Part One:
The Purpose of Your Life

Chapter 1: Life at the Next Level   17

Chapter 2: Using Goals to Expand Your Consciousness   27

Chapter 3: Using Goals to Increase Your Personal Capacity   39

Chapter 4: Using Goals to Make a More Significant Personal Contribution   47

Part Two:
Your Comfort Zone

Chapter 5: The Curse of the Comfort Zone   53

Chapter 6: The Cost of Staying in Your Comfort Zone   61

Chapter 7: The Overrating of Certainty   65

Chapter 8: Lessons From the Comfort Zone   73

Part Three:
Building Goal Foundations – Values and Vision

Chapter 9: The Importance of Your Personal Life Values   79

Chapter 10: Identifying Your Personal Life Values   91

Chapter 11: The Value of a Personal Life Vision   103

Chapter 12: Creating Your Own Personal Life Vision   113

Part Four:
Preparing for Goal Creation

Chapter 13: An Introduction to Personal Goals   123

Chapter 14: The Three Levels of Goals   127

Chapter 15: The Two Basic Types of Goals   133

Chapter 16: How to Work Out What You Want in Life Even if You Have no Idea   137

Chapter 17: Top Tips for Creating Goals   143

Part Five:
Creating Your Goals

Chapter 18: Goal Creation Exercise 1: The 'Non-Stop Writing' Technique   155

Chapter 19: Goal Creation Exercise 2: The 'Roles and Goals' Exercise   157

Chapter 20: Goal Creation Exercise 3: The 'Six Questions' Exercise   161

Chapter 21: Goal Creation Exercise 4: The 'Dream Day' Technique   169

Part Six:
How To Create Goals That Are Most Likely To Succeed

Chapter 22: Top Tips to Consider Prior to Selecting Your Final Goals   177

Chapter 23: Finalizing Your Goals and Making Them S.M.A.R.T.   183

Chapter 24: Goal Creation Checker – Top Tips for Forming Your Top Goals   199

Part Seven:
Give It the "G.A.S."- The Goal Achievement System

Chapter 25: How to Achieve Your Goals. Step 1: Craft the Perfect Goal   213

Chapter 26: How to Achieve Your Goals. Step 2: Create a Winning Strategy   217

Chapter 27: How to Achieve Your Goals. Step 3: Take Affirmative Action   227

Chapter 28: How to Achieve Your Goals. Step 4: Align Your Inner World   233

Chapter 29: How to Achieve Your Goals. Step 5: Align Time to Outcomes   239

Chapter 30: How to Achieve Your Goals. Step 6: Build a Structure of Review and Accountability   243

Chapter 31: How to Achieve Your Goals. Step 7: Practice 'Sensory Sensitivity' and 'Strategic Suppleness'   253

PART EIGHT:
TOP TIPS FOR ACHIEVING YOUR GOALS

CHAPTER 32: TOP TIPS FOR ACHIEVING YOUR HEALTH GOALS – WEIGHT GOALS … 267

CHAPTER 33: HOW TO INCREASE YOUR ENERGY LEVELS – THE 2 HUMAN FUEL TANKS … 273

CHAPTER 34: TOP TIPS FOR ACHIEVING YOUR HEALTH GOALS – FITNESS GOALS … 277

CHAPTER 35: TOP TIPS FOR ACHIEVING YOUR HEALTH GOALS – MENTAL GOALS … 281

CHAPTER 36: HOW TO LEVERAGE THE LIKELIHOOD OF PERSONAL CHANGE … 291

CHAPTER 37: TOP TIPS FOR RELATIONSHIP GOALS – VALUES AND YOUR LIFE PARTNER … 299

CHAPTER 38: TOP TIPS FOR RELATIONSHIP GOALS – IDENTIFYING WHAT LOVE LOOKS LIKE … 307

CHAPTER 39: TOP TIPS FOR RELATIONSHIP GOALS – COMMUNICATING EFFECTIVELY … 313

CHAPTER 40: TOP TIPS FOR RELATIONSHIP GOALS – THE VALUE OF A LIFE PARTNER RELATIONSHIP … 323

CHAPTER 41: TOP TIPS FOR MONEY GOALS – USING WORK TO HELP YOU FULFILL YOUR LIFE PURPOSE … 329

CHAPTER 42: TOP TIPS FOR MONEY GOALS – GROWING YOUR INCOME … 335

CHAPTER 43: TOP TIPS FOR MONEY GOALS – WEALTH CREATION … 339

PART NINE:
THE SOFT SCIENCE OF GOAL ACHIEVEMENT

CHAPTER 44: THE SOFT SCIENCE OF SUCCESS - INTRODUCTION … 351

CHAPTER 45: REPROGRAMMING YOUR MIND FOR SUCCESS … 353

CHAPTER 46: HOW TO BUILD YOUR COMMITMENT AND PERSISTENCE MUSCLES … 375

CHAPTER 47: HOW TO STAY MOTIVATED … 381

CHAPTER 48: 'GETTING OVER IT:' HOW TO HANDLE UNWANTED EMOTIONS … 391

CHAPTER 49: CONSCIOUSLY WHAT TO DO WHEN IT ALL GOES PEAR-SHAPED … 405

CHAPTER 50: HOW TO FIND SOLUTIONS TO EVERY PROBLEM … 409

CHAPTER 51: HOW TO REALLY ENJOY THE JOURNEY PART 1 – DEVELOP 1ST CLASS GOALS … 419

CHAPTER 52: HOW TO REALLY ENJOY THE JOURNEY PART 2 – PRACTICE MINDFULNESS … 429

CHAPTER 53: How to Really Enjoy the Journey Part 3 - Stay Committed but Not Emotionally Attached   437

CHAPTER 54: Positive Thinking Versus Reality Thinking   445

CHAPTER 55: How to Deal With Survival Reactions   451

CHAPTER 56: How to Push Through Discomfort   455

CHAPTER 57: Understanding the True Nature of Personal Change   459

PART TEN:
THE EXTRA-ORDINARY PERSONAL GOAL

CHAPTER 58: The Extra-Ordinary Personal Goal (EPG)   479

CHAPTER 59: Types of Extra-Ordinary Personal Goals   487

CHAPTER 60: My Personal EPG Examples   491

CHAPTER 61: Choosing an EPG   499

ABOUT THE AUTHOR   503

PREFACE

"Life is a daring adventure or nothing. To keep our faces toward change and behave like free spirits in the presence of fate is strength undefeatable."

—Helen Keller

WELCOME TO THE WORLD OF THE EXTRA-ORDINARY

THIS IS A world where you go places that only 1 in a 1,000 humans will ever venture. It's a place that will test you and expand the very limits of your potential. It's *where* you get to meet your nemesis and to beat him or her at their own game. And frankly, it's mostly a very uncomfortable place.

The reason that this book has the potential to produce discomfort in your life is that it's about choosing to create an Extra-Ordinary Life. And that, in turn, requires time spent out of your Comfort Zone. There is no growth without effort.

Unfortunately though, the opiate of the masses these days isn't religion, it's pleasure. As the "standard of living" increases, billions of bored and stifled souls have chosen to swap their Freedom for certainty and have consequently cocooned themselves in a collective huddle within the safety of a stupefying Comfort Zone.

Developed countries have the highest standards of living across more socio-economic levels than at any other time in history. Many of the routine, time-sucking and energy-sapping tasks have been automated or outsourced, and what we are left with is more choice and supposedly, more Freedom.

And yet ironically, at the same time that we bear witness to this plethora of pleasure and this cornucopia of choice, the world is also experiencing a vacuum of Happiness, a dearth of Fulfillment and a massive increase in the swallowing of antidepressants.

So what's gone wrong? Surely more money, more toys, more choices must mean more Happiness, more Freedom and more Fulfillment? Apparently not.

The problem is that our ability to manufacture and deliver pleasure and comfort to the marketplace has outpaced our ability to alter the intrinsic human needs of growth, challenge and Fulfillment.

Creating, distributing, and branding larger and more pleasurable Comfort Zones may be all well and good when it comes to building fat corporate profits, but it does nothing for the human spirit which needs to grow and experience life outside of the Comfort Zone in order to feel Fulfillment.

In a world obsessed with making life easier and more pleasure-filled, I am advocating a different approach. My observation is that most people are primarily motivated by securing certainty around their cocoon of comfort. I propose that we each replace that primary driving force for the Goal of being Extra-Ordinary.

My observation is that the very act of proactively choosing to create "A Life Extra-Ordinary" leads one to all manner of obstacles and challenges that, when overcome, produce character growth and a sense of Fulfillment besides which the value of pleasure pales by comparison.

There is no growth and no Fulfillment within a Comfort Zone. Without challenges and obstacles and effort and achievement, there is no Fulfillment and no lasting Happiness.

> *"It takes courage to push yourself to places that you have never been before ... to test your limits ... to break through barriers. And the day came when the risk to remain tight in a bud was more painful than the risk it took to blossom."*
>
> **—Anais Nin**

When my grandson learned to swim, we gave him some ""water wings." That gave him more confidence. One day he'll take them off and then he'll be able to swim faster and have even more fun.

Today it's like the populace have forgotten to take off their water wings. They are metaphorically traveling through life being propped up with the twin water wings of pleasure and comfort.

Not that there is anything wrong with a piece of pleasure or a slice of comfort. When my father was born in the Depression years of the 1920s, there was very little choice and even less comfort. Hard work, if you could get it, was your only hope of eking out a little pleasure. But in our haste to put some distance between ourselves and those decades of deprivation, we have swung the pendulum of pleasure far too far the other way.

We have sold our souls for the price of a trinket of technology and a few shiny things with fancy brand names. We can, however, buy our lives back by taking a leap of faith outside our Comfort Zone, by collecting our courage and reinvigorating our spirits with the challenges and experiences that are all a part of Consciously creating "Your Extra-Ordinary Life."

This is a book for people who refuse to settle down and be ordinary. God forbid that anyone should come to my funeral and say that I lived a sensible and normal life. I'd throw up in the casket. And then I'd haunt them until they recanted. As Peter Garret of Midnight Oil so succinctly sung, "It's better to die on your feet than live on your knees." I'm hopeful that when my body dies, they'll then have to beat my passion to death so my soul will finally let go. Until then, it's "game on."

Every day you have a choice. Live or exist. Give up or step up. My wish for you is that you may live every day for the rest of your life. This book shows you both why you need to do this and how to do it.

As you read these pages, I hope you'll find some stirring in your spirit and join in the greatest adventure of all: to live "Your Extra-Ordinary Life."

> *"It was not for small things but for great that God created men, who, knowing the great, are not satisfied with small things. Indeed, it was for the limitless alone that He created men, who are the only beings on earth to have rediscovered their infinite nature and who are not fully satisfied by anything limited, however great that thing may be."*
>
> —Marcilio Ficino

You'll notice that throughout the book I type the first letter of each important concept or word as a capital letter, e.g. Goal or Life Purpose. This is simply to emphasize the importance of these words and concepts.

PART ONE:

THE PURPOSE OF YOUR LIFE

"The purpose of life is a life of purpose."

—ROBERT BYRNE

Chapter 1:

Life at the Next Level

This book is a declaration of independence from the mainstream mindset of mediocrity that simply seeks an easier, more comfortable and safer life. I've written this for every courageous Being that recognizes a need deep inside of himself or herself to go beyond the safety of their Comfort Zone and to pay the price that Fulfillment asks of us, rather than the cost that is demanded and paid by millions when they cocoon themselves in a warm world of no risk, no pain, and consequently, no gain.

My belief is that human potential has the capacity to continually expand to new levels of achievement in both the physical outer world as well as the Inner Worlds of the mind and the soul.

I further believe that true Fulfillment can only be experienced by those individuals who make a lifelong quest out of experiencing "life at the next level." And there is always another level.

Fulfillment is the experience of continual growth. By its nature, Fulfillment is not a destination, it is a journey. When we choose to experience Fulfillment by achieving at continually higher levels, we swap the cocoon of our old ordinary life for the wings of "Your Extra-Ordinary Life."

A Goal is a vehicle that has the capacity to transport us to that next level, again and again. Goals get us out of our Comfort Zone and into a whole new world of adventure, achievement, and growth.

What's Important to You About Your Life?

So what does "Your Extra-Ordinary Life" look like to you? In other words, what are the Goals that are important for you to achieve before your soul leaves your body?

In general terms, I know the type of Goals that most people set because I have devoted over a decade as a full-time professional to helping my high-achiever clients both set and achieve Goals. I've done this either through the coaching programs that I've developed (see www.espcoach.com) or through working with clients one on one.

The Goals that my clients have set include Goals to improve health (physical, mental, emotional, spiritual, cultural, and sport), to improve relationships (Life Partner, children, family, friends, and community) as well as money-related Goals (income, profit, investment and philanthropy).

On the face of it, we are motivated to set Goals so that we can create… a better-quality life. Experiencing the reality of life at the next level comes about through the simple, but challenging process of setting and achieving Goals. Nothing new in that.

THE PURPOSE OF A GOAL

But what you might find disturbingly new and unsettling is the primary reason why we set Goals and go about the journey of attempting to create a better life. Read this next part slowly and carefully and most importantly read it with an open mind.

'The primary purpose of a Goal is to create obstacles.'

And now re-read that statement even slower and more carefully and with even more of an open mind. Ponder it and let it take a little while to sink in. See if you can work out why I would write such a thing before you go on and read my explanation which follows. This process of contemplation is healthy.

Now, before you throw this book away and call for the men with white jackets to come and take me away, let me explain why I believe that the ultimate purpose of a Goal is to create obstacles.

OUTCOMES AND INPUTS

A Goal can also be referred to as an Outcome. Essentially, life can be divided into Outcomes and Inputs. An Outcome is the result of some Inputs. If you want a different Outcome such as better health, better relationships, or increased wealth, then you need some different Inputs. Insanity is defined as "doing the same thing (Input) over and over again and expecting a different result (Outcome)." Clearly not an especially productive strategy but it still amazes me how many people, including myself from time to time, want a different result but continue to act the same way. If you refer back to the Goals listed previously, you will see that one person's set of Goals can contain many different Outcomes and even more ways of achieving those Outcomes.

But every worthwhile and progressive Goal will have one common characteristic. Each of these Goals will represent an Outcome that you will not have experienced previously. And a different Outcome will demand a different set of Inputs. For example, the Inputs that got you to a $100,000 income will not get you to a $1,000,000 income. Eating habits that created 20 kilograms of excess fat are clearly not the Inputs that you need to get down to your naturally lean self. And the person who has just been divorced for the third time is heading for number four unless he or she tries something different the next time around. I'm sure that you get the picture: you get out what you put in.

So how does the concept of different Goals demanding different Inputs lead to my statement that the ultimate purpose of a Goal is to create obstacles?

Simply put, whenever you create a new Goal (Outcome) you then have to try a bunch of new things (Inputs) in order to achieve that Goal. And in doing so, you will create obstacles. These obstacles will come in the form of both known challenges as well as unforeseen setbacks. You will need to develop new ways of thinking, new habits, new skills, new knowledge and lots of new actions. All of these things are in themselves obstacles and thus the Goal will take you out of the familiarity of your Comfort Zone and into the twilight zone of the uncertain and the unknown. Your capacity to be comfortable with discomfort will in large part determine your capacity for success.

Each obstacle that you create as a result of pursuing your Goal will demand that you apply intelligent effort to Overcome the obstacle before you can reach the prize of achieving the Goal.

To Those Who Overcome ...

John is an old friend of mine. He is a Christian minister. Interestingly, in talking about these concepts, John reminded me that there is a passage in the Book of Revelation where it states: *"To him who Overcomes, to him I will give of the hidden manna, and I will give him a white stone, and on the stone a new name written, which no one knows but he who receives it."* John keeps a white stone on his desk to remind himself constantly of the need and benefit of overcoming the obstacles that are a natural consequence of attempting to achieve Extra-Ordinary results.

How Do Others Know Who You Are?

Some people think that their beliefs define who they are. I disagree. A person can be clinically diagnosed as an alcoholic but still not believe that they have a drinking problem. Their refusal to believe the reality of their alcoholism does nothing to alter the fact that they are an alcoholic. It's also possible for someone to believe that they are generous but to only give with selfish motives, or worse, to never give to those in need. Clearly, our beliefs do not define who we are.

I'm going to suggest that who you are is more dramatically and clearly defined by what you achieve than by anything else. The bigger the achievement, the bigger the obstacles that had to be Overcome. For thousands of years, our heroes have been people who have Overcome formidable obstacles against the odds. Our heroes may be soldiers who risked their lives for the Freedom of a nation, or a paraplegic who won a gold medal. Heroes can be triumphant entrepreneurs or a Mother Theresa, but they all have one thing in common: they are all Overcomers who achieved something Extra-Ordinary. We are inspired by the capacity to Overcome.

Extra-Ordinary Is as Extra-Ordinary Does

People know who you are not by who you say you are, but by what you achieve in life. Actions speak louder than words. And if words are a whisper and actions are a shout, then your achievements are a heavily amplified loudspeaker.

Your Goals therefore tell the world what you Value in life. And your ability to turn those Goals into reality is a living demonstration to the world of who you really are. In the creative sense, your capacity for power is reflected in your achievements and communicates to others the characteristics that you have developed, such as astuteness, perseverance, patience, etc., and your capabilities in areas such as your habits, skills, and knowledge.

It's said that Buddha instructed his disciples to spread his message of Happiness and compassion to the world and that he added that *"when necessary you may even use words."* Your message is not in the words you speak as much as it is in the Goals you have achieved.

When asked how a person could identify his disciples, Christ answered "By their fruit you will know them." He didn't say that you could tell because they would all be wearing white gowns or by what their beliefs were or even by the way that they acted. It wasn't how hard or how long they worked that was most important or even how nice they were to others. Christ said that you will be able to tell who a person was by what they produced. Their Outcomes would show the world who his disciples were. In other words, *what you achieve defines who you are.*

GOALS ARE NOT ONLY EVIDENCED EXTERNALLY

When I say that your Goals and achievements define who you are, you may tend to think primarily of your external achievements such as a new career or business, a new house, or having climbed a new mountain. But I'm actually referring as much to your inner achievements as I am to your outer ones. Inner achievements may include reigniting your passion for life, developing your capacity for tolerance, compassion, astuteness, or love. I suspect that in the long run you'll value these inner achievements even more than you value your outer ones.

CHARACTER DEVELOPMENT

So what happens when you Overcome obstacles and achieve a Goal? Two things happen. Firstly, you get to experience whatever it was that resulted from the Goal: the new Porsche or a debt-free home or a new career or a better relationship or improved health. That probably sounds pretty cool but wait… there's more, a whole lot more.

I've already alluded to the second thing that happens when you Overcome obstacles and achieve a Goal. It has to do with your own personal metamorphose into someone greater than who you were yesterday. By "greater" I'm referring to the development and growth of personal characteristics such as courage, patience, persistence, wisdom, resourcefulness or any number of other personal Values.

> *Anais Nin said that "Life is a process of becoming, a combination of states we have to go through. Where people fail is that they wish to elect a state and remain in it. This is a kind of death."*

THE ULTIMATE GOAL

That brings us to the Ultimate Goal, otherwise known as your Life Purpose. I've long held the belief that starting something is always more productive once we are clear as to what we want it to look like when we have finished. As Covey suggested: *"Begin with the end in mind."*

It doesn't matter if it's starting an e-mail, a phone call, a meeting, a day, a week or a year. It could be starting a relationship, some exercise, a holiday or a project. Starting with a clear Outcome focuses our efforts in a more effective way and is also a prerequisite for success in that, if we don't know what we want, we can never achieve it.

It makes sense then to give some thought to what you want your life to look like, at some point prior to your death! I have thought deeply about the questions of Life Purpose and have taught on the subject for many years now. I sum it all up in three areas which are listed below and in what I believe is their order of priority:

Your purpose in life can be summed up in the following three categories:

1. Consciousness

2. Capacity

3. Contribution

I have spent literally a lifetime attending workshops and seminars, reading all manner of books from east to west, listening to teachers, philosophers, religious leaders and gurus live, on tapes and CDs, and more importantly, being a daily student in the observation of my own life and the lives of others. I have found that anyone who is making progress toward all three of these areas will create and become the living definition of an Extra- Ordinary life. Let's look at each one of these areas in a little more depth.

CHAPTER 2:

USING GOALS TO EXPAND YOUR CONSCIOUSNESS

Life Purpose Model: 1. **Consciousness**
                      2. Capacity
                      3. Contribution

EXPANDING PERSONAL CONSCIOUSNESS is all about learning how to live a life of true and total Conscious choice. This not only means the ability to choose what you will create as your reality in your physical world or Outer World, but also to choose what you experience in the Inner World of your thoughts, emotions, and character development.

LIVING UNCONSCIOUSLY

Socrates referred to mankind as being asleep, which he said was the opposite of being Conscious. If we follow Socrates" teaching, we learn that most people are not living their lives Consciously. People who are "sleep-walking" through life have little or no power to change their emotional and mental states at will. They fall victim to unwanted feelings and emotions and are powerless to shift by choice from one state such as anger, to another such as Happiness. They feel stuck in stress and while they may long for peace of mind, they hang onto the very actions that perpetuate their anxieties. Their unconscious mind is full of mental patterns that create the exact opposite of what they want and yet they have no idea how to change it.

Additionally, sleep-walkers find themselves stuck with unwanted physical conditions such as excess weight, or low energy, or with an ongoing illness or injury. Sleep-walkers often feel trapped in their relationships and generally feel that they lack options when it comes to creating a life of their own choice.

In fact, many sleep-walkers are so unconscious that they do not have a clear idea what they really want in life. By not being clear on what success looks like they end up feeling like a pinball in the giant pinball machine of life and they stay that way until they wake up and begin to live Consciously.

In summary, any form of emotional or mental suffering is a symptom of being unconscious. Nightmares are the domain of those who are asleep.

Conscious Living

Like any other skill, our capacity to live life Consciously and therefore choose both our Inner and Outer World realities can be strengthened with practice. Moving from an unconscious state in life to a Conscious one takes time and commitment. But the Rewards are well worth it.

The characteristics of a person who lives their life in a fully Conscious state are:

1. People who live Consciously are aware that they have choice. They feel that they are free and in fact they are truly free.

2. Because they are aware of their capacity for choice, they understand that at some level, they have created every one of their experiences, either Consciously or unconsciously.

3. Because they are awake, Conscious people are aware of how they are feeling and can choose to experience a different emotion at will. Most of the time they choose to be happy. The state of authentic (as opposed to contrived) "24/7" Happiness is the mark of a truly Conscious person. This is why Socrates claimed that attaining the state of continuous Happiness was the most important Goal in life.

4. In addition to having power over their Inner World, a fully Conscious person can create any Outer World experience or result that they choose. They can create deeper and more satisfying relationships, improved levels of health and well-being as well as increased levels of financial wealth, should they choose to do so. This ability does not come in the form of a magic wand or pixie dust. Success for Conscious people still takes time and intelligent effort; it's just that they have total certainty around the final result.

5. Fully Conscious people do not suffer. People who are awake do not have nightmares.

6. Fully Conscious people are never the source of making other people suffer. They operate from a motivation of loving kindness, compassion and wisdom. They make decisions based on the principle of "highest and greatest good," as opposed to operating from fear or ego-centricity. There are occasions however that a sleep-walker will feel insecure or threatened in the presence of a more Conscious person. The unconscious ego does not want to give up control.

LEVELS OF CONSCIOUSNESS

There are very few beings on this planet that have increased their Conscious capacity to the point where they have lived in that space continuously. Examples would include historically validated people such as Buddha, Christ, Paramahansa Yogananda (author of *Autobiography of a Yogi*) and others.

There are, however, many others who have lived a life in a higher state of Consciousness than average and examples include Albert Schweitzer, Mahatma Gandhi, Mother Teresa, Helen Keller and some of the more successful world leaders.

Levels of Consciousness can be measured and the work of David R Hawkins (*Power Versus Force* and *Qualitative and Quantitative Calibration of the levels of Human Consciousness*) have added significantly to our understanding of Consciousness.

But no matter who we are, it's important to bear in mind that almost all of us have some degree of Conscious ability and we also spend time in an unconscious state. The name of the game is to spend more of our time in a Conscious state because that is where true choice or Freedom exists. Additionally, increased feelings of love, Happiness and peace of mind are all hallmarks of Conscious living. And in addition to those Inner World attractions there are the Outer World advantages of Conscious living that include the power to create the reality of your choice.

Have I got your attention yet? You see, the concept of Consciousness is not just for Eastern gurus. It has practical application in your everyday experience of life, from brushing your teeth to closing that multi-million-dollar deal. Consciousness is cool.

> *Technically speaking there is a difference between the "Subconscious" mind and the "unconscious" mind. The Subconscious is the repository of all those instincts and functions that we were born with, such as the capacity to run our cardio-vascular system and innate drivers such as the avoidance of pain. By contrast, the unconscious stores the collected experiences of our lives; every sight, sound, taste, smell, and touch is stored in the unconscious. The unconscious stores our beliefs and other thought patterns. At the risk of over-simplifying, we might say that everything in the Subconscious was there prior to our birth, and the unconscious began to store all of our experiences after birth. The programming in the Subconscious is innate and the programming in the unconscious is learned.*
>
> *For the sake of simplicity, I make no distinction in this book between the two terms and so you will find I use the terms "unconscious" and "Subconscious" interchangeably to mean "that which is below the level of Conscious thought."*

A life that is lived Consciously is a life of choice and power. By "power" I mean the "power to create at will," as opposed to "power over others." And it's a curious but powerful side effect of achieving your Goals that your capacity for Consciousness increases. Let me explain.

STAYING ON THE STRAIGHT AND SUFFOCATING

For most people, Subconscious pleasure and survival-motivated reactions will keep them from venturing far from what they have always done in the past. Many people continually destroy their relationships, their health, and their wealth with actions that self-sabotage their dreams. This happens when their unconscious programming noted at some point in the past that there was a pay-off for this behavior even though it is evident to the rest of the world that the behavior ceased to pay dividends many years ago.

The obese person who continues to over-eat or the alcoholic who continues to drink too much, both in the face of a diminished quality of life, are a living and twisted testament of the power of the unconscious over the Conscious. The person who destroys the love in their life by continually arguing with their Life Partner instead of putting their ego aside and really listening does the same, as indeed does the person who spends more than they earn and destroys their financial future. These are just a few examples among dozens where people sacrifice what they truly want out of life on the altar of their Subconscious.

The successful life is a life that is lived Consciously. Show me someone who is happy, and I will show you a person who in that moment is living Consciously. Show me someone who is persistently suffering from unhappiness or anger or resentment and so on and I will show you someone who is living unconsciously. Only a demented person would Consciously choose suffering over Happiness. But of course people don't Consciously choose suffering; unhappiness and other emotional pain come from the unconscious. They simply lack either the awareness or the knowledge of how to transform suffering into Happiness.

True Happiness and Freedom only comes as you increase your ability to live life Consciously. That means building the strength and power of your conscious "Mind Muscle" to the point that your Conscious mind has control over the unconscious.

> *Freedom*
>
> *There are of course different types of Freedom including physical Freedom, financial Freedom, and political Freedom and so on. For the purpose of this chapter though, I am referring to the type of Freedom that is the most important of all. Without this type of Freedom, none of the others are worthwhile. I am referring to Mental Freedom. This is the ability to choose what we think and as a consequence of that to be able to choose what we do and therefore to choose what we achieve.*

Allow me to make the point a little further through a time-tested analogy from Armenian philosophy Gurdjieff. Imagine a horse and carriage with a driver and the Master, the latter who would sit inside the carriage. The horse represents your emotions, the carriage represents your body, the driver represents your Subconscious mind and the master plays the part of your Conscious mind or soul. The question is: who is in charge?

In Gurdjieff's story, the master (Conscious mind or soul) has an important meeting in town. The driver (Subconscious mind) has lingered in the bar too long and gotten drunk. In fact, he is so drunk that he now thinks that he is the master. In the meantime, the horse (emotions) has been left to its own devices and is wandering around dropping messes all over the place and is unfed and uncared for. The carriage (physical body) has sadly fallen into a state of disrepair and is slowly disintegrating. The master (Conscious mind or soul) becomes aware of all this but feels powerless to take charge and decides to do so only when the driver has sobered up, the horse is properly harnessed, and the carriage repaired. Fat chance. If your Subconscious mind, or the driver, is in charge then you will find yourself constantly reacting to life's various situations. To "react" means to act again and again in the same way to the same sensory input. For example, your Life Partner tells you about something that you could do better, and you find yourself defending your actions instead of listening and learning. This can happen many times over many decades despite the wishes of your Conscious mind (the master) to do otherwise. Any situation that you react to over and over again, is a situation that your Subconscious is in charge of. In short, if your Subconscious is in charge you will find yourself often doing the things that you have always done in your past, and unless you change to a more Conscious state, this is probably a fair indication of what your life is going to look like in the future. Take a good look at your life and if you'd prefer a different Outcome then keep reading.

If the horse of your emotions is in charge, then your life is ruled by whatever emotion you are feeling in any given moment. These are the people who experience radical mood fluctuations and act accordingly without thinking about the consequences. In the context of this analogy, their lives are literally being driven by their emotions. Their "horse" is out of control and is taking them in a direction of random destruction. Again, not a great option.

When the carriage or physical body is in charge, however, it's like your body has a mind of its own and is taking your whole life wherever it wants to go. For example, if you find yourself addicted to pleasure in the form of food or alcohol to the point where you are overweight or ill, then your body is in charge. Likewise if you are obsessed with creating "body beautiful" to the point where you are compromising the quality of your health, wealth, and relationships, you again have a body in charge.

Please understand that I am a firm believer in the benefits of physical exercise and an even firmer believer in enjoying great food and wine or other alcoholic beverages. What I am writing about here, though, is the excessive indulgence in these things to the point where the gratification erodes quality Outcomes in other areas of your life, imbalance, in other words. This is what happens when your body takes you in a direction that your mind didn't Consciously want to go. Eating the extra slice or two of pie, having the extra glass or two of beer or wine and so on. This leads to a life packed with regrets and guilt. Not much fun the morning after.

The other possibility is that your Conscious mind or Soul is in charge. If this is the case, then you think and feel what you want to think and feel, you will do exactly what you decide to do, and you will make progress toward the sort of Outcomes that represent success in your life. Instead of reacting to situations, you will Consciously choose a response that takes you in the direction of your Goals.

So, who is in charge of your life? Your "Subconscious driver," your "emotional horse," "your physical carriage," or your "master mind?" The reality for most of us is that we experience moments of being led by all four forces. On a good day, I can normally experience the tug of each driver before morning tea! The trick is to increasingly move toward having the Conscious mind, or soul, in charge of the Subconscious, the emotions and the body. This is living Consciously.

> *The Subconscious is the mind of habit, whereas the Conscious mind is the mind of choice.*

THE SUBCONSCIOUS CAN BE YOUR BEST FRIEND OR WORST ENEMY

Some people get the wrong idea at this point. It's not that the Subconscious is bad or even that it's good for that matter. The Subconscious is not good or bad, it's just your Subconscious. The point is that the Subconscious mind, which often drives the emotional and physical, is a powerful ally to your Goals when it's "Second in Command." But it's as destructive as it is powerful when it's being "Master and Commander." Let me explain.

If you want to repeat an action over and over, then you'll do well to delegate it to your Subconscious mind. We call this establishing a habit. I call those habits that create the future that you Consciously want "Creative Habits." "Destructive Habits" are those that destroy the future that you Consciously want. Creative Habits include simple things like flossing your teeth, exercising and eating healthily, whereas Destructive Habits might include spending too much money, eating too much junk food, arguing with others, or working too many hours and in the process eroding the quality of personal relationships and lifestyle.

Here's the point to get: Overcoming obstacles and achieving a Goal requires the exercising of your Conscious will. During this process, you will increase your capacity for Consciousness.

This is because when you set a Goal to achieve something new you will need to learn new ways of doing things, take new actions, and think at a higher level than you did previously. In its natural state, the Subconscious resists such change simply because it associates effort and uncertainty with pain. The only way to Overcome such resistance is with Conscious will power. Pythagoras said that *"No man is free who cannot command himself."*

So in exercising your Conscious mind to achieve a Goal, you automatically strengthen your Conscious mind. And you can use this increased Conscious capacity to not only create success in your Outer World. but also your Inner World with the Conscious development of Happiness and Freedom.

That's not to say that everyone who is a Goal-achieving machine is necessarily happy and Free. It simply means that as they have developed the ability to Consciously create a reality of their choice, their capacity to Consciously choose Happiness and Freedom also increases. Whether they choose to apply their enhanced capacity for Conscious living to the development of Happiness and Freedom is another matter. Some do so and as a result become truly well-rounded and Extra-Ordinary beings. Others don't make the leap from using their power to create Outer World success such as career or business success, money and its associated toys, beautiful houses and cars and so on, to Inner World success such as Happiness and Freedom.

In summary, achieving Goals and overcoming the associated obstacles increases the power of your Conscious mind to create Inner-World realities such as Happiness and Freedom as well as Outer-World realities such as better health, relationships, or more wealth.

> *"The true value of the human being is determined by the measure and the sense in which one has attained liberation from the self."*
>
> **—Albert Einstein**

Chapter 3:

Using Goals to Increase Your Personal Capacity

Life Purpose Model: 1. Consciousness
                                       2. **Capacity**
                                         3. Contribution

You may be wondering what I mean by increasing your personal Capacity. Normally when we talk about capacity it might be in the context of "engine capacity," "tank capacity," "power capacity" or "production capacity" and so on. Capacity therefore has to do with the amount a thing can contain or its size. How big is your Capacity for Love for example? How big is your Capacity for courage, or for patience, or for any one of a thousand Values that are important to us as human beings? In addition to increasing our emotional and mental Capacities, I am also talking about the growth and development of new skills and abilities.

Our Capacity for Consciousness forms a part of this concept of course and, while there is an overlap in each of the three parts of my Life Purpose Model, increasing our Capacity for Consciousness on its own does not lead to a fulfilling life.

The development of increased Capacity for highly valued personal characteristics as well as for new abilities and skills is a large part of Life Purpose. And note that there is a difference between Personal Growth and Personal Development. When it comes to Life Purpose, the distinction between Growth and Development is a an important one to consider.

GROWTH VERSUS DEVELOPMENT

Outside the window of my office I have an Australian Eucalyptus tree. It's some 30 meters tall. Since the day that it was planted as a seed, it has done only one thing. It has grown. It has never developed. As humans, we have both the capacity to develop as well as to grow. When you grow, like the Eucalyptus tree, you get more of what you have already got. Physically speaking, you become taller and organs such as your heart and lungs grow as well. Personal Growth means that you can become more of who you already are. If you are already patient, then if you need to or want to you can become even more patient. That's growth.

Development has more of an emphasis on changing and becoming different. Unlike the Eucalyptus tree, humans have the capacity to change. For example, I was once a very impatient and selfish person. But the people that matter tell me that I have begun to develop patience and generosity in some small measure. I still have a long way to go, but the point is that I have the Capacity to develop new characteristics.

VISITING YOUR DEATH BED

To understand the concept of Personal Development and Growth more deeply, I will need you to come with me into a very precise place and time in the future. Specifically, the place is your bedroom and the time is a few seconds prior to your death, which is hopefully many fulfilling years away from now.

I want you to imagine the scene. You're about to gasp your last breath and around your bed are your loved ones. I don't know whether you believe in an after-life or not. Personally I choose to believe in multiple after-lives because I am having such a good time that I would love to come back. But let's be a little pessimistic though and assume that you only get one crack at this life, but let's also add just a pinch of optimism into the mix and say that we think there is another experience waiting for us beyond death. In survey after survey, most people say that they believe in an after-life of some description.

So picture yourself lying there in your bed and ask yourself this question about your soon-to-be experienced "crossing over:" *"What do I get to take with me?"*

Clearly, you don't get to take your health with you. That's gone, big-time. If you had any vestige of good health left, you wouldn't be about to "kick the bucket." What about the people standing around the bed? Do you think that they will want to come with you at this time? I don't think so. Chance are that they won't volunteer to join you on your very special journey. Don't get me wrong, I'm sure they are going to miss you, but not so much that they will be prepared to do a "Romeo and Juliet."

So of all the things that you value, the health and the relationships are about to disappear forever. That only leaves the money you've accumulated and its various bi-products such as houses, cars, cash, and various assorted toys. I read a biography of Howard Hughes who, when he died, was the richest man in the world. Have a guess at how much money he left behind. Any idea? Here's the answer: all of it.

So you don't get to take your health, the people you love, or your money when you die. The only thing you will get to take with you is in fact who you have become. That's it. That's the ball game right there. Your character, brilliant or flawed as it may be, is what you get to take with you. Some people imagine that when they die, they ascend into heaven where an angel waves some cosmic dust over them and creates a perfect being. I disagree. As someone once said "If you're a dipstick in this life you're gonna be a dipstick in the after-life."

Every time you create and achieve a Goal, you grow personally. In achieving a new Goal, you expand your Capacity and fulfill, in part, your potential. When you set a Goal to achieve something new, its very nature takes you into unchartered territory and presents obstacles and challenges previously not experienced. As you Overcome those obstacles, you expand your Capacity into something greater. As a truly successful human being, this process of expanding and fulfilling your potential will be repeated a thousand times or more in one lifetime.

Note that you can use different names for the obstacles that you create such as "problems" or "challenges," but whichever term you prefer to use, there is always one common theme. In order to Overcome an obstacle you will need to firstly think, which exercises your Consciousness, and secondly, you will need to make an effort, which will expand your Capacity.

If you get the first part right (thinking), then your effort will be more effective. If you don't get the first part right, or worse still you don't do any thinking prior to acting, then your effort will be considerably increased and, in all likelihood, it will be wasted. I hate wasted effort. I hate it with a passion. Always remember:

> "Ignorance + Effort = Failure
> Knowledge + Effort = Success"

So what are we left with? We know that the achievement of your Goals defines who you are. We know that the final and ultimate result of your entire Goal-achieving prowess is the development of your Capacities in the form of character and abilities and that this is all you get to take with you into the after-life. And we also know that you would never have expanded and fulfilled your potential Capacity without the obstacles that you created when you first set out to achieve a Goal.

That's why the ultimate purpose of creating a Goal is so that you can experience obstacles. Without the obstacles there would be no thinking and there would be no effort and there would therefore be no personal growth or development.

THERE IS NO GROWTH WITHOUT EFFORT

"The art of living is more like wrestling than dancing."
—**Marcus Aurelius**

This is a universal principle which no-one on the face of the earth gets to violate. You make an effort and you get to grow. And then you get to feel fulfilled. For a while. And then you need to make another effort so you can grow some more. And then you get to feel fulfilled again. And so on. It's the great game of life where success is not a destination but a journey. There is no growth without effort. End of story.

As a human being, you are wired to want Fulfillment and you never get to experience that sense of Fulfillment until you begin to fulfill your potential. I didn't write the rule book on this, and I'll let the evolutionists and their religious counterparts argue about whether humans are like this as a result of a God-inspired genetic infusion or simply the product of evolution. Either way, we are who we are, regardless of how we came to be wired like that.

THE 1-800 LIE

The sooner that people stop buying into the "quick and easy" message of the 1-800 ads the better The world is full of people who find it convenient to believe that they can increase their Consciousness and expand their Capacity for only six easy payments of $19.95 per month. The 1-800 ads often promise that fame and fortune will be delivered to your door complete with simple instructions and easy actions. Guaranteed.

Many 1-800 ads are the living embodiment of the proverbial "short cut to success" lie. "Buy my product (book/seminar/pill/equipment/food/holiday/property/enlargement) and you too can look like these happy, smiling, successful (actors) on your screen."

I'm here to tell you that when it comes to Fulfillment, peace of mind, Freedom, Happiness or any other aspect of personal development, none of those shortcuts work. Anyone who believes that you can have abs like Arnie in only four minutes a day or that you can make 100% in the markets every week is choosing to believe a lie that is robbing them of any chance that they have of experiencing life to the max.

Success and the growth of personal Capacity requires effort.

CHAPTER 4:

USING GOALS TO MAKE A MORE SIGNIFICANT PERSONAL CONTRIBUTION

Life Purpose Model: 1. Consciousness
                                      2. Capacity
                                        3. **Contribution**

IN BROAD TERMS, making a "Contribution" is all about making the world, or a part of it, a better place. Your Contribution probably occurs in the form of your chosen career, job or business, or indeed in being of service to your family, friends, and community. The fact that you may get paid for making a Contribution in no way makes it less significant or less worthwhile than unpaid or voluntary work, which can also be included under this category. While it's not the primary subject of this book, I will very briefly explain a few key points in relation to Contribution.

We are all born with some measure of talent for something. My mother used to remind me about this when I was a developing the discouraging and depressing habit of failing my high school exams with predictable monotony. "God gave each of us special gifts Tom," she would say, "and you are no different than everyone else in this respect." Once when I asked what she thought mine might be, she seemed lost for words for a few seconds and then declared that I was good at cleaning the bath. I must say that, at the time, the thought of spending my life as a bath cleaner didn't do a lot for lifting the personal sense of deep gloom that I was experiencing. However, as we have all come to know, Mother knows best. Examine where your talents lie and use them to serve others.

Passion Is the Key to Purpose

However, what you are good at will invariably be the result of spending a lot of time on that type of activity and that in turn will come about as a result of wanting to do it. This leads us to the issue of Passion. Putting it the other way around, your mission is to make the world a better place for having lived here by:

1. Identifying what you love to do, i.e. your "passions pastimes.

2. Focusing on your passion pastimes by investing increasing amounts of time in this area.

3. Becoming a genius at what you do and using that to be of greater service to others.

The Marriage of Choice

Some people get this horribly wrong by focusing on their Passion to the exclusion of life's practical realities, such as needing money to pay for food and accommodation. Don't just do something because you love to do it. And don't just do something because you can make some money out of it.

Create a marriage between Passion and profit. To me, that is the best of both worlds. Why not have it all? If you carefully choose a profitable Passion and follow it with thoughtful persistence, then the pennies will follow.

GIVING SOMETHING BACK

I believe that there is a lot of benefit for each party when a person acts in a way that helps another human being. The act of service may result in alleviating suffering or to making someone's life easier and more enjoyable. It may be around helping animals or improving corporate results. Whatever the Outcome, we all have a Contribution to make to the world.

We can of course do this professionally and get paid for it. In fact, I highly recommend this as a career strategy! But in addition, if you've been fortunate and clever enough to experience some success in your life, then I recommend that you set aside a portion of both your time and money to help others who have been less fortunate.

It's not so much a matter of giving people a handout, but rather a hand up. And while self-interest should not be the primary motivator for charitable acts of kindness, it helps that a generous heart is a prerequisite for peace of mind and Happiness.

I much admire the life of Helen Keller, the deaf and blind woman who, through Extra-Ordinary achievements, became a role model for millions. When it came to the subject of Contribution she once said: *"I am only one, but still I am one; I cannot do everything, but still I can do something; and just be-*

cause I cannot do everything, I will not refuse to do the something that I can do."

GOALS — THE MASTER KEY TO FULFILLING YOUR LIFE PURPOSE

Better health, wealth, and relationships are all highly desirable and as mentioned when we set about to achieve these worthwhile Goals, we will invariably create obstacles. As we Overcome these obstacles with mindful and persistent effort, we get the real gift in the Goal, which has less to do with the specific Outcome that we were after (new car, better relationship and so on) and much more to do with our learning how to Consciously choose our Inner (emotional and mental) realities as well as our Outer realities (health, wealth and relationships). Choice is true power and true Freedom.

And as you come up against obstacles and push through them, you'll also grow your Capacity for any number of Values such as persistence, patience, courage, and so on, as well as developing new skills and continuing to grow existing ones.

Finally, your increasing levels of Consciousness as well as your enlarged Capacity enables you to more powerfully serve others via Contribution, and thus your Life Purpose is being fulfilled.

Remember that Life Purpose is not a destination. By its very name, the Fulfillment of a Life Purpose only ceases as we draw our last breath. Until then, it's "game on" in the greatest adventure of all time — the continual expansion and Fulfillment of your potential in the form of Consciousness, Capacity and Contribution.

PART TWO:

YOUR COMFORT ZONE

Chapter 5:

The Curse of the Comfort Zone

I'm typing this with a broken wrist. It's uncomfortable.

The reason I have a broken wrist bone is that I have a Goal to race a Superbike. During practice, I had an argument with gravity after parting company from my bike at turn two of Eastern Creek raceway in Sydney. Needless to say, I lost the argument and the broken wrist was the result. If I'd stayed in the safety of my Comfort Zone, I'd have an arm that was still in one piece. No pain either.

Coincidentally, my partner also has a broken arm at the moment. Despite being a grandmother, she set a Goal to learn to ride a motor bike. She achieved her Goal and then she and the bike she was riding had a small disagreement with a low-lying brick wall. The final score was: Wall: 1. Bike and rider: 0.

So we've both got broken right arms and as we go for our regular walk along the beach with our matching casts, we are a real sight. People have literally stopped us and asked us what happened. We just tell them that there was "a two for one sale!"

As mentioned, if we had each stayed in our respective Comfort Zones, we would not have the discomfort of experiencing a broken arm. So why didn't we stay in our Comfort Zones? And why do millions of others choose to take unnecessary risks with myriad different sports and other challenges every day of every year when they could stay safe and secure in the pleasure dome of the Comfort Zone?

While it's true that if we had stayed in our respective Comfort Zones we would almost certainly not have experienced the pain of broken bones, we would also have never experienced the feelings of Freedom, fun, and Fulfillment that we've had countless times over decades of "going for it."

A Time and a Place for the Comfort Zone

Before going on to look at the concept of the Comfort Zone in more detail, let me just point out that there is a time and place for being in the Comfort Zone. We all need a degree of certainty in our lives. It provides a clear space in which you can take time to plan, to think, and to rejuvenate, and a place where you can complete important but routine actions.

Your Comfort Zone consists of known thought patterns and experiences that are stored in your Subconscious mind. And, when properly used, your Subconscious mind can automate all of those actions that you routinely want and need to complete in order to create the foundation on which to build a successful life.

For example, this morning I got out of bed, weighed myself, brushed my teeth, exercised, showered, meditated, had a nutritious breakfast, and planned my day. All of these things are within my Comfort Zone because I have habitually completed them for many years now. And all of them are important in terms of creating a platform on which to achieve my Goals.

So when I'm giving the Comfort Zone a bad rap later in this chapter, please bear in mind that what I am referring to is its overuse, not its proper use.

What's in Your Comfort Zone?

Within your Comfort Zone you will find a whole bunch of stuff that is familiar to you. Actually, staying in your Comfort Zone is a great way of maintaining the level of success that you have achieved to date. Unfortunately, it's also a great way to keep you at the same level. The only way to experience "Life at the Next Level" is to get out of your Comfort Zone. If nothing changes, nothing changes.

In your Comfort Zone you will find:

- Thoughts that you have always thought.
- Actions that you have always done that require little or no mental effort.
- Pleasure in the form of enjoyable experiences such as certain food, certain drinks, and (hopefully!) sex.
- Outcomes that you always get.

In short, the Comfort Zone is where everything is easy. It's all of the Outcomes you routinely experience and all of the Inputs, or actions, that you routinely do. It's the sum total of what you know that you can do and achieve without significant stress or undue mental effort. And as mentioned, it is a really great place to stay, unless you are interested in experiencing Freedom and Fulfillment.

YOUR ADVENTURE ZONE

If there is a Comfort Zone, then there must also be a place outside of that. Logically, this would be a "Discomfort Zone," but I prefer to call it the "Adventure Zone." In my experience, most adventures are uncomfortable to some extent, either physically, emotionally, or mentally, or all three. In fact any physical discomfort is normally exceeded by the mental discomfort. However, there is a risk that some people might misunderstand what I mean by the Adventure Zone. The Adventure Zone means different things to different people. Examples of "sampling" the Adventure Zone might include the following:

- Telling someone what you really want to say instead of holding back for fear of a reaction.
- Getting out of bed earlier than you normally do.
- Breaking out of your normal routine, e.g. going to a movie mid-week after work, on your own.
- Wearing something that's a little "out there."
- Singing at a karaoke club.
- Learning a new sport or hobby.
- Striking up a conversation with strangers at the café.
- Doing a course with a group of complete strangers.
- Climbing a mountain.
- Singing a song.
- Writing some poetry.

- Meditating.
- Sitting with an ill or dying person.
- Going for a promotion.
- Starting your own business.

… I suspect that the list could quite literally be endless.

You see, creating an adventure by moving out of your Comfort Zone is as much about an internal experience as it is about an external one. Colin Sisson, author of the classic self-published book *Inner Adventures* (available from www.iap.org.nz) claims that the best adventures are the inner ones. I agree, although I would add that in my experience, it's impossible to have an "Outer Adventure" without experiencing an "Inner Adventure."

Remember though that when it comes to getting out of the Comfort Zone, it pays to start small, grow your confidence, and then build from there. If you've made that a habit in your life to date, then it's time to take on even bigger adventures. Yahoo!

THE CLAN OF THE COMFORT ZONE DWELLERS

Socrates used to tell the story of a group of cave dwellers whose fearful disposition kept them virtual prisoners within their cave. Apologies to Socrates as I paraphrase a little.

Due to their superstitions and ignorance, the cave dwellers were so fearful that they would even cringe at the sight of their own shadow. After years of living in darkness with damp, cold, but familiar surroundings, one brave soul decided that he had nothing to lose in venturing out into the light of day.

Once out of the dark and damp cave, he experienced the beauty of green valleys, blue skies, clear running rivers, and snow-capped mountains as well as feeling strong and a sense of finally being free and alive. Excitedly, he ran back to the cave to share the joy of life outside. Instead of sharing his enthusiasm however, his clan told him that he was a deluded fool and not to talk such nonsense. After all, the cave had served them well over the years and who was he to suggest that it was better somewhere else?

Did he dare to question the wisdom of his ancestors with this foolish talk of Freedom and a new life?

Socrates' story of the cave dwellers has many meanings to it, but one that I take from it has to do with the price we pay for living too long within our Comfort Zones.

THE COMFORT ZONE DEFINED

When overused, there is nothing more insidious than your Comfort Zone. It's the place we all retreat to when we give up. It's the default setting that our Subconscious is programmed to return to should we ever be brave enough to explore life outside of our current level of experience.

One of my client, described people who live too much of their lives in their Comfort Zone as *"those who are happy in their misery."* The intriguing nineteenth century philosopher and essayist Henry David Thoreau claimed, *"The mass of men lead lives of quiet desperation. What is called resignation is con-*

firmed desperation." A tad bleak of old Henry perhaps, but not far from the mark I suspect, in terms of people being safely tucked away in the warmth of their Comfort Zone.

My definition of a Comfort Zone is a little stronger than my client's definition. When I speak to audiences about the Comfort Zone, I describe it as *"the place where you are happy to lie in the toxic vomit of our own mediocrity."* I don't want to make the Comfort Zone sound too comfortable!

A Late Check Out From Your Comfort Zone

As mentioned previously, it's not that being in your Comfort Zone is a bad thing; it's simply that there is a price to pay for staying there too long. It's like staying in bed for too long in the morning. It's warm, safe, and secure and nothing is required of you in terms of mental or physical effort. So you hit the snooze alarm and then hit it again and then finally turn the clock off and go back to sleep for "just a little longer." And nothing happens.

For what seemed like eternity but in fact was a brief period of time, one of my teenage daughters was "in between jobs" (read "unemployed') and started to make a habit of "getting up at the crack of midday." We agreed that she could continue to live in the family home without paying board on the condition that she would look for a job until she found one. To increase the odds of this Goal being achieved, we agreed that she was to be out of bed by 8:00 a.m. One morning, she was still languishing in bed at 9:00 a.m. and so I passed onto her a true pearl of wisdom, as we parents are inclined to do: "The most important lesson in life, my dear," I began as I figuratively stood on my soap box outside her bedroom door, "is that nothing happens until you get out of bed." As long as we lie in bed too long, nothing changes, everything stays the same. And it's exactly the same with our Comfort Zone. Like being in bed, we need some time in the Comfort Zone but the cost of staying or oversleeping is simply way too high.

Chapter 6:

The Cost of Staying in Your Comfort Zone

To use another analogy, overstaying in your Comfort Zone is a bit like arranging for a late check-out at the hotel, and then a later one still, and then a later one still. Before you know it, you've over stayed a week and the mini-bar bill is out of control and there's one hell of a price to pay! All kidding aside, that's a fairly accurate analogy because it makes the point that there is a cost to staying in the Comfort Zone too long and too often. The price is too high. You can't afford it. The cost is loss of Freedom and adventure, loss of learning, loss of growth, loss of development, and loss of progress, loss of self-respect, loss of Fulfillment, and in fact loss of life.

Loss of Freedom and Adventure

It may come as a surprise to you to learn that many people have a fear of Freedom. Being free to think, decide, and act means that we are also responsible for the results of that Freedom. If we are free and make a mistake, then we are accountable for that mistake. Some people are not prepared to pay the price for being free, which is to be accountable for one's own thoughts, actions, and results.

For several years, I was in prison. I love saying that and seeing people's reaction. However, I don't mean that I was an inmate or that I was there in any other than a purely voluntary capacity. The fact is that I choose to teach a program that I developed to show inmates in a maximum security prison how to go about getting their lives back on track. I teach on subjects such as how to set and achieve Goals, how to master emotions (without breaking something or hitting someone!), how to build Self-Esteem and also, what was for convicted criminals, the rather delicate subject of personal responsibility. Teaching personal responsibility in prison is always interesting given how many of my students stated that they "didn't do it !"

Escape from Freedom

One such prison facility was located in a country area and one day as I was driving out to take the program, my car was "buzzed" by a helicopter. Down the road a little farther I came to a roadblock, and a police officer told me I had to turn my car around and go back to where I came from. It turned out that a prisoner had escaped and that the prison was in "lockdown" mode, which meant that all inmates were confined to their cells and no one was going in and certainly no one else was getting out.

Most prisons have a pre-release system nowadays where an inmate will be given progressively increased levels of Freedom prior to their release so that they get mentally adjusted to the idea of Freedom. So they may be moved from a maximum security cell block to a medium security cell block and then to a pre-release house that is still within the prison parameters. It turns out that the escapee was a prisoner who was about to be released and he was on a working party in the fields near the prison as a part of his pre-release program. He had served some four years for armed robbery and was due to be released in ten days' time.

Freedom or Security?

I was initially astounded that someone could be so stupid or impatient that they would not serve out the last ten days of a four-year stretch. However, the next time I visited my inmate students, I learned that the escapee was in fact, neither stupid nor impatient. He was, in fact, simply full of fear. You see, after two nights and three days of false sightings throughout the country, our escapee friend was finally located — about 500 meters away from where he had been working. He had simply climbed over a few fences and sat down under a tree waiting to be recaptured.

The obvious question is "why would he do such a thing?" The answer is that he preferred to have the security of his Comfort Zone rather than the experience of Freedom. Strange though it may seem, he preferred the routine and certainty of prison to the uncertainty of Freedom. In prison, he may have had zero choice in terms of what he ate or when he ate, over what time he woke up or what time the lights went out, when he could shower, or when it was time for exercise, but he did have certainty. Like this prisoner, too many people choose the certainty of unhappiness over the uncertainty of Freedom. In this respect, they are also prisoners.

Chapter 7:

The Overrating of Certainty

That the Comfort Zone brings certainty is undeniable, and it is equally undeniable that we need some routine and certainty in our lives. But again, we can have too much of a good thing. Think about it. Of all the people on the planet, which groups would win the prizes for having the most certainty? The first group would be all of those people occupying space six feet below the earth's surface: dead people. The second-place getters would be prisoners, and then in third place would be monastics (nuns and monks). Still keen on certainty?

I remember listening with fascination to a speaker who was relating his story of being one of three New Zealanders who were the first group to kayak the length of the Antarctic Peninsula (**www.adventurephilosophy.com**). Mark Jones said that there were no detailed maps or descriptions of the area. This was fine by him, he said, since he wanted an adventure. In his terms, an adventure meant going into the unknown and having detailed maps would have meant less of an adventure.

With too much certainty we trade off Freedom and adventure. If these are important Values to you and you're not experiencing enough of them, then it's time to get out of your Comfort Zone. Become an escapee and stay that way; stay free.

Loss of Learning, Growth, Development and Progress

As mentioned earlier, it's a universal principle that there is no growth without effort. And since the Comfort Zone is an effortless place in which to stay there is no growth or progress within your Comfort Zone. Because "Life at the Next Level" requires an effort, making progress towards that Goal also requires an evacuation of your presence from the Comfort Zone.

Loss of Self-esteem

It seems to me that we human beings are wired to feel good about ourselves when we have a Goal, make an effort, and make some progress. Let's look at those three things.

Without the ongoing sense of purpose that Goals provide, people can easily become bored, lethargic, and apathetic. The Goal provides the motivation to make an effort.

One of the best cures for low Self-Esteem is the straightforward act of "make a list, take some action." The list is simply those actions that you need to take in order to change your current situation. It's like a series of simple mini-Goals and provides you with a sense of purpose and direction. Once you make an effort and Overcome the dreaded inertia, you will feel good about yourself. But having a Goal and making an effort will not keep you motivated forever. You will need to develop two skills that most people are bereft of. They are two of the best-kept secrets for increasing self- esteem. They are the twin skills of first becoming aware of your progress and secondly appreciating that progress.

Awareness of Progress

Most people are so focused on what they have yet to achieve they cannot see how far they have already come. It seems to be a human condition that we find it easier to exclusively focus on how far we have yet to go rather than pausing occasionally to reflect on how far we have already come.

Last year, I had a client who set Goals for his health, his relationships, and his business and had written down a list of one dozen actions that represented progress toward these Goals. At our first review a fortnight after the Goals were set, Sam began earnestly and thoroughly putting himself down because he had only completed a couple of the actions that he had committed to achieving. Once he stopped his self-flagellating, I asked Sam if his creating a list of Goals, identifying aligned actions, and completing two of them represented progress for him. Was it something that he had not done in the past? With some reluctance, he agreed that what he achieved indeed represented progress.

But instead of recognizing his progress, he compared what he had done to the ideal of perfection and as a consequence, enrolled himself into the largest club in the world, the "Self-beaters Club," simply because he had not perfectly executed all of the actions. Always remember this motto: "Progress, not perfection'

Appreciation of Progress

Appreciation has to do with highly valuing a thing. When a property increases in value, we say that it has "appreciated," and as a consequence, it's worth more; it's more highly valued.

If I make an effort to help someone and they really appreciate it, then I am much more likely to repeat my assistance for that person. But if I spend time and energy helping someone who does not appreciate my support, then I'll take it elsewhere. Why make an effort to help someone who doesn't really care? To me, this has nothing to do with needing to be thanked, but it has a lot to do with wanting to know if the recipient of my efforts valued the effort that I made and the result that I created. As mentioned, if they don't value or appreciate my contribution, then I would be better off taking my efforts somewhere else where my service was valued higher.

I think that most of us would agree that we wouldn't bother to make an effort to help someone unless that effort was appreciated. Let's face it, to continue making an effort with no appreciation being shown would be de-motivating, right?

So when you fail to appreciate your *own* efforts, your Subconscious is equally lacking in motivation to continue to repeat them. Thankless ingratitude is hardly the recipe for inspiring yourself to persist through difficult obstacles.

People who don't appreciate their progress are like the climber who, after much risk and effort, finally summits the mountain, but instead of pausing to admire the view, rushes down the other side in search of another mountain to climb.

On the subject of mountaineering, when I climbed Mount Cook in New Zealand, it was a big effort. The mountain is so big that at times I could literally be climbing for hours and yet, when I looked up, the summit appeared to be just as far away as ever. That was a discouraging feeling until I stopped and looked behind me to see how far I had come.

The Overrating Of Certainty

The appreciation of progress adds fuel to the furnace of motivation.

In Chapter 30, I'll go into more detail about how to create a simple structure that will raise your awareness and appreciation of the progress that you make. Why is it important that you feel good about your progress and more importantly about yourself? Because the simple fact is that people who feel good about themselves invariably produce great results.

Loss of Self-respect

Because of the way that I treat people (with courtesy and respect) and what I have achieved, I know that I have earned the respect of my children, my Partner, my friends, my business colleagues, my clients, and even some of my business competitors. But none of this is important to me compared to earning the respect of the "man in the mirror." And I get self-respect when I get my butt out of the Comfort Zone and do what I said I was going to do. I also know that I lose self-respect when I quit too soon and retreat back to the seductive warmth and security of my old patterns.

Loss of Fulfillment

Many years ago, I founded a company that is still going strong today. It's called the Entrepreneur's Success Programme (ESP). You can check it out at **www.espcoach.com.** I created EPS's internal Vision statement to focus my team on what we were all about as an organization. Our Vision refers to "the expansion and Fulfillment of human and business potential, globally." The interesting thing about human potential is that no one has found the limits yet. Which is why I referred to "the expansion and Fulfillment" of human potential rather than simply "the Fulfillment." To be more accurate, I could have written "the expansion and Fulfillment and then the expansion and Fulfillment again and then the expansion and Fulfillment again and then the expansion ...'; you get the idea. The point is that no one has ever yet found the limits of human potential. After many thousands of years, or millions depending on whether you believe the creationists or the evolutionists, we still have not found the place where we exhaust our ability to learn, grow, and achieve the Extra- Ordinary.

So the great game of life is this: create an experience of what I call "Life at the Next Level," and then to get to that next level and then the level after that and so on. The reality is that there is no final destination in the journey of life. There is, as they say, only a journey. That's because there are no known limits on human potential.

This means that the only way to experience a sense of Fulfillment is to keep learning, keep growing, and to keep developing. We do that by continuing to explore and create adventures and of course all of these things are non-existent within our Comfort Zone. What it comes down to is this: the only way for you to grow and expand your potential is to experience life outside the Comfort Zone. There is no Fulfillment within your Comfort Zone.

Loss of Life

I find it morbidly fascinating how often people will retire and then be dead within a couple of years. It's changing a bit now as the retirement industry breathes life into our more mature years, but for a few decades there were a whole bunch of people, primarily men, who retired then set about dying with alarming efficiency. When they were working in their career or business, they had Goals, a sense of purpose, and were constantly being challenged to achieve. In short, they spent significant chunks of their time outside of their Comfort Zone. All too often, when they retired, they found themselves inside a "purpose vacuum." My theory is that because there was no Conscious purpose and no new challenges created, the soul decided that there was no point in hanging around and consequently left the body.

Getting out of your Comfort Zone is a life-preserving act. In fact, not only is it life-preserving in terms of the length of your life, but it's also life-preserving in terms of quality of life. By that I mean that life is lived more fully when it's lived outside of the Comfort Zone. As someone once said: *"live life on the edge, it's less crowded there."* There is no adrenaline rush, no exhilaration, and no peak experiences within a Comfort Zone.

Time to Take Stock

Take a Comfort Zone inventory of your life. How much of what you did in the past week was spent inside your Comfort Zone? For most people, the answer would probably be "all of it." A healthier answer would be "most of it" or "some of it." As mentioned above, we need some routine, some certainty, and some periods of quiet rejuvenation where nothing is demanded of us. It's when we get too much of the routine and too much of the certainty that our soul, our psyche, our being, starts to shrivel and shrink from under-nourishment.

In fact, it may be easier for you to complete a stock take on your experiences *outside* the Comfort Zone. So, make a list of the times in the last week when you *chose* to put yourself in the Adventure/Discomfort Zone. It could be the time you gave your boss some feedback about his or her operating style, or it could be getting out of bed earlier than normal to exercise. You might surprise yourself at how talented you really are at creating Adventure Zone experiences.

COMFORT ZONES ARE A MOVING TARGET

What happens when we choose to go into the Adventure Zone is that we expand our Comfort Zone. I remember completing the excellent Technical Mountaineering Course, or TMC that was run by Alpine Guides (see www.alpine-guides.co.nz) in preparation for climbing Mt Cook. Later I was recalling the experience with a fellow course member. Sam, my guide, overheard us excitedly talking about some of the experiences. "Anyone would think that doing TMC was some sort of adventure" he said. I told him that to us it was a very big adventure indeed. Falling down crevasses, walking along a frozen mountain ridge with a 1,000 meter drop just a meter away, and learning how to climb vertical ice walls was very definitely an adventure for me. But to Sam, one of New Zealand's most experienced guides, it was the equivalent of a Sunday afternoon stroll in the park. One person's Comfort Zone is another person's Adventure Zone.

Chapter 8:

Lessons From the Comfort Zone

What are the lessons here? Everything is in the Adventure Zone until it's in the Comfort Zone. Look at how kids learn and grow from the instant they are born, if not before. Probably the only Comfort Zone activities they experience are sleeping and suckling. The rest of their life is one huge Adventure Zone. And look at how much they learn and develop and how much they really live. What starts out as an effort becomes effortless once you have mastered it. Everything is hard until it's easy. That means that like the newborn, once an activity moves from the Adventure Zone into the Comfort Zone you have grown.

So the point is this: as you expand your Comfort Zone, don't settle. It's all too easy to be seduced by the promise of pleasure and to find yourself sinking slowly into the suffocating numbness of normality. As the quite brilliant 20th century female author Anais Nin (see **www.anaisnin.com**) said *"I postpone death by living, by suffering, by error, by risking, by giving, by losing."* That's my kind of gal — in a "glad she's not my wife" sort of way.

Always remember: The size of the Comfort Zone changes with success. It's a never-ending journey. Never settle. Never stop. Just a pause now and then will suffice.

MAKING FRIENDS WITH DISCOMFORT

As alluded to above, it's possible to become comfortable with discomfort. It's said that the East German rowers who went on to win gold at the 1980 Moscow Olympics would train to the mantra of "I love pain, I love pain." I'm not suggesting anything as extreme as becoming masochistic, but there is some merit in making a friend out of discomfort.

There are certain habits that I have in my life, some of which I have practiced for over half of my lifetime. I maintain these habits as a way of making friends with discomfort. Most people don't "get" why I do these and simply shake their heads in dismay.

For starters, I typically have two cold showers per day. Depending on the weather, I may start the shower with hot water, but I invariably finish it with a couple of minutes of cold water. Also, I practice not bracing or grimacing when the cold-water hits, but simply experiencing it without judgment. I do the same thing after my twice-daily sauna when I dive into the swimming pool in the winter. And with an overnight low of three degrees last night, I can assure you the water was cold this morning. Obviously, check with your doctor to make sure your heart is up to the rigor of cold showers and swims before you try this. I do these things to train my Subconscious that discomfort is OK.

I have to give US literary giant Mark Twain all the credit for the other habit. He advised that *"If you have to eat a frog, don't look at it too long."* In other words, if you have something that you would prefer not to do, then do it sooner rather than later. Such a simple lesson and yet seemingly for many people, such a hard one for them to learn. For example, if you are going to have a conversation with someone who you think may be difficult, do it sooner rather than later. If you have news for someone that you think they may not like, then face them up to reality today rather than tomorrow. If you have a creditor that you can't pay, deal with it immediately — don't wait for them to call you. Keep "short accounts" of messes such as physical messes, relationship messes, unfinished business matters and so on. Keeping short accounts of messes means that you don't let them hang around too long. Clean them up. Choose to experience a little discomfort up front rather than a great deal of pain at some point later in time as the mess accumulates.

For example, if I am traveling early in the morning, I pack the night before. If I am parking my car or one of my motorbikes, I will back it in so I can drive or ride straight out when I leave. I have made a habit of sitting and planning before I act, and I can tell you that did not come naturally for a long time. Always take the pain up front. It's normally a lower voltage dose than if you leave it until later!

By the way, Mark Twain also said *"If you have to eat two frogs, eat the biggest one first !"* If you have two messes, deal with the most unpleasant one first.

Last Thoughts on the Adventure Zone

I have noticed that the times of greatest Fulfillment in my life, the *"yes!"* moments, the peak performances, have without exception been those times when I got out of my Comfort Zone. I experienced more Fulfillment on the playing field than I ever did sitting in the grandstands. And although I've enjoyed watching races of all descriptions over the years, I've never felt the buzz the same as when it was me crossing the finishing line.

> *"To know what you don't know you have to go where you never go."*
>
> **—Anon**

PART THREE:

BUILDING GOAL FOUNDATIONS – VALUES AND VISION

Chapter 9:

The Importance of Your Personal Life Values

Life Planning Pyramid

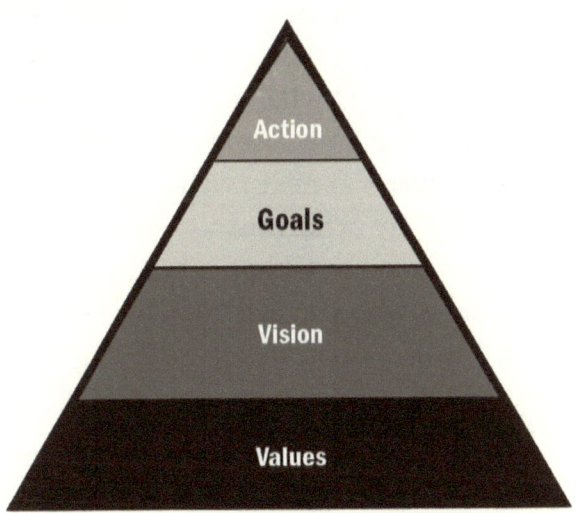

THE FIRST PLACE to start with planning your Extra-Ordinary Life is with your Values. I want to take a little time to explain why I don't recommend going straight into your Goals. Jumping into forming your Goals prior to working out your Values can result in feelings of frustration and lack of Fulfillment. Too many high-achievers never experience a sense of Fulfillment because they fail to understand that their Goals are more to do with *being* than with *having*.

Many unfulfilled high-achievers succeed with a Goal of more income or a better career, but fail to realize that the ultimate purpose of the Goal has more to do with the development of their "Being" than it does to do with the development of their "having."

The key to Fulfillment is not only to achieve your Goals, but also to value the parallel increase in your levels of Consciousness, Capacity, and Contribution. So before you embark on the process of setting Goals (what you want to "have") it's best to first work out your Values (who you want to "be"). Once you have worked out the big picture of who you want to be (Values) and what your perfect life looks like (Vision), then we can go on to the detail of what you want to achieve (Goals) over the next twelve months or so. Stephen Covey quite rightly exhorts us to "start with the end in mind" and as mentioned in Chapter 1, all you will have at the end of your life is who you are; your Being, your Values.

STEP ONE: IDENTIFY YOUR VALUES

At conferences where I speak on "Achieving the Extra-Ordinary," I sometimes tell the story of *Sophie's Choice*, which is a novel by American author William Styron that became a movie starring Meryl Streep as a Polish woman who stood at the gates of the concentration camp Auschwitz with her two young children. Sophie is forced by an SS officer to choose one of her children to be sent to the gas chambers. The other child is to be spared and sent to the children's camp. Of course, Sophie refuses to choose and the SS officer orders a guard to take both children to the gas chambers. The anguish that Sophie must have felt is unimaginable. However, just before the SS guard snatches both of the children out of her arms, Sophie, in a moment of blind panic, pushes her little girl into the arms of the guard. The scene changes and the little girl is seen being carried by the guard toward the chimney stacks with her arms outstretched toward her mother, pleading with her mother to be rescued, while Sophie, in abject anguish, can only stand and watch. The movie goes on and we learn that Sophie survives the holocaust only to take her own life afterward, as she cannot bring herself to live with the consequences of her actions.

Needless to say *Sophie's Choice* is an emotional rollercoaster of a movie. So why do I tell people about it?

What *Sophie's Choice* and movies like it do so well is to push the pause button on our otherwise busy lives and cause us to reflect on what is most important to us. If you are in business or in a career, you'll have noticed that technology and competition has forced the pace of life to increase significantly over the last three decades. Pressing decisions, deadlines, and demands can create a maelstrom of activity that acts as a snowstorm on the mental radar scope of our minds. We no longer see the big picture of our life; all we can see are the 67 e-mails, 10 client meetings, 3 reports, and a list of 45 "to-do" errands and projects that make up our day.

If we're not careful to stay proactive, we end up feeling like a pinball in the great pinball machine of life. I suspect that, like me, you'd rather feel like the flipper than the pinball.

Sophie's Choice brings us back to our Values. What's the most important thing to you in the world? Let me give you some choices. In working with top achievers, prisoners, business leaders, and my own family and friends I've found that all their Goals can fall into one of three categories. I've listed these three categories in order of priority.

1. Health

If you are anything like my clients, you'll want to improve your health, perhaps lose weight or cut down on addictions to substances such as nicotine or alcohol or caffeine. You'll probably also be quite keen on increasing your energy levels and improving your emotional life so that you feel more Happiness and more peace of mind. In addition, you may also have cultural or spiritually related Goals and Goals that relate to sports, hobbies, and other interests. I summarize all of these Goals under the broad heading of "Health Goals" as they all relate to personal well- being.

2. Relationships

Next on the list are people-orientated Goals. You may have personal Goals to find a Life Partner or to develop a deeper and more enjoyable relationship with your existing Life Partner, to support your children, and to cultivate some worthwhile friendships. Goals that involve supporting other people through the giving of your time in charitable acts with clubs, societies, or associations would also fall under the category of a Relationship Goal.

3. Money

Financially-focused Goals may include Goals for your career or business, personal wealth accumulation, and hopefully some Goals for philanthropy. Your money Goals may also include new houses, renovations, or landscaping plus new toys such as cars, motorbikes, boats or what I call "shiny things."

So what's this have to do with *Sophie's Choice*? Well, it's all about sorting out what you Value the most. In order to explain what I mean, I am going to personify the above categories by asking you to imagine that you have three children: Health, relationships and money. So I invite you to imagine that child number one is called "Health," child number two is called "Relationships" and child number three is called "Money."

Now let's put you in the queue at Auschwitz just behind Sophie. You've just witnessed the horror of her decision and now the SS officer turns to you and your three "children" and faces you with a similar choice: "Choose one to die and two to live!."

What would you do? Which "child" would you choose to die? Fortunately, none of us has to face such a challenging decision. But if you were forced, like Sophie, to choose to sacrifice one "child" (your Health, your Relationships or your Money) in order to secure the others which one would you choose?

Would it be your Health child? Probably not. You can't really enjoy your Relationships or your Money if you are stuck in some hospital bed with tubes sticking out of every orifice in your body! Loss of mental or emotional well-being is equally unthinkable. In fact, I've put this scenario to literally of thousands of people over the years and I've never had one person yet who would consciously choose to sacrifice their Health in order to preserve their Relationships and Money.

So I think it's reasonable to assume that Health stays.

That leaves us with a choice between keeping the love in your life, your Relationships, or the Money. Which one would you choose to sacrifice, if you had to? At this point, someone once asked me, jokingly, "How much money are we talking about?" At least I hope that he was joking.

Almost everyone agrees that, if they had to, they would sacrifice the quality of their financial life before they chose to destroy their Relationships.

So you can see how *Sophie's Choice* can shine the spotlight of awareness on our Values. Most people value their Health first — physical, mental, emotional, spiritual, and cultural well-being. Next on, most people's list of Values comes their Relationships. Money-related Values come last.

That's not to say that money is not important to most people; it's just that it places third on the list. A bronze medal if you like. Important, but not first place.

If you are like ninety-nine percent of humans, the test of *Sophie's Choice* confirms what you Value the most. So when you are sitting on your rocking chair, aged 99 and you are looking back over your life, you are going to score yourself on how you did by measuring how closely aligned your actions were with your Values.

Are you living your life in accordance with your Values? It's easy to figure this out. Simply ask yourself two questions:

Question 1: "Do I use my time in a manner that is aligned with what I Value?"

For example, if you say that your Health is important to you but don't invest any time keeping fit, then you don't have an alignment between your Values and your time. If a deep and satisfying relationship with your Life Partner or child is something you Value but you don't invest time in this area, then you are not "walking the talk." This is normally referred to as a lack of integrity. You may be horrified to think of yourself as lacking integrity, but the truth is that any time that any of us fail to align our use of time with our deepest-held Values, then we are in "integrity deficit." Worth contemplating, isn't it?

If you are experiencing this lack of alignment, then chances are you feel some inner tension. All does not feel well within, in relation to your Health value. Self-Esteem, or how we feel about ourselves, increases when we create an alignment between our deeply held Values and how we use our time.

Question 2: "Do I behave in a manner that is aligned with what I Value?"

Your Goals are normally a reflection of your Values. They represent what is important for you to achieve and are like a more detailed description of your Values.

So it's a very similar proposition to the first question, but instead of focusing your mind on Values-aligned use of *time*, I am asking you to consider if your *behavior* is Values-aligned.

If the answer is "yes," then congratulations, you are one of very few. Chances are though that some of your behavior is spent in an aligned manner and some is spent non-aligned. For example, if you value high energy but eat junk food for lunch, then you are not demonstrating Values-aligned behavior. If, however, for dinner you eat Cajun-grilled fish with healthy salad (go easy on the mayo!), then you're aligned again. It's darned hard to lead a one hundred percent aligned life, but the aim is to get closer and closer to total alignment.

> *Aligning your life with your Values*
>
> *When your car's wheels are out of alignment, it normally means that one or both of the front wheels want to pull in a different direction to the rear wheels. This creates unnecessary friction on the tires, thus reducing their life expectancy as well making it harder for you to keep on the road as you struggle with the steering wheel.*
>
> *It's the same with the alignment of your Values and how you use your time and how you behave. If you don't have enough Values alignment, then you will feel a lot of tension through the "steering wheel" of your mind and life will seem like an overwhelming effort. And like the front tires that are pulling in the wrong direction, there is a fair chance that your life expectancy will dramatically shorten. And if the length of your life does not reduce through non-Values-aligned living, the quality of it certainly will and you will struggle to keep your life on track.*

The way that a person behaves is in fact the clearest indicator of their Value priorities. For example, if someone says that they value generosity but never gives their time or money without thought of return, then they do not value generosity. Their actions indicate that they value selfishness.

Again, if someone says that they value having high energy, but they repeatedly fail to get enough sleep, then they don't really value high energy. At the very least, they value something else (e.g. working late, watching television) more than they value high energy.

We are human "beings." "To be or not to be?" was Shakespeare's question. We can "be" patient or impatient, wise or stupid, reckless or careful, loving or hurtful, flexible or inflexible, strong or weak, brave or cowardly. Who are you being at the moment? Perhaps you are being "open-minded" or you are being "contemplative." In fact, we are capable of being any one of a thousand Values.

But here's the kicker: who we choose to "be" will determine what we "have." Hence, behave (be-have). Here's the sequence: being – doing – having. The "doing" part refers of course to the way that we "be-have." How we "be-have" forms the bridge between "being" and "having." Perhaps that's what Christ was referring to when he was asked how his disciples could be recognized; *"By their fruit you will know them,"* he said. We know what we truly value by the fruit that our "Being" and the consequent "doing" or "behaving" brings forth.

Most people get themselves all screwed up when they get the starting point wrong. They start with what they want to Have (Goals) and work backwards through what they will Do and then they figure out who they have to Be in order to Have what they want. They believe that once they "Have" enough (normally money), then they can "Do" what they want and "Be" the person they want to be: happier and freer. The reality though, is that even those people who end up Having more than enough money still end up "Being" insecure and driven until they change their old mental patterns by developing new mental Capacities such as peace of mind and confidence around financial matters.

The bottom line is this: people who achieve their Goals by starting with "Have" often acquire the outer show of success, but find that it's disproportionately matched by inner feelings of inadequacy and scarcity. They achieve the outer trappings of success but still feel unfulfilled and inadequate on the inside, if not Consciously then certainly at a Subconscious level. Self-esteem stays low and the show of material success such as cars, property, and label clothes become a mask to cover inner feelings of frustration and emptiness.

"Behave" or "be-have" explains what "Doing" is all about. It invites us to start at the beginning, at the point of our Values or who we are Being.

This is why I like to preface Goal-creation with a session on Values clarification. What is most important for you to Be? What do you Value most in life?

Goals are still critically important. They give our lives meaning and provide the raw material for increasing Consciousness, Capacity, and Contribution. Putting it another way, Goals are not an end in themselves; they are the means to an end of fulfilling your Life Purpose (Consciousness, Capacity, and Contribution).

Always remember, if you are going to experience a life of inner-success (Love, Happiness, Freedom, Fulfillment, and

Peace of mind) as well as outer-success (physical well-being, financial independence, career, family, friends, and community), then you need to make sure that there is an alignment between your Values, where you invest your time, and how you Behave. Additionally, you will want to start work now on Being (Happy, Free, etc.) as a priority ahead of Doing or Having.

Happiness is a daily decision so you can begin by stating your intention at the start of every day to simply "Be" Happy.

Chapter 10

Identifying Your Personal Life Values

Values Identification Exercise One

This exercise is very simple. Go down the list of Values and tick up to seven Values that you feel are important for you to develop. I suggest that at this stage you don't stop to rationalize your choices; simply tick the Values that you feel drawn to. Of course, you could tick all of the words on this list as most people will Value all of these states to one extent or another. However, limit yourself to the ones that really leap out at you. Remember, no more than seven. If you find it easier, you can tick more than seven and then cull some out.

Acceptance	Authenticity	Challenge
Accomplishment	Automony	Charity
Achievement	Awareness	Children
Advancement	Balance	Clarity
Adventure	Belonging	Cleanliness
Aesthetics	Broadminded	Commitment
Affection	Business	Community
Altruism	Camaraderie	Communication
Appearance	Career	Compassion
Art	Caring	Competency
Astuteness	Certainty	Competition

Confidence	Health	Peace
Congruency	Helping others	Peace of mind
Consciousness	Homemaking	Persistence
Contribution	Honesty	Personal development
Control	Incomparable	Personal growth
Cooperation	Independence	Persuading
Courage	Indomitable	Physical exercise
Courtesy	Integrity	Philanthropy
Creativity	Influence	Physical change
Culture	Innovative	Physical independence
Decisivness	Insight	Physical work
Dignity	Inspiration	Pleasure
Desire	Integrity	Politics
Determination	Intellectual stimulation	Potent
Discovery	Intuition	Power to change myself
Economic Return	Joy	Power to change my reality
Ectasy	Justice	Precision
Education	Kindness	Prestige
Energy	Knowledge	Problem solving
Enlightenment	Leadership	Progress
Emotional independence	Learning	Public attention
Ethics	Legacy	Recognition
Equality	Leisure	Relaxing
Excitement	Leverage	Religion
Fairness	Life partner	Research
Faith	Love	Resolve
Fame	Loyalty	Resourcefulness
Family	Management	Respect
Fast Pace	Marriage	Risk
Financial Independence	Material status	Romance
Flexible	Medical independence	Routine
Focus	Mental change	Security
Forthright	Moral Fulfilment	Selectiveness
Freedom	Morality	Self awareness
Free time	Motivation	Self belief
Friendship	Music	Self confidence
Fulfilment	Nature	Self esteem
Fun	Orderliness	Self expression
Genius	Organisation	Self honesty
Giving	Ownership	Self image
Growth	Own space	Self preservation
Guided	Passion	Self respect
Happiness	Patience	Self worth

Service to others	Supportive	Variety
Sexual Fulfilment	Team work	Vision
Simplicity	Tidiness	Vocation
Solitude	Time flexibility	Wealth
Sport	Transformation	Win-win
Spirituality	Travel	Wisdom
Stability	Truth	Work
Strength	Truthfulness	
Succeeding	Understanding	

VALUES IDENTIFICATION EXERCISE TWO

Get yourself a separate piece of paper on which to write the answers to the following questions.

Question 1: Imagine that you only had *one year* to live. How would use that time? What would you do differently? What behaviors would you change? Write down the answers before going on to the next question.

Question 2: Imagine that you only had *one week* to live. How would use that time? What would you do differently? What behaviors would you change? Write down the answers before going on to the next question.

Question 3: Imagine that you only had *one day* to live. How would use that time? What would you do differently? What behaviors would you change? Write down the answers before going on to the next question.

The answers to these questions will reveal what you Value the most because, as mentioned previously, how you use your time and how you behave is a reflection of what you truly Value.

VALUES IDENTIFICATION EXERCISE THREE

Imagine that it is many years from now and that you are in fact dead. Not a pleasant thought, maybe but bear with me for a moment! You are going to witness your own funeral in Spirit form and even stranger still is the fact that you have been asked to write the eulogy that your Life Partner is going to deliver.

To summarize:

1. You are now dead.

2. You get to witness your own funeral in Spirit.

3. You are going to write the eulogy that your Life Partner is going to deliver.

So here's the question: If you had lived your life perfectly, in one hundred percent alignment with your Values, what words would you want your Life Partner to use to describe you?

For example, would you want your Life Partner to say that you were strong, compassionate, supportive, and funny, or that you had integrity, were reliable, or that you were challenging in a positive sort of way? I'm sure that you get the idea. Without referring back to the Values list above, what words come to mind that would describe the ideal you?

Remember, we are not talking about how your Life Partner might describe you now, but rather after you have lived the perfect life by your own standards. Finally, as you make your list, remember the Values to note are the ones that are important to you, not necessarily to anyone else.

Limit your list to seven Values or character traits (the latter also being Values). Note that if you don't currently have a Life Partner then you could imagine a future Life Partner. If you don't want a Life Partner in way shape or form, then imagine a close friend whose opinions you really respect.

Once you have finished writing down up to seven words or phrases, then repeat the exercise from the perspective of one of your children. If you don't have children, you could imagine a future child. If you don't want children in the future, then imagine this from the perspective of one of your parents. Again, limit your list to seven words or phrases.

Values Prioritization Exercise

Now you have completed three Values Identification Exercises and will have a list of up to 28 Values, although in all likelihood some will be repeated so you may have fewer.

Now, cull the list down to twelve Values. This won't be easy, but remember that while all Values will have some level of importance to you, we are interested in ones that are supremely important.

Once you have your list of twelve Values, then prioritize them. So place a "1" next to your most important Value and then a "12" next to the twelfth most important value. Then do number "2" and then number "11" and so on until every Value has a number next to it from 1 through 12.

These top twelve Values are what I call your Primary Life Values. The prioritization of these Values is important as it will help you to resolve dilemmas when you find that you have two Values in conflict.

For example, two of my Values are "Family" and "Adventure." I worked out that Family is a higher-prioritized Value to me than Adventure, so when my family was younger I would plan my adventures in such a way that I would have enough quality time with my Life Partner and the children. I made sure that I was there for most of the kids' sporting events and we had plenty of family holidays and so on.

Once you have completed the prioritization of your Values, type or write the list up along with a brief explanation of what that Value means to you. See the inset box for some examples.

The following is a list of Values along with a brief explanation.

Adventure:	Growth via challenge, adventure, new experiences, exploration, travel, sport, adrenaline.
Freedom:	Mental, financial, physical, emotional, medical, Conscious choice.
Consciousness:	Personal development, enlightenment, Happiness, ego-free.
Love:	Unconditional acceptance and giving, togetherness, sharing, friendship, respect, courtesy.
Authentic communication:	Truth, honesty, openness, self-expression.
Energy:	High levels of physical, mental, and spiritual energy.
Legacy:	Make a difference, impact, inspire, role model, philanthropy, volunteer, contribution.
Fun:	To enjoy the journey, every bit of it regardless of the experience.
Fulfillment:	To fulfill my life purpose, to be happy, help others to be free, and to realize their potential.

The following is a list of Values along with a brief explanation.

Strength:	Persistence, endurance, choosing to be strong.
Astuteness:	Wisdom, being smart, making intelligent choices, using "reality thinking."
Contribution:	To make a difference in the lives of others.
Consciousness:	Happiness, Freedom, ego-free, power to change my reality.
Integrity:	To walk my talk and to integrate my values.
Family:	To provide support, love, and to be a great role model.

Congratulations, if you have completed the exercises above, you now have a list of your Primary Life Values listed in order of priority and a brief description of what each Value means to you.

You may find that your list of Values changes over time, but it's probably not going to change a lot. In all likelihood, the order of priority will change as your circumstances change. For example, if you value "Financial Independence" and you then go on to create it as a reality, it may drop down the list. It's not that Financial Independence is no longer important; it's just that now that the need has been satisfied there may be other Values which increase in importance. Scarcity tends to increase the importance of a Value and the opposite is also true.

Now that you have your Values sorted, it's a matter of ensuring that you spend your time and behave in a Values-aligned manner. And of course, having become clear on what you Value, you are in a position to create Goals that are aligned with those Values. In turn, as you set about achieving your Goals, you will naturally be investing your time and behaving in a Values-aligned manner. This is one of the secrets to Fulfillment.

Store your set of Personal Life Values somewhere that lets you refer to it often. You may choose to have this on your PC, but also print it out and place it in your planner, your diary or scheduling device so that you can continue to work on it and also to stay Conscious of the person that you want to become.

If you want a place to store these Values as well as your answers to the rest of the exercises in this book, you can visit **www.tompoland.com and download** my "Goal Creation and Achievement Planner" from the "Online Shop."

Remember too that when you hit an obstacle on your way to achieving your Goals, you'll be able to "see the gift" in the obstacle much clearer when you can relate the challenge that you are facing back to the development of one or more of your Values, such as courage or persistence.

But before we get to the Goals, we need to do a little work on creating a motivational and inspirational Vision of what your life will look like in the future.

And before we get to the vision, I want to make some distinctions between Wasting time, Spending time and Investing time. As you read on, you'll see how the way that we use time is analogous to the way that we use money.

WASTING TIME

Wasting time is what we do when we spend energy on activity that is not taking us toward the Fulfillment of our Goals. It's similar to Wasting money by buying things that we will never use. Wasting time actually takes us away from our

Goals and not towards them. For example, I Wasted time last weekend going to the racetrack with my motorbike and practicing when I was too tired. I failed to listen to my body and my intuition. I forced myself to do it because I thought "I should." After the fourth time I rode off the end of the track and into the gravel pits, I packed it in and came home. That was Wasting time. Or it could be that you are a compassionate soul who tries to rescue other people from their suffering by trying to do everything for them. Some parents suffer from this pattern of Wasting time. The reality is that there is no point in caring more about someone else's suffering than that person cares themselves.

Classic time-wasters include most television viewing (except for the footy!), gossip-type magazines, procrastination, over-analyzing, sleeping in beyond what you need, taking a wrong direction in life, not listening to your intuition, and the list goes on.

Note that when I talk about Wasting time, I am not including the proper use of "time out" from expending energy for the purpose of rejuvenation. Lazing around in a hammock by the pool is not Wasting time if you need to recharge your mental batteries.

SPENDING TIME

Spending time is what happens when we engage in activities that satisfy short-term demands but do nothing to create a return in the longer time. Using money again as an analogy, we often Spend money on necessary and important items such as groceries or petrol. We need to Spend the money on items such as these to maintain our quality of life.

It's not a Waste of money to pay for such items; it's just that it does little in terms of building a better future.

Similarly, we Spend time when we eat to keep blood sugar levels up, when we sleep, or when we brush our teeth. Spending time is primarily about maintenance. Important and necessary, even vital, but it's not at the same level as Investing time.

INVESTING TIME

What makes Investing time different is that it provides us with a return on our efforts which we can "reinvest" to create an even better future.

The comparison with money is again self-evident. When we Invest money wisely, as opposed to wasting or spending it, we gain a return on that Investment which we can then reinvest and then gain an even greater return and so on. That's why the first million is always the hardest.

We Invest time when we engage in activity that is not mandatory for daily living but will increase our capabilities in the longer term. For example, if you learn a new skill at work, you are of more value to your employer or the marketplace, and so you can use that skill to help you get your life to the next level of financial success and career Fulfillment.

Financial Investments do not normally provide an immediate return and it's the same with Investing time. We need to learn to take some of the time that we would normally Waste or Spend, and set it aside so that we can Invest it into building a better future.

Provided that there is some Goal-related value, the following are all examples of Investing time:

- Exercising
- Changing to healthier eating
- Quality time with a loved one
- Meditation
- Attending courses or workshops
- Learning new skills or capabilities
- Planning and thinking
- Listening to audio teachings on CD or from digital files
- Studying or reading

Just the same as Investing money, most people have difficulty in coming to grips with the need to Invest time. The ability to really leverage your results only comes when you learn to take a portion of what you are Wasting or Spending for short-term gratification and put it aside so that you can benefit in the longer term.

So have a think about your last seven days. How many hours did you Invest? That's the crunch. How many hours did you put aside with no thought of immediate return, into activity that will help you experience greater success in the future? A bias toward Wasting and Spending time is otherwise known as the P.I.G. syndrome: the "Problem of Instant Gratification!"

Chapter 11:

The Value of a Personal Life Vision

Let's Revisit my Life Planning Model
Life Planning Pyramid

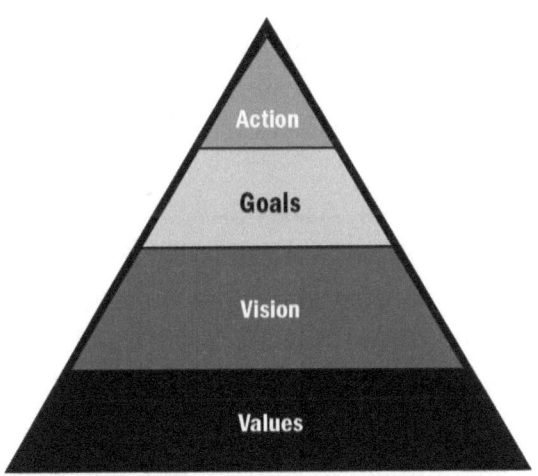

So now we can tick off Values. In terms of the planning phase, they are well and truly "done and dusted."

The next step prior to creating Goals is to work out what your perfect life looks like. I refer to this outline of your perfect life as your "Vision." A great Vision statement paints a picture of what your one hundred percent ideal life will look like when it's done.

There is a story concerning Michelangelo and the statue of an Angel that is today on display in Venice. If you take the appropriate tour, the guide will tell you that after Michelangelo had chiseled this exquisite statue, he was asked by an awestruck admirer how he had managed to create such a masterpiece out of an ordinary block of solid marble. Michelangelo is said to have replied, *"It was easy: I first saw the angel in the marble and then I simply chiseled to set it free."*

Vision is like seeing your Angel in the marble of your life. It's imagining your life as a masterpiece — a Van Gogh or a Rembrandt. To work out what your masterpiece will look like when you've finished chiseling, ask yourself this question: "If I had no shortage of money, no shortage of time, and no fear of failure, what is it that I would dare to achieve, what sort of life would I create?" Once you have answered that question to your satisfaction, you have your Vision.

In the remarkable book, *Man's Search for Meaning*, Austrian psychiatrist Victor Frankl describes both his experience as a Jew during the holocaust and more specifically some of the lessons he learned from those unimaginably difficult Concentration Camp years.

Just for a moment imagine yourself as a witness at the gates of Auschwitz as the Nazis are processing a queue full of fearful families of Jews. Which ones would do you think would survive the experience? Frankl said that if we had tried to guess which fortunate few in that queue would endure, we would most likely have picked the strongest ones, or the best-looking ones or the ones with skills that the Nazis valued the most. And as Frankl says, we would have been wrong.

The Value Of A Personal Life Vision

Frankl states that after a few months of living in subhuman conditions, with horribly long forced marches over frozen winter wastelands and inhumane forced labor, after routine torture and witnessing indiscriminate killings, after months of sleeping six to a bunk with one blanket in sub-freezing temperatures and a bowl of watery soup and a stale piece of bread each day to sustain each person, all of the good looks, the previous physical and even the mental strength, and any skills were good for nothing as each person was reduced to a shell of their former self.

What Frankl discovered is that the common denominator among those who survived the concentration camps was that they had a powerfully compelling picture, or Vision, of what their life would look like after the war was over. Each soul who survived had a dream that they would cling to that motivated them to keep going.

Frankl himself made several decisions when he found himself in the living hell that we now call the Concentration Camps. Firstly, he decided that he would survive the experience. Secondly, he made a commitment to help as many of his fellow captives to do the same, and lastly, he vowed to learn as much as possible from the holocaust experience so that he could use what he learned to help others once the war was over.

What Frankl discovered was that a person's will to survive was totally and completely destroyed unless that person had a powerful reason to continue living. He describes how, on occasions, he would come across a pair of prisoners who had made a suicide pact. He would talk to each one and uncover something important to them about their future after the war; something that was worth living for. It may have been an author's book that was unfinished, or a daughter waiting for the war to end back in Vienna. Frankl himself would imagine lecturing in a warm and brightly lit auditorium to a group of well-dressed students, eager to learn about his theories of what he termed "logo-therapy."

In his book, Frankl touches on a concept that has not only assisted many individuals to survive the worst experiences known to mankind but has also affected the course of whole nations: the power of Vision.

Lee Kuan Yew, Prime Minister of Singapore from 1959 to 1990, set a Vision of an orderly, prosperous, tightly run society where the lifestyle and financial security of citizens was assured to continually improve. The Vision was created in 1959 and over the next three decades it set the course of a whole nation.

Martin Luther King started a similar phenomenon when he stood on the steps at the Lincoln Memorial in Washington D.C. on August 28, 1963. With words that still echo down the corridors of power in the USA, King declared *"I have a dream that one day this nation will rise up and live out the true meaning of its creed: We hold these truths to be self-evident: that all men are created equal."*

Martin Luther King's dream was a Vision.

Earlier in the same decade and in the same country, John F Kennedy planted a Vision in the minds of all Americans when he challenged the scientific community to put a man on the moon prior to the end of the 1960s.

That Vision, in the form of a challenge, did what only Vision can do. It gave the minds and hearts of millions a sense of purpose and a clear direction. It was the catalyst for transformational change, the legacy of which lives on today in the United States NASA space programs.

Vision is a remarkably potent concept that not only has the power to transform the lives of individuals but can also galvanize and motivate families, communities, and as mentioned, whole countries into aligned action through a common sense of purpose and direction. And if Vision can do all of that for whole nations, think for a moment of what its power will do for transforming your life.

TIME TO THINK BIGGER THAN BIG

An effective Vision Statement needs to be powerfully motivational. And in order to be motivational, it's critical that you free your mind from the shackles of reality. The time for reality thinking is when you work on creating Goals, but practicality has no place in the realms of Vision Creation. This Vision needs to be a "wow." Let go of the "buts," "shoulds," "can'ts," "won'ts" and hook into the untapped potential of your imagination. Einstein is quoted as saying *"imagination is everything."* If it worked for him so well, it's just possible that thinking big might help you too!

To help set your imagination free, you will need to forget about the past. Your past is in the past. It's over. Whatever failures or successes you had are now history. That was yesterday. Both past successes and failures can be handicaps when forming a clear picture of the perfect future. If you focus on the failures, you can easily increase insecurity and low Self-Esteem, and if you focus on successes, you can limit your thinking to a simple extrapolation of those victories, i.e. "more of the same please."

Note also that in addition to your Vision of the future being unshackled from your past, it should also be free of the restraints of the present. How much time, energy, money, skill, or other resources and capabilities at your disposal need to completely put aside when it comes to shaping your Vision. All of these may be considerations to use when it comes to creating your Goals, but for now we are going to leave them out of the picture because they will restrain you from thinking big.

Have you ever gone for a walk or driven along a familiar path and instead of seeing what you have always seen, you've looked up and seen what's on the horizon? Possibly a whole new panorama of beauty that you had never previously noticed; possibly a whole mountain range you had never seen before, or a beautiful stand of tall trees. Vision is about lifting your gaze above where your feet normally tread and seeing new possibilities that are exciting and motivational.

In his 1994 inaugural speech as incoming President of South Africa, Nelson Mandela quoted from *A Course in Miracles*, by Dr. Helen Schucman, as follows:

> *"Our deepest fear is not that we are inadequate. Our deepest fear is that we are powerful beyond measure. It is our light, not our darkness, that most frightens us. We ask ourselves, who am I to be brilliant, gorgeous, talented and fabulous? Actually, who are you not to be? You are a child of God. Your play-*

ing small doesn't serve the world. There is nothing enlightened about shrinking so that other people won't feel insecure around you. We are born to make manifest the glory of God that is within us. It is not just in some of us; it is in everyone. And as we let our own light shine, we unconsciously give other people permission to do the same. As we are liberated from our fears, our presence automatically liberates others."

That sort of attitude is right on the money when it comes to forming your Vision Statement. Unfurl your Superman or Superwoman cape and dare to be outrageous in terms of how high you can fly. Back yourself; believe in miracles just for a moment and imagine you had a magic wand.

What sort of life would you create? That's the stuff of which a powerful Vision is made.

Values Aligned

The next point to note is that parts of your Vision should reflect your Primary Life Values. For example if "Family" or your "Life Partner" is on your Primary Life Values list, then include in your Vision statement a description of what that relationship looks like when it's perfect. Likewise if "Financial Independence" is an important Primary Life Value, then a description of what that might look like will also be important to include. It's by no means mandatory that every one of your Primary Life Values is elaborated on in your Vision, but certainly some of the "biggies" will need to be included. Someone else should be able to read your Vision statement and have a reasonably accurate idea of what your Primary Life Values are, based on what they have just read.

Once you have a succinct statement of what your life will look like when you are perfectly successful, I call that statement your Primary Life Vision. Here's an example of a Primary Life Vision to give you a bit of an idea what it might contain:

> *"I enjoy abundant energy levels and total Freedom from illness and injury. I am lean, fit and well-toned. I enjoy a full range of healthy emotions including feelings of love, Happiness, peace of mind, and Freedom. I make regular progress towards fulfilling my life purpose and constantly feel grateful for the opportunity to serve others both professionally and personally. I continue to create and enjoy a wide range of adventures which challenge me, expand my capabilities, and inspire others. My partner and I experience continually deeper levels of love while at the same time we have fun as well as continually working together to grow and develop personally. I spend time supporting my children and encourage and inspire them to be all that they can be. I enjoy more than enough passive income to support our lifestyle but choose to continue working as it is my passion and provides high levels of Fulfillment and satisfaction. I live in a beautiful home with wide sea views and easy access to the beach. I continue to enjoy success with my writing and speaking career and this business grows every year. I spend increasing amounts of time working with a non-profit organization that works with children on breaking the cycle of poverty and crime. I continually feel grateful and happy to be experiencing such a fulfilling life."*

Yahoo! If that was your Vision, would you find it motivating as a dream to move toward? Would it motivate you enough to put your feet on the floor in the morning on a cold dark winter's day so that you could get out of bed with enthusiasm to go make it all happen?

Note that the Vision statement is written in the present tense and in the first person so that your mind can more easily visualize this as being real. *"What the heart can believe the mind can achieve."*

Finally, before we get into the Vision creation exercise, it's important to mention the last reason we want to create a Vision statement for your life. A good Primary Life Vision gives a frame of reference for forming Goals. It's like locating a town or city on a map. First of all, you have to locate the right State or region and then you drill down to the city. The State or Region is analogous to Vision and the town or city in analogous to the Goal. When you create a Goal and then pour time, money, and energy into it you want to make sure that it's taking you in the right direction. Creating a Values-aligned Vision will do just that. When you get to the next part of this book and begin to create your Goals, you'll see how much easier and more effective it is when you can use a clear and powerful Primary Life Vision as the backdrop.

Chapter 12:

Creating Your Own Personal Life Vision

Vision Creation Exercise 1:

First of all, put on some really uplifting "power music" to turbocharge your confidence levels. One of my personal favorites is "Search For The Hero" by M People. Women seem to also like "I Believe I Can Fly" by R Kelley from the Movie "Space Jam." Choose your own song, but make sure that it has an uplifting energy. Having listened to your "power song," grab a pen and a piece of paper and answer the following questions:

Question 1: If you knew that you could not fail what one great service to mankind would you perform?

_____

_____

_____

Question 2: If you had no shortage of time, money, or power, what great project would you complete?

_____

_____

_____

_____

Question 3: If money were not an issue and you could make a difference with your current talents by doing something that you enjoyed, what sort of work would you involve yourself in?

_____

_____

_____

_____

Question 4: If you were now aged 95 and were sitting on the deck in your rocking chair, and you looked back on a life of total and complete success, what one achievement would you be most proud of?

_____

_____

_____

_____

VISION CREATION EXERCISE 2:

The following is a simple exercise in creative writing. Simply write a paragraph on each of the following categories. Wherever possible, make your statement broad rather than specific: e.g., rather than writing "I play golf three times a week" write something like "I have all the time I need to play my chosen sport."

Remember to use the present tense and to write your statements using the first person, e.g. "I."

Category 1: Describe your ideal state of Health. Comment on leisure activities, energy levels as well as your mental, emotional, spiritual, and cultural well-being.

_____

_____

_____

Category 2: Describe what your perfect Relationships will look like. Describe the ideal life partner relationship, as well as the ideal relationships you have with friends, family, and community.

_____

_____

_____

_____

Category 3: Describe your ideal Money situation. Be sure and include income (passive or otherwise) as well as assets, lifestyle, and philanthropy.

_____

_____

_____

_____

Once you have completed the exercises, prepare your final draft Personal Life Vision statement and place a copy behind your Personal Life Values in your diary, scheduler, or planner. Along with your Values, this will keep your Vision "top of mind" as you read it regularly and remind yourself of the future that you are headed toward. Remember, if you want to put all of your plans on a simple electronic system then visit my web site at www. **tompoland.com** and download my "Goal Creation and Achievement Planner" from the "Online Shop."

A Final Note on Vision

I have many clients who completed their Primary Life Vision and never seriously believed that they would achieve it. That was never the intention. As you now know, the idea was to set up a big-picture, long-term dream to provide context and direction for Goal-setting. But like them, when I wake up and look at my life, I am now "living the dream" as I have come to achieve large parts of my Primary Life Vision.

Just under a decade ago, I wrote my first Vision statement. My dream was to be a professional writer and speaker, to live near the sea, and exercise on a beautiful beach in the mornings. I wrote that I would have plenty of time off to pursue my personal passions. I specified that I would have leveraged my income so that money was banked into my account even when I was on holiday and that I would have a wonderfully deep, intimate, and satisfying relationship with my Life Partner, and that my relationships with each of my four children was one of friendship, trust, open communication. I wrote about high levels of energy, about passion and profit, and about fulfilling my purpose in life.

And as I sit here typing this, I can run my pen down the page and go "tick, tick, tick." I am now living the dream. I'm not writing this to impress you, but rather to impress upon you how powerful Vision is for transforming your life from a dream into a daily life experience.

So the first point is that, while you may have written large parts of your Vision without serious thought of ever actually achieving it, the reality is that if you follow my system you will end up living the dream in many areas of your life. That's way cool. And that brings me to my second point.

Yes, it's true that I am living the dream. Every day is rather terrific. And in addition to that, I have problems. The problems are what I see when I take my eyes off the opportunities. And the problems are all I see when I let all the great things that I have created drop off the radar scope of my mind. The very act of continuing to create and achieve Goals create these challenges in my life.

So point number two is this. Develop the "Attitude of Gratitude" so that when you turn your Vision from some dry ink on a piece of paper into your daily reality, you can truly appreciate what you have created. Otherwise, you'll be like so many unfulfilled high-achievers who get to the summit of their success and never take the time to appreciate how far they have come up the trail of life.

To assist you in developing the Attitude of Gratitude as well as a penchant for appreciation, let me give you a recommended habit to be completed once a day, preferably right at the start of the day when you are going for your walk or brushing your teeth. Ask yourself this question:

What do I really appreciate about my achievements yesterday?

The key is to focus your mind on what you achieved that was worthwhile. What efforts did you make that you can be proud of? This is the time to proverbially pat yourself on the back. All too often in our culture, we are too quick see where we have fallen short, to instantly identify what we have *not* done, to put ourselves down and to beat ourselves up. So if you ask yourself this question and you hear yourself mentally reacting with something like, *"I didn't do my exercise, and I was grumpy with one of the kids,"* then simply take a breath and with a small smile say to yourself, *"Welcome, my old friend self-criticism."* Then ask the question again and keep asking it until you have three or more actions that represent progress in your life. Sometimes I've had to dig pretty deep with this question: *"Well I got out of bed and I remembered to floss !"* Mostly though, you'll be surprised and gratified at how much of what you did took you a step closer to fulfilling your Vision and achieving your Goals.

The reason for asking this question is two-fold. Firstly, you will *"enjoy the journey"* more if you take time to appreciate your progress as you travel along. Secondly, you will feel better about yourself and people who feel better about themselves produce better results.

PART FOUR:

PREPARING FOR GOAL CREATION

Chapter 13:

An Introduction to Personal Goals

Life Planning Pyramid

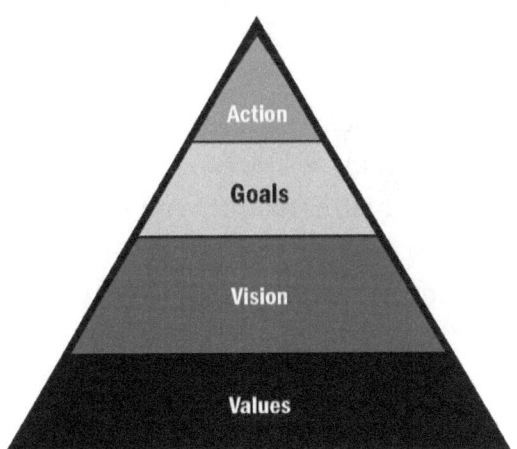

As mentioned previously, Goals are the stuff of which life is made. What you achieve speaks more about you than an infinite number of words. Who you are "Being" is reflected in what you are "Doing" and the result is what you "Have" (what you achieve).

What inspires you? What are you passionate about? What represents the essence of you? What do you stand for and what will you not stand for? What excites you? What lights up your eyes when you talk about it? Where is the thing that lifts your whole energy when you think of it? The answers to these questions will provide the raw material for forming at least some of your Goals.

This is vital stuff. There is nothing more important in your life than who you are, what you do, and what you achieve. And this is what Goals are all about. I know we've taken a while to arrive at this part of the process, but my philosophy is that if you are going to create some Goals, it has to be done right. It's like laying the foundations for a magnificent building. It's too important simply to mess around with it or to pay it lip service or to rush it and to have it become just another tick on a list of things to do.

So here we are, at the heart of this book. You're going to set some Goals. These Goals will have the potential to change your life forever. As I sit here and type these words, I have to say that I feel excited for you. In fact, I even want to go back and have another look at my own Goals because I feel so much positive energy flowing through me about this subject of sculpting a masterpiece of a life through the Conscious creation and achievement of Goals. It spins my whizzer to think of the power that each one of us has to create something that never existed before and would never have existed unless we had the idea and made the effort. The creation and achievement of Goals are the ultimate expression of creativity.

GOALS ARE NOT JUST EVIDENCED EXTERNALLY

When I state that your achievements define who you are, you may tend to think primarily of external achievements such as a new career or business, a new house, or having climbed a mountain. But remember that I'm referring to your internal achievements as well as your external ones such as reigniting your passion for life or developing your capacity for tolerance, compassion, astuteness, or love. I suspect that over time these inner achievements will be more valued by each of us than the external ones.

Chapter 14:

The Three Levels of Goals

The mind is a Goal-creating machine. We are constantly either creating Goals to move away from something such as being broke, sick, lonely, or bored or we are creating Goals toward something such as better health, wealth, love, or Happiness. Our Goals may be "away from" or "towards" something; they may be Conscious or Subconscious , they may be written down or simply an intention, but they are always resident 24/7 in every human being. The psychology of Goals is probably the most proven and well-researched of all psychologies.

While there are many different types of Goals, we can place them into one of three different levels. This concept is based on American psychologist Abraham Maslow's famous *Hierarchy of Needs* so my apologies to Dr Maslow for the simplifying and paraphrasing that follows.

Level One: Survival Goals – the Avoidance of Pain

If your physical existence is threatened by lack of food, shelter, or warmth, your Goals would consist entirely of having these basic survival needs met. If you've been on a mountain for three days and you're scared, tired, cold, and hungry, you're not thinking about whether you're going to buy that new "5 series beamer." Your Goals will be related to getting warm, getting food, and getting safe. That is all that will fill your Consciousness. Likewise, those poor souls who live in poverty and famine-racked countries care even less about a new car.

LEVEL TWO: LIFESTYLE GOALS – THE PURSUIT OF PLEASURE

Once we begin to experience daily certainty about being warm, sheltered, nourished, and safe our mind then begins to create Goals directed at improving our living conditions. Getting yourself a job or having your own business, finding a Life Partner to walk through life with, buying an even better car or house or yacht. And of course, if you're a guy then your Lifestyle Goals will almost certainly include upgrading your toys and gadgets, whatever they may be. All of this is good fun so long as we don't take any of it too seriously and we keep expenditure in balance so that it doesn't negatively impact on other Goals, such as wealth creation or our relationships. Please remember my earlier point that it's vitally important that you learn to be happy regardless of how successful you are at acquiring these "shiny things."

LEVEL THREE: FULFILLMENT GOALS – THE PURSUIT OF PURPOSE

I was on holiday last month and stopped at a motorcycle museum in Tamworth, New South Wales, Australia. I got talking to the curator, an older weather-beaten man who spoke slowly with words that dripped with homespun wisdom. He looked like he had been riding bikes for at least a quarter of a century before I was born.

The Three Levels Of Goals

The curator asked me what sort of bike I had. *"I've got four bikes,"* I replied with some pride. *"Too bad you've only got one bum then,"* he responded!

Later, as I rode away from the museum, I had time to ponder his comment. He made a fair point. How many cars can one person drive? How big or flashy does the house have to be? How much money is enough? For those people who have not yet learned that ultimate Happiness and Fulfillment are found beyond Level Two – "The Pursuit of Pleasure," no amount of money or things is enough. Buying and owning things is different from enjoying Freedom, Fulfillment, and Happiness.

Purpose-sourced Goals are those that you take on for reasons other than ensuring survival or improving your lifestyle. They may still be financially related as in a business Goal, but the critical difference is that the money is not the prime motivator. Fashion designer Trelise Cooper is a great example of someone whose Goals are at Level Three. Starting from zero five years previously, Trelise created a business that turns over ten million dollars a year and she exports to some of the finest fashion retailers in the world.

> *"I've always had a passion for clothes, but I've never had formal training, so I don't do anything in a conventional way,"* she says, *"and I have a Freedom in that. I don't compromise. If I want to buy fabric because it's beautiful, I do. If I want to add detail, I do. It's not about price, it's about want."*
> *"I don't do this to sell clothes,"* she says. *"My whole aim in setting up this business was to have self-expression as a woman; to create a woman's space in my working and selling environment; to do what I absolutely, passionately love which is creating clothing. If you emphasize the right things, the money comes naturally."*

You may get a sense now about what I mean by Goals that are at Level Three – the "Pursuit of Purpose." Trelise has moved beyond Survival Goals and is not motivated by Lifestyle Goals. For her it's about passion, expression, creativity and being the essence of who she wants to be.

I firmly believe that one of the reasons that Trelise is so successful is that she has not compromised her Values in building her business. The world is drawn to Trelise's authenticity because most people have starved themselves of that particular Value in order to be accepted by conformists. I further feel that when people wear Trelise's creations they experience the essence of her spirit and it inspires their own soul to be faithful to their authentic self. It's as though Trelise's authenticity gives others a "permission slip" to likewise express the essence of their own true inner self.

Like Trelise and others like her, we will all eventually move beyond Level One and Level Two Goals and come to value Level Three Goals. It's just a question of how many lifetimes it will take. The Fulfillment of our Life Purpose is the destiny of each and every one of us.

So the point of this chapter is this: by all means have some Goals that are Lifestyle-related, but make sure that at least one of your Goals is at Level Three: Purpose.

Your Level Three Goals are going to be expressed in the form of either expanding your personal Capacity (for Freedom and Happiness, etc.), or in the form of Contribution Goals such as career, business, or possibly even volunteer work.

In regard to business and career, certainly have a Goal to make a profit; that's vitally important. In addition, however, ensure that you understand that the real purpose in career or business is increasing the effectiveness of the Contribution you make toward improving the lives of those you serve – your colleagues, clients, and suppliers.

These twin areas of continually expanding your Capacity and Contribution will be the source of your ultimate sense of Fulfillment.

Chapter 15:

The Two Basic Types of Goals

We've dealt with the three levels of Goals: Survival, Lifestyle, and Fulfillment. Within each level there are two types of Goals. This chapter explains what those two types of Goals are.

Some people write Goals and some don't. However, everyone has Goals, all of the time. The difference is that some people devote all their time to "Maintenance Goals" while others create space in their life to also focus on "Progressive Goals."

Maintenance Goals

Maintenance Goals are those that help to maintain the quality of life that you have achieved to date. For example, if you are fit and you have a Goal to keep that level of fitness, then you have a Maintenance Goal.

By way of a further example, I have a Maintenance Goal to keep my weight and body fat levels below a certain figure. I achieved significant weight loss over fifteen years ago and I want to stay at that weight. I keep this as a Maintenance Goal because even after all these years, I find it easy to put weight back on again. Having this as a Goal keeps me Conscious of what I want and Committed to achieving it.

So the purpose of a Maintenance Goal is to keep you Conscious of what is important to you so that you don't "take your eye off the ball" and relapse into old patterns.

Remember that there is nothing wrong with having Maintenance Goals. In fact, these Goals involve actions that helped you get to where you are today. It's just that if that's *all* you do, the same actions that got you to where you are today will keep you where you are today. Maintenance Goals and maintenance actions are not the same as the Goals and actions that will take your life to the next level.

PROGRESSIVE GOALS

As mentioned, we all need Maintenance Goals, but we also need to develop the habit of investing time each week for "Progressive Goals." Progressive Goals are those that move your life up to the next level, whatever the "next level" is for you. When you have Progressive Goals in your life, you are investing significant portions of your time and energy into the achievement of some very big Goals such as health improvements, deepening of personal relationships, wealth creation, or philanthropy. If you really want to get your life to the next level, you are going to need a system for creating and achieving Progressive Goals.

TIME ALLOCATION INVENTORY

Grab a pen and paper and make a note of how much of your waking time last week was spent on maintenance activity.

Remember, these are Goals that help you to keep what you've already got. Then make a note of the amount of waking time that you invested in "Progressive Goals." You may find it's not much. And that's OK. You now have a starting point and the game is to build on what you have already achieved and are maintaining, by increasing the amount of time you invest on Progressive Goals. This may mean you need to delegate or outsource some of your Maintenance Goal related activities (e.g. domestic chores) in order to create the time and energy needed to invest in Progressive Goals.

Make a list of all the activities that you perform every week including household chores. To free up time and energy in your life for the achievement of Progressive Goals, work out which of these activities you will delegate or outsource to people who specialize in those areas. For example, if you are still involved in maintaining your grounds and you don't enjoy that process, then invest in a grounds person to complete the lawn mowing and gardening. Of course, if you love doing these tasks then keep them as part of your weekend recreation routine.

Invest the extra time and energy that you gain into Progressive Goals and the return on your investment will far outstrip the money spent on the grounds person. That's leverage.

Chapter 16:

How to Work Out What You Want in Life Even if You Have no Idea

BEFORE WE GET into the steps for creating Goals, I want to deal with a major hurdle that prevents a significant number of people from creating the life of their dreams.

The number one reason why people don't get what they want in life is because they don't know what they want. This point is well illustrated in Lewis Carroll's *Alice in Wonderland* when Alice comes to a fork in the road. *"Which road do I take?"* she asked. *"Where do you want to go?"* responded the Cheshire Cat. *"I don't know,"* Alice answered. *"Then,"* said the cat, *"it doesn't matter!"*

Don't Know What You Want?

I've noticed over the years how easy it is for some people to sabotage success by Subconsciously creating a mental pattern of never knowing what they want. I've met quite a number of these genuine but frustrated people over the years. They have a very real problem in that they don't know what they want, and they are often desperate to work out what it is they do want. Their desperation is only matched by their incapacity to create clarity around their desired future.

For ease of explanation, let's personify all of these people into one person who we will call Bobby (not his real name). Bobby doesn't know what he wants to achieve for three reasons:

- Firstly, at a Subconscious level, there is a big pay-off for Bobby not knowing what he wants. It's likely that earlier in Bobby's life he knew exactly what he wanted, and he didn't get it. What he wanted may have been to pass an exam, score the new girlfriend, or get the new car. When he failed to achieve the desired Goal, he felt pain in the form of disappointment or rejection.

   One of the functions of Bobby's Subconscious is to protect his Conscious mind from pain and it normally does this without Bobby being aware, hence the term "<u>Sub</u>-conscious ." So now Bobby has a Subconscious that associates *"I know what I want"* with pain and it does a great job of protecting him from potential pain by making sure that he will never come up with a Goal again. To Bobby's Subconscious mind, "no Goal = no pain."

- Secondly, it didn't take Bobby's Subconscious long to figure out that there was an additional payoff in creating the *"I don't know what I want"* programming. Not only does Bobby minimize the likelihood of feeling more disappointment (or rejection or whatever), he also never has to get out of his Comfort Zone again. No more making an effort, no more risk, no more discomfort. When the Subconscious mind reviews these benefits, each one gets a big tick.

This, of course, makes for one very frustrated Bobby. Often people like Bobby are go-getters who are sick of under-achieving. Consciously, they badly want to have something worthwhile to live for and they can't understand why they seem to be incapable of working out what they want.

- And that brings us to the third reason why Bobby doesn't know what he wants. Let's say Bobby hears me speak about the wonders of Goal creation and achievement and on the one hand he's motivated but on the other hand he senses another bout of bewilderment around what it is that he wants to do with his life.

So here's what happens: Bobby comes up to the front of the auditorium after I have completed my talk and he shares his problem with me. And being the compassionate soul that I am, I agree to have a coffee with Bobby to discuss his blockage.

If I let Bobby talk and simply ask some questions, then I'll count seven to ten occasions within the first twenty minutes of conversation where he tells me that he doesn't know what he wants. So my first recommendation to Bobby is that he change his language. *"Every time that you tell someone else that you don't know what you want, there is a second person eavesdropping. That second person is your Subconscious mind who happily complies with your command,"* I explain. When the Subconscious hears *"I don't know what I want"* it responds internally with something like *"OK boss, I got the message again and I will comply with your instructions to ensure that we will never know what we want."* In this respect, the Subconscious is simply following orders.

If you find yourself in a similar place to Bobby, then get this: you can reprogram the way that you think and feel. You are not stuck with your current mental and emotional patterns; you do not have to be a prisoner of your own mind. The moment that you are Conscious of what you are thinking and feeling, you are at what I call the *"point of power."* All you need to do to reprogram your Subconscious is to simply create an affirmation that states how you want to think and/or feel and repeat it with real depth of concentration as often as you can. For example, if you notice that you are programming yourself up with statements like *"I never know what I want,"* then simply repeat the opposite as an affirmation of your intent: e.g. *"Every day and in every way I am clearer about what I want."* There is great power in such statements when they are repeated consistently and with concentration. My recommendation is that you repeat the affirmation once for each breath cycle for 21 breaths. In other words, breath in and out, in a full but relaxed way and repeat the affirmation once during that breath cycle and again for a total of 21 times. Do this every time that you notice your mind thinking a thought that you would like to change (e.g. "I don't know what I want') and it's possible to totally reprogram that thought within a few days, or at worst a few months.

'Fake It 'Til You Make It'

Some people have a problem with repeating an affirmation like this when they feel that it is not true. If this applies to you, then just remember that all that you are doing is retraining your Subconscious mind to lead you to a solution. We all create our own reality by the thoughts that we think.

If someone does not know what they want, then that person has created that uncertainty as their reality by thinking that thought so often that it is ingrained in the Subconscious. The Subconscious then simply follows the orders. So issue another set of orders by repeating the new thought 21 times during 21 breath cycles. You will find more on this subject under the "Thought Transformation Technique" in Chapter 48.

Now that we have dealt with the issue of *"I don't know what I want,"* let's move a little closer to actually forming some Goals that will take your life to the next level.

Chapter 17:

Top Tips for Creating Goals

So Anyway, What Is a Goal?

A **Goal is something** that you want to achieve; it's a specific Outcome. All of life can be divided into Outcomes and Inputs. What separates the successful from the unsuccessful is their ability to Consciously and effectively align Outcomes and Inputs. In other words, successful people achieve real clarity about what they want to achieve in their life (Goals/ Outcomes) and then they ensure that their actions (Inputs) are creating those Outcomes.

Before we get into specific exercises for forming your Goals, it's important that I give you my Top Tips for creating Goals.

Top Tip 1: Forget the Past

We want the first cut of your Goals to be formed without the limitations of what you have succeeded at or failed at in the past. It's especially important that your Goals are not limited by what you have achieved previously.

For example, at the time of going through one of my "midlife chrysalis" experiences, I was working with a large international corporate. I had been involved with re-structuring work and I like to think that I had become pretty good at my specialty.

The company I was with had its faults, but then so did I and in general I was happy with the relationship. However, after many years of mutual benefit, it was time for a change. I wanted to get back to owning my own business and so I set about on a "Vision Quest" to work out what it was that I would do with the next part of my life. However, I initially handicapped the planning process by attempting to take my past and project it into the future. I made the mistake of limiting my thinking to what my successful past experience had been. As a result of this error, I concluded that I would start a consultancy practice in marketing and restructuring. While this was logical, it never felt quite right. I felt a little like I was trying to force a square peg into a round hole. While I was comfortable with this scenario at a rational level, it never felt right intuitively.

So instead of proceeding with a new consultancy business, I shifted my thinking perspective from the past and into the future. In other words, I started thinking about the issue more from the angle of what I really wanted to do as opposed to what I used to do.

I decided that what I really wanted to do was to speak and to write and to use those two mediums as a means to help others live life more fully. I had a natural affinity with small- and medium-sized business owners and hence the Entrepreneur's Success Programme was born (see **www.espcoach.com**). And it would never have even been so much as a twinkle in my eye had I not shifted my perspective from the past to the future. If I had let my past dominate my thinking and planning, I would have severely limited my future potential and the lives of thousands of people would not have benefited from their contact with the ESP Programme and its various forms.

The same principle of forgetting your past applies if your past contains a lot of failure. If you want to be fit and lean but your idea of strenuous exercise used to be to resist the current as the water runs out of the bath while you sip your beer, then it doesn't matter. It's what you want in the future that really counts, not what you were in the past.

And if you've burnt out all of your relationships through being too selfish, too impatient, too fussy, or too anything, it doesn't matter one iota (that's a really small amount!) in respect to what you can achieve tomorrow. Your heart's desire for the future is what you need to tap into. Passion Overcomes past patterns.

So hopefully, we've agreed that we will leave past failures where they belong — in the past.

Although we have agreed to not being limited by past success, I do want to encourage you to use the memories of those successes to boost your confidence. While it's true that whatever successes you had in the past are gone, you can use that success to feel good about yourself and build confidence. Just don't cross the line into arrogance and think that you are bulletproof simply because of a success in the past. That was yesterday and it was with a specific set of circumstances that will never come together again in precisely the same way. The best Goal achievers have a small but very healthy level of paranoia in them.

In summary, your past is called the past because it has passed. Apart from the strength and feelings of confidence you can draw from your past successes, when it comes to creating new Goals, leave the past where it belongs: in the past.

As mentioned, we really want to start the process of Goal-creation with a future-based perspective. It's like you get to create your life from the perspective of looking back from the future.

TOP TIP 2: FORGET THE PRESENT

Likewise, for the *first* draft of these Goals, I want your mind to be free of the present. That is to say, I want you to disregard your present resources such as available time, money, energy, capabilities, and relationships when you form the first draft of your Goals.

The time to be mindful of which resources you are short of and what you can do about it is when you are finalizing your Goals. If what you want to achieve is clearly not possible with the resources, you have two options. You can either get more resources or adjust the size of the Goal to a level that is achievable with your current resources.

The point is that you can really limit yourself if you are mindful of resource constraints when you first set about creating Goals. Become mindful of resources later when you are considering if the Goal is achievable in its original form.

So during the exercises that I am going to give you, let your mind think in terms of creating a "future history." That's as if you are looking back from the future and assuming that everything worked out perfectly.

TOP TIP 3: FORGET THE PEOPLE

By this I mean that these are Goals for *your* life. Other people may have their ideas about what you "should" do and what you "have" to do. But when you're sitting on that rocking chair aged 95 and reflecting on what you achieved, it's unlikely that you'll be thinking *"Thank God I did everything that everyone else wanted me to do !"* It's your life and it's up to you to choose what you want to do with it. So regardless of how well- intentioned other people may be, don't let them set your Goals for you.

Of course, when you set your Goals you should be mindful of not creating unnecessary conflicts with others. But if you are going to err at all, then you are better to err on the side of living your life your way as opposed to acquiescing to other people's ideas of success.

Friedrich Nietzsche said it best: *"The individual has always had to struggle to keep from being overwhelmed by the tribe. If you try it, you will be lonely often, and sometimes frightened. But no price is too high to pay for the privilege of owning yourself."*

This brings me to my second point which is the flip side of not letting others set your Goals: you cannot successfully achieve Goals for other people. Don't set Goals for your Life Partner or for your children. For example, don't try to push your child into a career that you think will be good for them unless they have a passion for it. And don't try and turn your Life Partner into someone they are not. Let them be who they want to be. After all, that's the person you fell in love with.

I know that you want the best for them; it's just that you can't do it for them. As I have said previously, it is futile to care more for someone else's future than they care themselves. It's just an exercise in wasted energy and frustration. It's like trying to milk a mouse: not only is it not worth the effort, but it's also quite painful for the mouse!

Clearly there is a place for supporting your loved ones and wanting the very best for them, but when you cross the line into coercion or manipulation you are trying to control another human being. History shows that all attempts to control end up in a bun fight. The "controller" loses the illusion of power that they thought they had and the "controllee" ends up angry and rebellious and strikes out on their own.

By way of another example, you may really Value being slim and you want your Life Partner to enjoy the same energy-enhancing benefits of carrying less fat. But "lean" is your Value and not necessarily their Value. They may in fact Value being lean but they may more highly Value being able to eat whatever they want, when they want to eat it. If you attempt to control their eating habits, they will end up resenting you and you will destroy the quality of your relationship. Setting Goals for others is dysfunctional. End of story.

Mostly, Goals for others are not written down, but they are top of mind when you are talking to the person concerned. I've done it and so have most people who have been in any kind of relationship. People have to want something for their own reasons in order for them to be motivated enough to achieve it.

When you think about it, having Goals for others is actually quite arrogant, because we are saying that our Values are better than their Values. We think that we've got it right and they've got it wrong. Personally, I've had too many instances of "knowing" I was right only to find out later that I was wrong, to insist that anyone else should swap their beliefs and Values for mine. Provided the pursuit of their Values is not violating agreed Shared Core Values in the relationship, then you are best to leave them well alone in respect to setting their Goals.

One of my clients is the Managing Director for a large multi-national organization. He is a loving Life Partner and a devoted father. We'll call him Sam. When Sam formed his first set of draft Goals, he had a couple of Goals that he set for his Life Partner and his kids. After talking with Sam, he repositioned his Goals and as a consequence became fabulously supportive and highly influential in the lives of his loved ones, but with not one ounce of controlling or manipulating.

Sam realized that his Life Partner and kids were not employees and were far more free-spirited. While he no longer has a sense of control over their lives, he now realizes that this was always an illusion anyway. His sense of frustration at their lack of response has gone and so too is their resentment of his overly assertive approach.

Sam has moved to a position of influence and trust. His son, who I suspect was previously getting tired of the weekly "message from Dad's soap box," now talks to him openly as a friend and even asks for advice. Over the last year, this same young man has transformed himself from a virtual high school dropout into a student who scores all As and Bs and has been accepted by a well-respected American university. I suspect that the son's transformed grade average is in part due to his increased self- esteem that came about from feeling accepted and valued by his Dad.

Sam is a terrific example for others. He's supportive, listening, understanding and he's there for his Life Partner and children when they need someone, but he's dropped the role of being Managing Director of their Universe.

The bottom line for this tip is to set Goals for yourself but never for others.

Top Tip 4: Trust Your Intuition

If you create a Goal and emotionally or psychologically it feels like it just doesn't fit, then drop the Goal. At least put it on the shelf for a while. The point is to trust your intuition. Don't create a Goal simply because it's the logical thing to do or because you feel that you "should" do it.

It may be that the timing is not quite right or that the need for the Goal will be superseded by an event that you are not yet aware of. Lack of trust in my intuition has cost me a lot of money and wasted a lot of time in my life for too many years. Now, if I am about to set a Goal, or even if I am going to spend some money or book a meeting, I stop and check how I am feeling about that idea. If I sense a tension in my body (normally in my gut), a feeling that I am forcing something, then I back off. Invariably I find out later why I felt like that and why the decision that I made was the right one. In those instances, I congratulate myself for moving from what used to be only a very incomplete approach to decision making (using only logical thinking) to becoming more balanced by listening to both my rational and intuitive minds. These days I need a green light from my rational mind as well as my intuitive mind before I proceed.

Top Tip 5: Focus on Passion

I maintain that we should organize our life around fun. There is "easy fun," which is what I do when I am goofing off on holiday or taking my bike along some mountain trail. And then there is "hard fun." That's generally what business is about. There's no doubt that business is competitive, and competitors will always be attracted like gazelles to an oasis whenever one finds a profitable niche. I love competition. I love the battle. In fact, I realize that I'm addicted to it. Being challenged and having to lift my game puts a grin on my face. It's hard but it's fun so long as I don't take it all too seriously. Sure, my grin may begin as a grimace when a competitor eats into our market share, but to quote Nietzsche again *"That which does not kill us makes us stronger."* I grin more than I grimace these days because I like getting stronger.

As a general principle, center your activities around things that turn you on. Don't compromise your Being by doing stuff that you weren't born to do. Most people will water down their Values to accommodate the rest of the world to the point where they forget what they stand for. At that point, they fall for anything. Always remember that the world is changed by unreasonable people.

If you set your Goals around Outcomes that feel like drudgery, then you will spend your time feeling like you are trying to force everything. Life will seem too hard, too tough. Everything will feel like a supreme effort. But if you focus your energy on Goals that inspire your soul and bring out the passion in you, then your efforts will have a greater sense of flow about them. Drudgery requires force. Passion produces flow.

Hard fun and easy fun. It's a simple philosophy to remember.

Part Five:

Creating Your Goals

Chapter 18:

Goal Creation Exercise 1: The 'Non-stop Writing' Technique

I'm going to give you several exercises to complete in order to help you clarify your thinking as to what your Goals are going to be. The idea here is to create a lot of Goals by completing all of the exercises. After you have created your list of Goals, then we will come back and select the most important ones.

The first exercise is one of my favorites for creating lots of potential Goals. Simply follow the instructions, to the letter, and you will probably be quite surprised at what you create.

The Non-stop Writing Technique

Step 1: Get several sheets of clean paper. Lined or unlined is fine. You will also need a pen and a watch. A stopwatch or countdown timer is ideal, but otherwise a normal watch with clear marking for every five minutes will suffice.

Step 2: Write at the top of each sheet of paper *"What's my heart's desire?"*

Step 3: Put on some "Power Music," shut your eyes, take a few deep breaths and listen to the beat and feel the energy of the song charging your soul.

Step 4: Once the music track stops, your time starts. You will be writing for fifteen minutes non-stop. The fact that you will keep your pen moving for the whole fifteen minutes is the key to this exercise. For fifteen minutes, write down any ideas for Goals that come to your mind. Any idea. I don't want you to edit the ideas at all as you write them down. Instead just keep writing.

If you get stuck for any idea simply write out the question that is at the top of each page: *"What's my heart's desire?"* and keep writing it out until the ideas begin to flow again. You can write short-term, medium-term and long-term Goals. You can write business Goals or personal Goals. You can write Goals for your health, your relationships, and for your money. It really doesn't matter at this stage. Simply keep writing; that's the key. We'll look at editing the Goals later, but in case I didn't make it clear before: the most important thing is to keep that pen moving!

Once you have finished the first exercise, go onto the next one. Remember, we will be coming back later to select the most important Goals for you to start work on.

Chapter 19:

Goal Creation Exercise 2: The 'Roles and Goals' Exercise

My clients often have a concern for maintaining balance in their life while at the same time experiencing new growth.

By identifying the main Roles you have in life, you will then be in a position to set Goals in a balanced manner.

On the following page, identify what you believe are the main Roles in your life currently. Limit the list to 7 by grouping some Roles together if necessary.

An example of roles follows:

1. Life Partner

2. Father or Mother

3. Sports lover

4. Friend

5. Community worker

6. Managing Director

7. Physical exerciser

For each role identified, write one or two Goals. For those readers who are in charge of running a business, you will need to have a separate business plan that details your objectives for the organization.

The following example may help you to understand what I am suggesting.

Primary Role	Primary Goals
1. Art Lover	1. To visit the Louvre in Paris.
	2. To have a painting displayed in an art gallery.
2. Father	1. Spend quality time weekly with my children.
	2. To have a great holiday with the family over Christmas.

Primary Role	Primary Goals
1.	1.
	2.
2.	1.
	2.
3.	1.
	2.
4.	1.
	2.

Goal Creation Exercise 2: The 'Roles and Goals' Exercise

Primary Role	Primary Goals
5.	1.
	2.
6.	1.
	2.
7.	1.
	2.

Remember that at this stage all we are doing is creating a pool or resource of possible Goals to select from a little later on.

Chapter 20:

Goal Creation Exercise 3: The 'Six Questions' Exercise

Goal Creation Exercise 3

Grab another sheet of paper or use the space provided below and take a couple of minutes to answer the following questions. It's important not to think about your answers too long with this exercise, so make sure that you write down the first response that comes to your mind for each question.

Question 1: What is there in my life (not the lives of others!) that frustrates me?

_____
_____
_____
_____

Question 2: What inspires me? What captures my imagination or lights the fire of passion in my heart?

_____

_____

_____

_____

Question 3: If there was a question that I often ask myself what would it be?

_____

_____

_____

_____

Question 4: If I had a magic pill that I could swallow and change one thing about myself and my current reality, what would I change?

_____

_____

_____

_____

Question 5: What has to happen in the next 12 months in order for me to consider the year a success?

_____

_____

_____

_____

Question 6: If I was to die tomorrow, what is it that I would regret not having done? (Remember to focus on what you have not yet done as opposed to regrets about what you have done)

_____

_____

_____

_____

Now that you have answered the questions, let's go back and have a look at each one and see what they reveal about you are your destiny.

QUESTION 1: WHAT IS THERE IN MY LIFE (NOT THE LIVES OF OTHERS!) THAT FRUSTRATES ME?

This is an area to work on. It may be that you are stuck in a dead-end job or that you keep getting turned down for the employment opportunities that you really want. It could be that extra weight that you want to shift or that you are still smoking after trying to quit so many times. Look at the frustration as a gift. It's a niggle that won't go away because it's not congruent with one or more of your deepest held Values. Whether or not the frustration is about yourself or your situation, it still comes back to the cold hard reality that nothing will change in your life until you change. And changing the source of your frustration could make a great Goal.

QUESTION 2: WHAT INSPIRES ME? WHAT CAPTURES MY IMAGINATION OR LIGHTS THE FIRE OF PASSION IN MY HEART?

Is there a cause or an activity that you are drawn to? It could be musicor art or a specific sport. It could be an environmental or social justice issue.

I remember many years ago I created a situation where I was working too hard for my own good. Life had become very serious and at the time I didn't feel like I had my own space. It was all work and family. A lot of people share a similar experience when they have a young family. I felt guilty about wanting time for myself, but the reality was I needed some outlet in order to have a sense of fun and to recharge my batteries.

So I looked back over my life and started to think about what I had really enjoyed in the past. Tennis was the activity that came to mind, so I joined a tennis club, enrolled in the inter-club competitions and later set a Goal to become a First-Grade tennis player. When I started, I was in Fifth Grade (there were only five grades!) and I was ranked player number four (there were only four players!). I achieved the Goal of playing First Grade tennis some five years later. Setting the Goal opened up all sorts of growth opportunities as I took coaching lessons weekly and went to countless drill sessions. I met new friends, became president of the tennis club and generally added a whole new dimension to my life that all stemmed from the simple question above. Above all else, it put some balance back into my life and made me a better father and husband as a result.

QUESTION 3: IF THERE WAS A QUESTION THAT I OFTEN ASK MYSELF, WHAT WOULD IT BE?

People often ask themselves the same question over and over. For example I realized that I was constantly asking myself *"How can I make this better?"*

Here's some of the questions that others have come up with once they've thought for a while about their "Primary Question:"

- *"Why can't I make friends easily?"*
- *"Why do I always go quiet in a group of people."*
- *"How is it that I am always broke?"*
- *"Why can't I quit drinking so much?"*
- *"Why do I seem to lack confidence?"*
- *"How come I always screw up?"*
- *"What's the point?"*

Chances are that, if you contemplate this concept for long enough, you will identify one Primary Question that you ask yourself more than any other. Once you have identified your Primary Question, you may gain some clues for a worthwhile Goal.

For example, a person who keeps asking *"Why can't I make friends easily?"* would do well to make a Goal of creating and growing a close friendship. They'll also want to replace the old question with a new affirmation or question that leads their mind to a solution rather than focusing on the problem. For example, their affirmation might be something like, *"I naturally make friends with ease and grace,"* or *"What can I do to help this person?"*

Not all questions will lead to a Goal, but if, for example, your question relates to something that you are not happy about in respect to yourself or your circumstances, then it's a fairly strong clue that there is a Goal in there somewhere.

QUESTION 4: IF I HAD A MAGIC PILL THAT I COULD SWALLOW AND CHANGE ONE THING ABOUT MYSELF AND MY CURRENT REALITY, WHAT WOULD I CHANGE?

All too often we stall in our quest for Fulfillment because we think that the Goal will be too hard or that we don't have enough resources or the right capabilities. Remember, the obstacles are what you see when you take your eyes off the opportunities. If it was as easy as waving a magic wand, what would you change about your life? If you could change anything about yourself as easily as that, what would you change? Would you get rid of that nagging injury or that health issue? Would you clean up that debt? Would you sort out that mess in your relationship? Would you quit smoking? Would you go for that promotion?

The key here is to motivate yourself to get off your butt and to back yourself and go for it. You need to start and that's the hardest part. Once you've decided to go for it, you'll find that your fear turns into energy.

Here's what Goethe said about getting off your butt (from the play "Prelude at the Theatre'):

> *"Then indecision brings its own delays, And days are lost lamenting over lost days. Are you in earnest? Seize this very minute;*
> *What you can do, or dream you can do, begin it; Boldness has genius, power and magic in it."*

QUESTION 5: WHAT HAS TO HAPPEN IN THE NEXT 12 MONTHS IN ORDER FOR ME TO CONSIDER THE YEAR A SUCCESS?

Perhaps I have left the best until last! This question is so simple and has such a relatively short time frame that it focuses the mind almost immediately. It's a straightforward question that those with a high degree of rational thinking ability seem to relish. A variation of this question that can work better for those with a more creative approach to thinking may be to try the following variation of what is essentially the same question: Imagine that it is now exactly one year from today's date. You are looking back over those twelve months and your life has been a total and complete success. What was it that you changed or achieved over the last twelve months that made it so successful? Remember, you are looking back from the perspective of twelve months' time.

QUESTION 6: IF I WAS TO DIE TOMORROW, WHAT IS IT THAT I WOULD REGRET NOT HAVING DONE? (REMEMBER TO FOCUS ON WHAT YOU HAVE NOT YET DONE AS OPPOSED TO REGRETS ABOUT WHAT YOU HAVE DONE).

This question is terrific for giving you clues for future direction. What's so important to you that you would regret not having done it if you were to die tomorrow? Within 48 hours of my elder brother Hugh being diagnosed with terminal leukemia he was dead, aged 31. It was a sober reminder to me that none of us know with certainty that we will live until tomorrow. Carpe Diem. Seize the day.

CHAPTER 21:

GOAL CREATION EXERCISE 4: THE 'DREAM DAY' TECHNIQUE

Before we get into the process of selecting your first set of Goals to work on, let me tell you about another concept called the Dream Day. This concept will not only help you to form Goals, but you can also use it as a creative way of generating new ideas for any area in your life.

I created this concept when I was in search of a mind-opening experience that could really free me from the blinkered thinking processes that I tended to use when I got into my work routine. There is a time for staying focused and operating in a routine and there's also a time for breaking free and coming up with an idea that has the power to radically transform your results in life and/or in business.

A Dream Day is a terrific way of coming up with ideas for new Goals because it is an "ideas" day. As mentioned above, you can use a Dream Day for ideas other than new Goals, but seeing we're on the subject of reshaping your life, I'll tell you how to create a Dream Day for that purpose.

The purpose of a Dream Day is to come up with the answer to a specific question that we will discuss soon. It's a way of developing new concepts, options, philosophies which in turn often morph into new Goals. In this case, the "big idea" relates to new Goals.

Here's how a Dream Day works.

First of all you need to go on holiday. I'm talking about the "blobby" kind like a week or two at the beach, by a river, in the mountains or wherever. Reading, walking, and generally just chilling out. Take the kids on outings or visit the local cafes or museums or historic sites and so on. The key thing here is to make sure that your mind and body are recharging. For this reason holidays where you are travelling a lot don't count and neither do holidays where you are having to mentally stretch yourself.

On the penultimate day of your holiday, in other words two days prior to returning to work, you put aside a day for your Dream Day. I recommend you do this once every three months, or every ninety days. Even having a Dream Day once a year can deliver Extra-Ordinary results.

Prior to your Dream Day, you will need to form a question that will lead your mind to a positive answer. For example:

- ✔ "How can I double my income and enjoy my work even more?"
- ✔ "Where would be the best place in the world for me to spend the next phase of my life?"
- ✔ "What is the most productive way for me to work?"

Goal Creation Exercise 4: The 'dream Day' Technique

- ✓ "How can I work a four-day week and increase my income at the same time?"
- ✓ "If I were to radically change how I live for the better, what would that look like?"
- ✓ "What can I do to dramatically improve my lifestyle while at the same time make a significant contribution to society?"
- ✓ "How can I experience a quantum leap in the levels of fun, Freedom, and Fulfillment?"
- ✓ "What could I do that would make me proud of my achievements and that I have a natural talent for?"
- ✓ "What can I do more of that makes me feel happy and worthwhile?"

As you can see, these are big questions that have the potential to transform your life.

The forming of the right question is critical to the success of this process and in fact it's a very special skill itself (see "Creative Questions" and "Destructive Questions" below).

Once you have your question formed, then you are ready for your first Dream Day.

On the morning of your Dream Day, start with a lined yellow pad and a blue pen and write your question at the top of the first page.

To create answers to your question, you can use any number of techniques. Everyone has their favorite way of generating ideas and answers. Use whatever techniques work for you:

- ✔ Brainstorming
- ✔ The non-stop fifteen-minute writing technique from Chapter 18
- ✔ Day dreaming
- ✔ Visualizing
- ✔ Doodling
- ✔ Mind mapping (buy a book and learn it)
- ✔ Yes/no technique (form a question that can only be answered "yes" or "no" and then meditate to still the mind before asking the question and then noting the first answer that comes to your mind)
- ✔ Journaling
- ✔ Meditating
- ✔ Contemplating

Write your answers onto a lined yellow pad .

As soon as you feel like it, leave the question and go for a walk, have a swim, go to a café or anything that relaxes your mind and takes your Conscious attention away from the question.

Come back to the question when you are ready and continue to create answers using the techniques suggested above.

Toward the end of the day, pick your best ideas and schedule time to start implementing them.

The three key points to really lock in on to make a Dream Day significantly successful are the following:

Goal Creation Exercise 4: The 'Dream Day' Technique

1. Clear the mind with a real "veg-out" type holiday.

2. Get the question right.

3. Spend time on and then off the question.

PART SIX:

HOW TO CREATE GOALS THAT ARE MOST LIKELY TO SUCCEED

Chapter 22:

Top Tips to Consider Prior to Selecting Your Final Goals

Congratulations, if you've followed my system so far you will have created a plethora of potential Goals. It's important to remember that when it comes to setting and achieving Goals, less is more and slower is faster.

What I mean by these cryptic phrases is that now you have done such a magnificent job of creating so many Goals you are going to need to be disciplined and patient and select only three to start work on. Yes, that's right; I recommend that you focus on only three personal Progressive Goals at any one time. In fact, it could be argued that in the perfect world you'd only have one personal Progressive Goal to work on at a time. However, the fact that you have read this far means that you are an "over-achiever" and you will never stick to having only one Goal anyway. So let's agree on three. But no more. You may however add some other "Maintenance Goals," but no more than three personal Progressive Goals.

The major mistake that almost everyone makes at this stage is setting far too many Goals.

I recall getting a question from a rather "on edge" gentleman in one of my workshop audiences many years ago. *"I'm having difficulty making progress on all of my Goals. What do you suggest I do?"* It was the word "all" that tipped me off to his problem. *"How many Goals do you have?"* I asked. *"Twenty seven,"* he replied. No wonder he looked stressed! Twenty-seven Goals! Full marks for trying, but zero points for strategy.

Let me illustrate the folly of starting with too many Goals. If you learn how to juggle, your instructor will start you off with one ball and will ask you to perform specific hand movements as you "juggle" your one ball.

Once you have mastered the "one ball juggling technique" your instructor will then give one additional ball. You'll then learn how to juggle two balls and when you demonstrate a reasonable level of competency with two balls you will be given a third. Sounds like common sense doesn't it?

Can you picture the instructor saying to you *"Here you go, start with these twenty-seven balls and see how you go!"* You can imagine the result. Chaos, frustration, and inevitable disillusionment. Eventually you might even be tempted to declare that "juggling sucks."

So why would you drop all the balls? Because your mind could not cope with all of the demands on it. It's the same with your Goals. If you set too many, then you will "drop the balls" and instead of achieving the Goals you'll experience frustration, disappointment, disillusionment, and eventually you'll give up on the lot. Goals will just become another item on your "it didn't work for me" list. And again, you would not have failed because having Goals is a bad idea, but rather because, metaphorically speaking, you simply had too many "balls in the air."

So you may now be asking why I had you come up with so many Goals in the first place. The reason is simple: selection implies choice. More selection means more choice and the more choice the more likely it is that the quality of your final Goals will be superbly high.

The Power of Focus

On many occasions during Goal-creation I have observed an interesting mental phenomenon in myself and others that I call the "Exclusion Illusion." What happens is that we spend so much time creating and focusing on our Goals and we get so passionate about them that Subconsciously we come to believe that this is now what we are going to do with the remainder of our lives. And this is all we are going to do. We forget about the day to day realities of our life which we believe will not happen.

But of course, life does happen. The boss makes extra demands, a client cancels an order, a competitor "ups the ante," the dog gets sick, the school calls and wants to talk about your kids, the washing machine breaks down, and amidst the 74 emails that came in yesterday, the 5 faxes and the 3 projects still needing attention, the Goal gets neglected. There's simply not enough space in your life left for it.

So what happens to your "steel like" resolve to follow through on your Goals? The steel begins to feel like old and brittle rubber that's being stretched to a breaking point.

The "Exclusion Illusion" leads us to believe that we are able to focus on our Goals to the exclusion of everything else. When "life happens," our composure gets rattled and we find it easy to quickly abandon the pursuit of our Goals.

In other words, we underestimate the amount of time and energy that will be consumed in the mere maintenance of our lives. Most people spend 100% of their resources on maintaining where they are at right now. Keeping your body and your "things" clean, tidy, and in working order gets 40% of your time. Work gets 50%. No one knows where the remaining 10% goes, it just goes. Successful people have mastered the art of setting aside 10% of their time to proactively pursue Progressive Goals for health, relationships, and money.

If, when you set your Goals, you allow yourself to develop an "Exclusion Illusion," then you will set too many Goals because you won't be aware that even to devote 10% of your time and energy to these new Goals will be a supreme challenge for you initially.

And always remember: the enemy of the good opportunity is the great opportunity. You are a limited resource. You only have so much time, physical energy, mental energy and only so much money. When it comes to committing to Goals, the solution is to commit to less quantity and to greater quality.

Choose fewer Goals and achieve them faster. You will be able to tackle the other Goals later on once you have nailed the higher-priority ones.

'Under-commit' and 'Over-achieve'

One of the reasons why people get so stressed is because they over-commit their resources. When you commit to completing six weeks work in two weeks, the result is a stressed and unbalanced life. Similarly, most people commit around 105% of their income and that creates stress. Bear in mind too that, if you are reading this book, it means that you are above average, so chances are you commit even more of your income than the average person. How's that working for you so far?

Learn to commit to less (under-commit) but to achieve more (over- achieve) than you commit to. Think of it as being like a UPOD gift (Under Promise and Over Deliver) to yourself.

In our ESP workshops, we use specific forms for planning Goals that ensures Goals are set in each of the three critical areas of Health, Relationships, and Money (see **www.esp-coach.com**).

As mentioned earlier, in an ideal world, we might have only one Goal at a time. We would give that Goal our full attention and devote all of our resources to the achievement of that Goal until it was completed and then we would turn our attention to another area of our life.

However, people who are attracted to taking charge of life tend to be over-achievers and to limit them to one Goal would simply create the human equivalent of a pacing caged lion.

So allow yourself up to two Goals for each section — health, relationships, and money. And I recommend that only one of those Goals be a Progressive Goal and the other, if there is another one, can be a Maintenance Goal.

For example, under my Health category I have one Goal that is a Progressive Goal that relates to increasing levels of Consciousness, and another Goal that is a Maintenance Goal that relates to fitness and weight.

I did the hard work on my fitness and weight many years ago and achieved my Goals in these areas. But I want to make sure that I stay fit and I especially need to watch my weight, so I keep the Goal on my planner as a Maintenance Goal.

Chapter 23:

Finalizing Your Goals and Making Them S.M.A.R.T.

Increasing your physical and mental energy levels are your highest priorities because energy is the raw material that you take into the process of "Goal achievement manufacturing." So you need to be fit, have the right amount of body fat, and preferably be free of illness and disease. And that means you need to take charge of your diet, your exercise, and your leisure time; the latter also helps with keeping mental energy levels high.

The next most important Goal relates to nurturing and growing your relationships with your Life Partner and children, if you have these relationships. If not, then I suggest you focus on doing the same for several close friendships.

Finally, you may want to have a Goal for growing your income, or for wealth creation.

The three areas mentioned above are the broad categories for what most people will want to start with in terms of creating Goals. However, do please take the time to review the Goal Creation exercises you completed a couple chapters ago and sort out your first three personal Progressive Goals.

In addition to Progressive and Maintenance Goals, I also have what I call "Shelf Goals." These are Goals that I really want to achieve, but they are simply not at the top of my priority list at the moment. In other words, I don't have enough resource of time and/or energy and/or money to take them on without creating imbalance in my life or without diluting my focus on my more important Goals. Therefore, I "put them on the shelf" until the time comes when it's appropriate to give them my attention. At the point when I have achieved one of my Progressive Goals, I can move that Goal to a Maintenance Goal status and then replace it with a Shelf Goal.

I know that it will be challenging for you to leave a lot of your Goals on the shelf for now, but remember that you will be able to come back to them once you have achieved your first, and more important, set of Goals.

Is My Goal a S.M.A.R.T Goal?

When it comes to setting Goals, most people set themselves up to fail by missing certain key characteristics that must be inherent in every Goal.

There is a way that you can write a Goal that will increase your likelihood of success. If, when you write a Goal, you fail to include any one of these five vital characteristics, you will probably never achieve the Goal. Setting the Goal up right in the first place is a bit like your ticket to enter the race. It does not guarantee that you will win the race, but it does mean you get to start.

The five key characteristics in creating an "odds-on" Goal are as follows:

1. Specific

2. Measurable

3. Achievable

4. Reasons

5. Time-bound

As you can see, we can create an acronym out of these points: S.M.A.R.T. Let me explain what I mean by each one of these letters.

Specific

In my native country of New Zealand, there once existed a bird called the Moa, or "Dinornis Giganteus" to be precise.

Standing up to 2.5 meters tall, the Moa was the world's largest flightless bird and having no natural predators, it roamed the country in massive numbers. Then man arrived in the form of the Maori and took a bit of a fancy to Moa stew and the like. As the old kiwi song laments, *"They're gone and there ain't no moa."* But had they really gone? When Europeans arrived in New Zealand, sightings of the bird persisted, and numerous Moa hunting expeditions were set up. You'd think that a flightless bird standing a massive 2.5 meters tall would be hard to miss, but New Zealand is blessed to have millions of hectares of lush and dense native bush, most particularly in the South Island where the alleged sightings occurred. No live Moa was ever found.

What's my point here? If one day you get the urge to go hunting for a Moa, then first you better make sure that you know what a Moa looks like. Similarly, if you are going to put a lot of time and effort into your Goals, make sure that you know exactly what the finished result will look like before you start.

For example, "get fit" is not a Goal. It is an idea. It's a worthwhile idea but it's still just an idea. If you were one of my clients, I would want to know what "get fit" looks like to you. Does it mean that you can walk ten kilometers in under 75 minutes? Or does it mean that you can bench press 80 kilos? Or both? What does "get fit" look like to you? On which days will you train? What time will you start and how long will you train for? What will you wear? How will you warm up and warm down? Now we're starting to get a little clearer. Specificity is power.

On a number of occasions I have had people say to me *"I'm going to lose some weight."* Great idea. But that's all it is: an idea, a concept, an intent. How much weight will you lose? And by when? What will you eat and just as importantly, what will you *not* eat? When will you start? What will you do on special occasions? What will happen when you go to a restaurant? If this was your Goal, I would want you to think long and hard about all of the different situations that you might face and I would want you to work out as precisely as possible how you were going to act in those situations. Until you are clear on not only the Outcome, but all of the possible Inputs, you are not in a position, either physically or mentally, to commit to the Goal. The disciple Luke recounts Christ's words: *"For which of you, intending to build a tower, sits not down first, and counts the cost, whether he has sufficient to finish it? Lest perhaps, after he has laid the foundation, and is not able to finish it, all that see it begin to mock him, saying, "this man began to build, and was not able to finish."*

Once you are clear and you can be specific about what the Outcome and the Inputs look like, you have something that you can consider before you commit. Always remember that Commitment is only possible once you have Clarity. Don't go Moa hunting until you know what a Moa looks like.

Measurable

This one is an extension of the idea of being specific. The reason that you need to be able to measure the Goal is in no small part due to the fact that the recognition and appreciation of progress is vital to your success. What can be measured can be managed, and progress that is measured is motivational.

Not being able to measure your progress towards your Goal would be a little like travelling by car to a city that was a long way away, only you have no idea how far away it is and at no stage on the journey do you know how far you've gone. You wouldn't know if you were 99% of the way there or still only 1%. The thing that demotivates people more quickly than anything else is sustained uncertainty.

There are however two valid ways that a Goal can be measured, and they are each quite different. The first is called "objective measurement" and the second is known as "subjective measurement."

Objective measurement means that progress can be measured free from any form of opinion. Objective measurement is based on facts, whereas subjective measurement is based on feelings or perceptions. We have been taught since the time of Aristotle not to trust our feelings (although his mentor and teacher Socrates was very big on trusting intuition), but to base our judgments purely on fact.

A sound rule of thumb is that where possible and practical, Goals should be formed so that progress can be measured objectively. This is easiest to do with Money Goals and with Physical Health Goals. It's more difficult to do with Emotional Goals (e.g. Happiness) and Mental Goals (e.g. peace of mind or creativity) and it's especially challenging with Relationship Goals.

Let me explain.

With Money Goals, you either have it or you don't. There is no argument about it. It's not based on an opinion (although one could argue that Profit is just that; an opinion). It's based on fact. Inarguable and clear.

With physical Health Goals objective measurement of progress is equally easy. For example, you can stand on the scales and see if you are on track to hit your weight Goal. If it's a fitness Goal, a stopwatch will tell if you can do the run in time. The stopwatch is not a subjective opinion; it is cold hard objective fact. Likewise, with a sporting event Goal, you either finished the marathon or you didn't. You either achieved the top ten finish in the yacht race or you didn't.

No opinions are required here. All of these Goals can be measured objectively.

But what about developing greater Happiness? That's one of the most important Goals of all. And yet you can't measure Happiness objectively. It's an opinion. You can certainly feel it, but you can't put it onto a spreadsheet or under a slide rule and there are no bathroom scales that have been developed for you to weigh it. So how do you measure your progress towards it? Simple: you measure your progress to it subjectively.

Paddi Lund taught me this. Paddi is a terrific human being and someone who has taken a serious interest in Happiness and especially in creating what he calls a "Happiness Centered Business." You can learn more about Paddi and his amazing story at www.solutionspress.com.au.

Paddi wanted to create more Happiness at work. So each morning he and his team would sit down, and they would score themselves on a scale of one to ten (zero being suicidal and ten being euphorically ecstatic) on how happy they were at work the day before. Over a few weeks, they all noted where they were, but the level of Happiness did not significantly improve until Paddi added the masterstroke.

In addition to scoring themselves, each person on the team was asked what the cause of their score was. Why were they unhappy or Happy. They quickly discovered that they could significantly influence levels of Happiness by being courteous to each other. So Paddi introduced his now famous "Courtesy System," which encouraged patience and tolerance along with considerate and polite behavior.

Paddi tapped into a simple concept that Hindus have known about for over four thousand years. The concept is called "contemplation" and is one of the most underrated and underutilized activities in the western world.

To effect a permanent change in any emotion or mental pattern, you first need to be aware of it. No awareness equals no choice. The more you are aware of how you are feeling or what you are thinking, the more choice you have in terms of what you do about it. Contemplation of how you feel or what you are habitually thinking is a highly effective method for increasing Consciousness around emotions, thought patterns, and their causes.

The Buddhists also practice the art of contemplation as the Buddha himself was a Hindu prior to his experience of Enlightenment and subsequent establishment of Buddhism. Hence the Dalai Lama also recommends contemplation of emotions, thought patterns, and causes as a way to alter Consciousness and reality.

Additionally, the Dalai Lama also recommends adding the contemplation of consequences, and this adds a powerful new dimension to the art of contemplation. As you contemplate the consequence of say, remaining unhappy, you bring to your Conscious awareness the suffering you experience when you are unhappy and also the impact of your lack of well-being on others around you. You may also decide that as a role model to others such as children and co-workers, unhappiness is not such a great look. As you contemplate your unhappiness together with its causes and consequences, you'll tap into a deep well of determination. Once you have completed your contemplation, making a note of your observations in a journal (otherwise known as "journaling') is an effective way of driving your newfound thoughts even deeper into your Subconscious.

Having completed your contemplation, you are then in a clear position to create an affirmation around how you would prefer to feel, think, or act in the future. See Chapter 45 for a fuller explanation on how to use affirmations and other tools for rewriting your Subconscious programming.

The bottom line is that Goals for mental and emotional health as well as Goals for developing deeper and more fulfilling relationships can be measured even though the methodology is subjective.

In the case of relationship Goals with children or a Life Partner, it's worthwhile involving the other person in the subjective evaluation of how they feel that the relationship is progressing. From experience, I can tell you this will in all likelihood open a real can of worms, especially with a Life Partner who has repressed their true feelings for many years! If there is suppressed resentment and a long list of behavior modification requests that follow, you're better off knowing about it rather than co- existing with someone who is thinking those things but not expressing them. What your Life partner is feeling about the relationship will be manifest one day, one way or another. Don't be like my friend Bill, who thought things were fine with the relationship until he came home one day and found his suitcase on the front doorstep, packed with a few of his personal possessions, and a new front door lock firmly shutting him out!

So if you are serious about developing a loving and nurturing relationship with those who are close to you, in addition to learning to accept them as they are and learning to give to them unconditionally, you're also going to have to learn how to make a meal out of "the breakfast of champions": feedback. See more in chapter 39 where I write about "Top Tips for Relationship Goals."

As mentioned before, some people will tell you that every Goal needs to be stated in such a way that it can be measured objectively (based on inarguable fact) and that subjective Goals are not valid. I disagree.

A case in point is a Goal to develop a better Life Partner relationship. Let's look at two different ways of stating the Goal.

Objectively measured method: *"I have a weekly date with Sue and once a month we take a long weekend holiday away together."*

Subjectively measured method: *"I enjoy a truly loving relationship with Sue that is continually increasing in fun, passion, and Fulfillment."*

I am OK with the Goal being stated either way, but I have a preference for the latter. The reason is simple. The first example does not actually state the desired Outcome; instead, for the sake of being able to be measured objectively, it specifies certain Inputs. In other words, it's not actually making it clear as to what the Goal actually is. It would therefore be possible to complete the Inputs — have a weekly date and have the long weekends away — and still not be making any progress toward the real aim of developing a more fulfilling relationship together.

Don't get too hung up on this though. There is no definitive right and wrong when it comes to how to state a Goal; the most important thing is that you have a Goal.

Achievable

I can never be the Queen of England or the President of the Ukraine. Not that I would want to be. These Goals are not achievable. No amount of "positive thinking" is going to Overcome knock-out factors such as not being a female (although it seems that can be changed these days) or not being born in Kiev (capital of the Ukraine) fifty years ago.

In addition to being achievable, your Goals need to be realistic. There is a school of thought that is often misunderstood around the concept of "positive thinking." Some believe that if one were simply to think positively, then all manner of impossible things will suddenly become possible. I don't agree. No amount of positive thinking is going to help me win the Australian Superbike Title in my first race, or frankly even in this lifetime! The guys who win the Australian Superbike Champs have been riding bikes since they were seven years old, have competed since they were ten years old, and are either young and fearless or slightly older but vastly experienced. They are also backed by professional factory race teams and they devote virtually every waking hour to riding. Everything, including their finances, their relationships, and their health has to fit in with their Goal of becoming number one. For me to set a Goal of winning the championship would not only be doomed to failure due to my lack of capability, but it would also destroy the rest of my life in the attempt.

Where positive thinking does help me though is when I line up for the start of a race alongside someone else of similar ability who is not thinking positively. I'll beat him every time. Positive thinking will help you perform better than someone else in the same circumstance who is full of fear and self-doubt. But it won't transform results into the miraculous on its own.

So make sure that your Goals stretch you to the point where you will be required to step out of your Comfort Zone and make an effort, but not so far out that you will lose your confidence and your balance in life. The problem with being a "Don Quixote" and tilting at windmills is that it will crush your confidence and murder your motivation. Far better to chunk the Goal down into something smaller and really nail it before stepping up to the next level.

Bottom line: make sure that your Goals are achievable and realistic and then you can successfully devote the necessary amount of time and energy not only to that Goal but also to your other Goals so that you maintain a balanced life.

Reasons

This is another big one. Reasons are fuel in the furnace of motivation. Having a stack of powerful reasons as to why you want to achieve the Goal adds a potent mix of motivation, drive, and discipline to your Goal-achieving resources. No reasons equals no go. When you hit the obstacles and progress slows down, you need to have powerful motivators to drive you forward. This is one of the reasons why it's important that your Goals are what *you* want and not what someone else either in your past or present thinks that you should want.

Let's take the example of quitting smoking. What sort of reasons could you stack up? In addition to the obvious health reasons, there are financial benefits to being smoke free as well as social benefits. Let's look at the list of reasons so far:

- ✔ I will probably live longer.
- ✔ Once I am over the withdrawal phase, I will be fitter and have more energy.
- ✔ I won't have to go outside during a restaurant meal to smoke.
- ✔ I can enjoy a more active sports role.
- ✔ I can use the money to fund my new set of golf clubs.
- ✔ I will increase my confidence levels and I can apply that to other Goals.
- ✔ I will gain respect from those I live and work with.
- ✔ I will gain respect from an even more important place when I look myself in the mirror every morning.

And the list could go on. But we can add another set of reasons that make the mix more motivational. The extra dimension of power comes from reasons that relate to others you care about. My experience is that most people will be prepared to sacrifice a lot more if they think that other people will avoid suffering. For example, imagine a smoker adding the following to his or her list of reasons for quitting:

- ✔ My children will have a smoke-free parent as a role model.

We've just added some jet fuel to his/her motivation tank!

You may have noticed another useful distinction that I made in the above list. In uncovering otherwise hidden reasons, it's useful to categorize the reasons into "Outer world" and "Inner world" reasons. In the "smoke-free" example, there were a bunch of Outer-World reasons such as not having to go outside to smoke at restaurants and using the money saved from cigarettes to buy a new set of golf clubs. But there were also powerful Inner-World reasons such as improved self-respect. These Inner-World reasons are often what people find the most motivational. Every successful salesperson knows that people buy on emotion (Inner-World) and justify with logic (Outer-World).

Let's say that you set a Goal that really was Extra-Ordinary (see Part Ten, "The Extra-Ordinary Personal Goal'). It may be climbing a mountain, sailing an ocean, or helping a worthy cause through a philanthropic contribution of time and effort. Here are some potentially motivational reasons:

- ✔ I will increase my levels of Consciousness by getting out of my Comfort Zone and overcoming new and challenging obstacles.
- ✔ I will expand my Capacity as I learn new skills and develop new abilities.
- ✔ I will experience a quantum leap in self-confidence and Self-Esteem: in short, I will feel good about myself.
- ✔ I will have some amazing experiences along the way and will learn and grow as a result of those experiences.
- ✔ I will form new friendships with some stimulating people and will be enriched in the process.
- ✔ I will be a great role model to my Life Partner, children and clients and may inspire them to get out of their Comfort Zones more and to really live life fully.

✔ I will create a legacy of achievement that will inspire my grandchildren and their children to go for greatness.

If you've gone for the philanthropy-based Goal, you could also add:

✔ I will make a significant contribution to my community/society and others will benefit in a way that would not have been possible otherwise.

Remember: reasons are the fuel in your furnace of motivation. Feed your motivation levels with lots of powerful reasons and they will be transform into more mental and physical energy.

Time-bound

The mind loves a Goal and until you put a time target on your Goal, it won't create the sense of focus and immediacy that you will need in order for you to communicate to your Subconscious that you are in fact serious about this Outcome.

So always put a time limit on achieving a Goal, but don't fall into the over-achiever's trap of making the deadline too tight. Cut yourself some slack when you date stamp each Goal. Remember to allow for the rest of your "life" to still happen while you go about the business of achieving your Goals.

Be mindful of being flexible with the time frame for achieving your Goal so that you don't destroy the quality of the result by rushing the final stage, and also so you don't create unnecessary stress or imbalance in your life.

Hurry makes waste. Wasted time, wasted energy equals a wasted life. Slower is faster. Less is more. Under-commit and over-achieve.

Remember that if you want a comprehensive planner to document and keep track of your Goals then visit www.tompoland.com and download my "Goal Creation and Achievement Planner" from the "Online Shop."

CHAPTER 24:

GOAL CREATION CHECKER – TOP TIPS FOR FORMING YOUR TOP GOALS

THERE ARE A just a few more points to consider before you finally commit to your Goals. Remember that it really pays dividends to spend enough time making sure that your Goals are really what you want and that they really are S.M.A.R.T. Goals. You are going to be investing a lot of time and effort into bringing these Goals to life, so you want to make sure that you are investing those resources in the areas of your life that you truly want to change for the better.

ALIGNING YOUR LIFE

Earlier I discussed the issue of aligning your Vision to Values. This concept also applies to the alignment of your Goals, so let's take a brief refresher on what I mean my alignment.

The word alignment has to do with placing items in a straight line. It can also infer that each item is pointing in the same direction. If the front wheels of your car are "out of alignment" it means that they are pointing in a different direction than your rear wheels. This results in you having to put more effort into holding the car on the road through the steering wheel to ensure that the car keeps heading in the right direction. Additionally, the front tires will wear excessively and even the engine will have to work that little bit harder, burning more fuel, as it pushes the slightly skewed tires forward.

Remember that just like your car, your life can also be out of alignment. For example, if your daily actions are not taking you in the same direction as your Values, you will feel "out of sorts." And just like trying to keep a car that's out of alignment on the road, you'll feel that life is a struggle and you'll be spending a lot of effort just to keep things on track. Also, you'll be wasting energy and time that could more profitably be invested into taking your life in a more Values-Aligned direction.

ARE MY GOALS ALIGNED TO MY VALUES?

For example, if one of your Values is "Family" or "Love" but you don't invest any time and effort toward a Goal targeted at developing relationships or you don't give selflessly to other people, then you will suffer from that lack of alignment. Similarly, if you Value "Balance" but have ignored my recommendations and instead end up with three Money Goals and no Health or Relationship Goals, then you will never feel fulfilled.

You will feel "out of kilter" or "out of whack."

When you act in a way that represents progress towards a Values- aligned Goal, then those actions will also fit your

Values like a glove on a hand. Your Self-Esteem will soar to new levels and so will your levels of productivity.

ARE MY GOALS ALIGNED TO MY VISION?

An aligned set of Goals also means that when you achieve a Goal you will have taken a step further toward fulfilling your Vision. Any Goal that you create that does not feature this characteristic is a Goal that you should promptly abandon, or if you feel that the Goal is valid, and aligned to your Values, then alter your Vision statement to reflect that.

> *Goal-aligned action*
>
> *Many people suffer in life from not having clear Goals. But for those who do know what they want, the problem then becomes doing what they know they need to do. Non-compliance is not just a problem that doctors have with patients, it's a problem that we all face. To align my actions, I have often asked myself a simple question. I have found it to be the most powerful action-aligning tool that I have ever come across. Its simplicity belies its power. I call it the "Creation Question" and it goes like this:* **"Does this action create the future I want, or destroy it? Nothing is neutral, everything counts."**
>
> *Using this question every day will help keep your actions aligned to your Goals.*

Are the actions that are required by this Goal aligned with my Values? Do I feel comfortable with these actions or do I feel that they would, in some way, compromise my Values?

ARE MY GOALS IN HARMONY OR DO THEY COMPETE AGAINST EACH OTHER?

It's possible to set up Goals that are aligned with Values and Vision but that fight each other for limited resources. For example, if you have a Goal to repay personal debt and another one to lease a new Porsche Carrera, then chances are you have two Goals each fighting for funding from the same source. Work out which Goal is the priority (I'll give you a hint: it doesn't have four wheels!) and then nail your highest priority Goal. You can always come back and do the luxury sports car thing once you're debt-free.

Another example of Goals that fight each other might be if you have a business Goal that requires you to work long hours, but you also have a Goal to better develop a relationship with your Life Partner or children. You don't have to be Einstein to see the conflict there. Both Goals are going to be competing for the same time resource and one or both of them will end up being starved of time. In this case, there may be a way that you can achieve both Goals. It's a matter of deciding that you are still going to hit your business Goals but that you'll find a way to achieve this using less time. In other words, work smarter and not longer. Learn to delegate more, learn to waste less time, and learn to focus your energies like a laser on only the most highly productive activities.

I'm a great believer in working hard, but I am not a believer in working too long. Working too long will end up damaging your personal relationships, your physical and mental health, and it is counter-productive to your Goal of higher productivity in any event. Learn to work smarter. Think twice, act once.

Is My Emotional Well-being Detached From Achieving This Goal?

You need to learn how to achieve at a high level and to be relaxed and happy at the same time. Too many people attach their emotional well-being to the realization of a specific Outcome:

- *"Someday when the kids are off my hands then I'll relax."*
- *"Someday when I've got that promotion then I'll feel more confident."*
- *"Someday when I've made my first million then I'll be happier."*
- *"Someday when I've got that new car then I'll feel more like a real person."*

"Someday" may never arrive. What if you only had today left? Would you choose to make it a happy one? Do you even know how to relax or to be happy or to feel good about yourself?

Being emotionally detached means that you will develop your emotional capacity independent of your other Goals. It means, for example, that you will choose to practice being Happy regardless of whether you are making progress with your Goals or whether you are going backwards. Anyone can be temporarily Happy when things are going according to plan. It takes a Master to be Happy, and to take appropriate action, when things are not going the way that was wanted.

BE FLEXIBLE WITH THE TIME FRAME

The purpose of setting a time target for each Goal is to increase the sense of immediacy in your mind and to give your mind a target. Once you date stamp your Goals, your mind will have a framework of time in which to focus and to "plot and scheme." Always remember though the purpose of the time target. It's to give your mind a frame of reference, a target to focus on. It's not to create unnecessary stress and imbalance in your life simply so that you can tick off the Goal on schedule.

For example, I set a Goal to have this book written before Christmas. It's now January the 3rd. I missed the self-imposed deadline. I could have worked all my weekends and nights around my business schedule and hit the Goal's target date. But I doubt if the finished result would be something that I would be proud of. And I doubt if my family would be feeling valued and well-supported if I had spent every spare minute of my life tapping on a keyboard.

If hitting a deadline means reducing the quality of your Outcome, it's not worth it. That finished result, whatever it may be, is a reflection of who you are — your Values. And if hitting a deadline means screwing up your health and neglecting your relationships, it's also not worth it. I mean, why do you think they put the word "dead" in the word "deadline?" Sometimes "deadline" becomes frighteningly close to the literal meaning of the word "dead:" "deprived of life."

Goals such as competing in a certain event have a predetermined time frame, so if that's the case, just make sure that you have budgeted for plenty of time to prepare.

Once you think that you have allowed enough time, then proceed with your Goal. But wherever possible, extend the time frame if you need to so that you can maintain balance between your health, relationships, and money.

Have I Set My Goals for Others?

I've mentioned this before but it's worth revisiting because it's such a common mistake. As a caring human being, we want the best for our kids and our Life Partner. We don't want to see them suffering and we believe that if we can just get them to change (and be more like us!) then all will be well with their world.

The fact remains, however, that you can lead a horse to water, but you can't make it drink. You can support your loved ones, but you cannot set their Goals for them. They have to genuinely and truly want not only the Outcome that you have in your mind, but they also must be prepared to commit to the required Input. And this all needs to take place without your coercion! Maybe you're a great salesperson at work but let me assure you that a person convinced against their will is a person who remains unconvinced. Despite their reluctant outer appearance of agreement, they will only develop the confidence and commitment they need if they really want the Goal for their own reasons.

The best advice I can give you as a parent who wants the best for their kids is to first of all love them for exactly who they are right now. You need to demonstrably show them that they have your unconditional love. This applies whether they are fourteen months old or fourteen years old. A child who knows that they are good enough right now, warts and all, for their mother or father is a child who has a foundation of a healthy mental state on which they can build a great life.

Loving your kids means that you invest high-quality time with them while they are still dependent on you. That's easier when they are younger because they can't get enough of you. You're their hero. It becomes a little more challenging when they get into their teens, so where possible it's important to create a common interest early on. One of my clients, whom I regard as a superb parent, has the challenge of trying to be a father to a son who lives in a different country. Because their time together is so limited, Alex wanted to give his son, who was around seventeen years old, a lot of advice as soon as he arrived in the country to visit.

Fortunately, Alex and I had a conversation prior to his son's arrival and instead of proactively giving his son a lot of advice, Alex simply hung out with him and did stuff that his son wanted to do. They ended up pumping a lot of weights which just about permanently disabled Alex, but it did create enormous rapport. After a pattern of such behavior, Alex rarely needs to offer advice; his son now asks for it.

In respect to Goals for Life Partners, you need to resign from trying to be "General Manager of the Universe" and let them be free. Some of their Values won't be the same as yours. You may want them to benefit from the extra energy you've found since you've become fit, but they may not care. And it is pointless caring more about someone else's suffering than they care themselves. Manage your life, not theirs. The best influence you can have on a Loved One is to be a great role model. "Be the change you want to see."

Of course you should be there to support your loved ones, but you need to earn the right to be asked for help. And you do that by loving them; by accepting them one hundred percent as they are and by unconditionally giving to them the things that they need to grow.

ARE YOU AS PASSIONATE ABOUT THE INPUTS AS YOU ARE ABOUT THE OUTCOME?

Imagine playing poker and betting on a pair of twos. How would your confidence levels be? How about if you held three Aces? Better? Once you have S.M.A.R.T. Goals you've got the first Ace. The second Ace comes once you have identified the right strategy and tactics.

The third Ace pays massive dividends when you get it added to the first two. But beware, without the first two Aces, the third one is as useless as a pair of twos. Once you have worked out what you want to achieve (SMART Goal) and how you are going to achieve the Goal (strategy and tactics), the toughest part is simply completing the appropriate Inputs (actions) diligently and with persistence.

Leveraging your performance comes automatically when you are as passionate about the Inputs as you are about the Outcomes.

For example, If you set a Goal to complete a marathon but really hate running, it obviously makes your ability to persist in achieving the Goal more difficult. If however, you love swimming then you can make the Goal more achievable by finding the swimming equivalent to the marathon.

Bear in mind, however, that any worthwhile Goal you select is still going to require effort and persistence. The Ironman Triathlon I completed meant that in addition to the swimming and running training, I needed to spend hours and hours cycling. Although I derive some masochistic satisfaction from cycling in smaller doses, I found the longer training sessions of up to six hours to be simply unenjoyable. The problem wasn't the degree of difficulty or even the need to push beyond the pain barrier; it was that I simply disliked long cycle rides – a lot!

By contrast, I can spend a day at the race track practicing on my motorbike and enjoy the process immeasurably more. While the same levels of physical endurance are not required like they were for Ironman training, the sessions are nevertheless challenging and still demand significant effort. The difference is that with racing a motorbike, I enjoy the Input a lot more than the cycle training. I guess I just prefer the form of two wheeled transportation that has a 160 brake horse power engine between my legs.

There are hard, unenjoyable and unsatisfying Inputs. And then there are hard, "enjoyable-in-a-painful-sort-of-way" and satisfying Inputs. I prefer to get my growth from the latter. So give yourself a break and where possible engineer the Goal so that you can enjoy the journey as much as you actually enjoy arriving at the destination.

ARE YOUR GOALS REALLY GOALS OR JUST AN IDEA?

At the ESP Programme (**www.espcoach.com**) we've found that some Members initially express their Goals more as an idea than a real Goal. As mentioned previously, the lack of specificity means that they have about as much chance achieving the life of their dreams as they have of choosing next week's winning lotto numbers.

To help you really get a handle on this, I've included below some examples of typical Goals that our clients have set over the years. You will notice that they can all be expressed as an idea, but that with a bit of polishing they can also be turned into S.M.A.R.T. Goals. Where practical, they have been worded in the present tense and in the first person. This makes the Goals easier to say as an affirmation and therefore easier for the Subconscious to accept as inevitable reality.

Examples of How to Turn an Idea Into an 'Odds On' S.M.A.R.T. Goal

Original Idea	S.M.A.R.T. Goal Equivalent

Health Goals

I'm going to get fit	I am able to run for 30 minutes without stopping before Dec 31. Or I have a VO2 max* of 3.5 liters/minute by Dec 31.
I want to lose some weight	I achieve & maintain a weight of 80 kg, 18% body fat and a 86cm waist before June 30.
I need to relax more and unwind	I take an average 2 full Leisure Days every week starting March 1st and I start a weekly yoga class commencing April 1st.
To play the guitar more	I play "Dueling Banjos" competently for my son at his birthday on August 22.

Relationship Goals

To spend some time together as a family	I invest every Saturday with my family totally devoted to them. I leave work for home by 6p.m. at least three times per week and we have a family holiday three times per year.

Original Idea	S.M.A.R.T. Goal Equivalent
Better relationship with my Life Partner	I enjoy a truly loving relationship with Sue that is continually increasing in fun, passion, and Fulfillment.
Get involved in the community	I coach a soccer team for the upcoming season.

Money Goals (Personal)

Reduce my personal debt	I am free of personal debt and have paid off all credit cards by December 31.
Get some passive income	I have $100,000 of passive income outside of business interests within five years.

Take some time finalizing your Goals but start by forming a first set of draft Goals for you to fine tune over the next week or so.

* Fitness can be measured by the volume of oxygen you can consume while exercising at your maximum capacity. VO2 max is the maximum amount of oxygen in milliliters, one can use in one minute per kilogram of body weight. Those who are fitter have higher VO2 max Values and can exercise more intensely than those who have a lower VO2 max value. You can increase your VO2 max by working out at an intensity that raises your heart rate to between 65 and 85 per cent of its maximum for at least 20 minutes three to five times a week. A mean value of VO2 max for male athletes is about 3.5 liters/minute and for female athletes it is about 2.7 liters/minute.

PART SEVEN:

GIVE IT THE "G.A.S."
THE GOAL ACHIEVEMENT SYSTEM

Chapter 25:

How to Achieve Your Goals. Step 1: Craft the Perfect Goal

A Science Not a Game of Random Chance

Achieving the life of your dreams needn't be like a game of pin the tail on the donkey. Goal Achievement is a science and, like any other science, it can be studied, learned and the principle applied. It's a little like knowing the combination to an unbreakable safe that contains treasure. If you don't know the combination, it seems impossible to get in, but once you know the steps, it's relatively straightforward. You just need to know what those principles and steps are, and the rest is a matter of time and effort.

By following my Goal Achievement System (GAS) you'll be taking a lot of the guesswork out of the process and you'll also speed up the achievement of your Goals quite markedly. The GAS system has been tested and proven by thousands of people. It has stood the test of time and experience. Learn to use it and it'll pay massive dividends. The power is at your fingertips, or actually more literally, it's between your ears and within your heart. I can supply the system, but you must bring the passion.

THE SEVEN-STEP GOAL ACHIEVEMENT SYSTEM (GAS)

Here's a summary of what I call the seven step Goal Achievement System:

1. Craft the "perfect" Goal

2. Create a winning strategy

3. Take affirmative action

4. Align your Inner world

5. Align time to Outcomes

6. Build a structure of accountability and review

7. Practice "Sensory Sensitivity" and "Strategic Suppleness'

Now that you have formed your Goals, go through each one of them one at a time and make sure that they are as perfect as they can be. This checklist is a summary of the main points covered in regard to forming Goals and if you can tick each point off, then you have what I call "The Perfect" Goal, which is Step 1 of the GAS system.

By following this checklist, you'll have created a Goal that is as near to perfection as possible. Think of it like creating a plan for a magnificent building. If the plan is ill-conceived, then the chances are the building is going to be less than magnificent. However, if the plan has been well thought through, then the building has the best possible chance of being successfully constructed. The checklist:

- ✔ The Goal is clear and **S**pecific.
- ✔ The Goal is able to be **M**easured.
- ✔ The Goal is realistic; it's **A**chievable with effort.
- ✔ You have powerful **R**easons for wanting to achieve this Goal.
- ✔ You have date stamped and **T**ime bound the Goal.
- ✔ Where possible, you are prepared to be flexible with the time frame.
- ✔ This Goal is for *your* life, not for the lives of others.
- ✔ You feel as passionate about the Inputs as you do about the Outcome.
- ✔ The Goal is aligned with your Values.
- ✔ The Goal is aligned with your Vision.
- ✔ Your Goal is in harmony with other Goals and will not fight against them.
- ✔ You are detached emotionally from this Goal.
- ✔ You will be able to find sufficient resources to achieve this Goal, e.g. time, money, energy.
- ✔ You have a maximum of three personal "Progressive" Goals (as opposed to Maintenance Goals).
- ✔ Your Goals are balanced, i.e. you have a Goal each for Health, Relationships, and Money.
- ✔ You are committed to achieving the Goal.

A friend of mine spent many years in the construction industry. David visited Japan as part of his quest to learn all that he could from other constructors around the world. He told me that in Japan you could walk past the same construction site day after day and week after week and all you would see was a big hole in the ground. In the western world, he said if such a thing occurred, everyone would be concerned about the lack of activity, but not so in Japan. Week after week, that site sits there with nothing happening. And then all of a sudden construction commences and a building takes shape and shoots up towards the sky at a breathtaking pace. What was happening for those weeks and even months of seeming nothingness? David said the plan was being prepared. And the plan was being prepared to the nth degree. One hour of careful planning will save you three hours of effort. As a carpenter would say, "measure twice and cut once." Most people rush their Goal-setting and then charge off in what they later decide was the wrong direction. Wasted time, wasted energy, and wasted money. Slower is faster, less is more. Think twice, act once.

Perfection is of course an ideal that may be impractical to achieve, but it will pay dividends for you if you can get as close as possible. Getting to within 90% of "The Perfect Goal" will be adequate. It will take you a lot longer to get to 100%, but you can get to 90% perfect in only 20% of the time that it will take you to get to 100%.

Of course, don't use over-preparation as an excuse for inaction either. Frankly, most people don't have a problem with over-preparation; it's normally woefully underdone. Get the balance right by working on the formation of your Goal until you are satisfied that you are ready to commit.

Chapter 26:

How to Achieve Your Goals. Step 2: Create a Winning Strategy

Strategy is all about the best way to achieve your Goal in broad terms or in big-picture terms. By way of illustration, imagine that your Goal was to travel from one city to another. Let's say that you traveled for a while and then you were able to get into a helicopter and fly straight up above the point where you were standing to such a height that you could now see both cities. You may not be able to see the building you started off from, but you can see "the big picture." This is like gaining a strategic point of view. Working out your route to the next city is probably going to be a whole lot easier now that you can see things from a larger perspective.

In summary, forming a strategy becomes easier when you go to the "big picture" before you get to the detail. Once you can see this larger picture then you are in a position to decide on your strategy.

If you were going into a physical battle against another army, you rely on a lot of things to Overcome your enemy. First of all, you would want to know the "big picture" in regard to your enemy's strengths and weaknesses. Then you would need to establish what sort of competitive advantage you will bring to bear against the forces arrayed against you. Will you rely on superior numbers, or better technology? Will your strategy be to dominate the air or to land lock your adversary by sea? Will you rely on a quick and powerful knock-out blow or will you want to out-last your opponent in a war of attrition? Fortunately, most of us are not faced with such difficult and unpleasant decisions in our lives, but the principle behind the example is the important thing. The question that strategy begs to have answered is this: "how will I win?'

In the world of sports, strategy is equally omnipotent. Targeting a perceived weakness in the opposition is a key to effective sports strategy. Will you attack the flanks or play it up the middle? Will you demoralize your opponents by a blistering start or save your best to last? Will you rely on superior fitness or greater technical skill or the experienced "old heads" to pull you through, or will you combine all three into a winning strategy?

Business, of course, has its parallels to both war and sport. There are competitors and there is a scorecard which is mercifully measured in profit and market share as opposed to body count. In business, organizations seek to gain competitive advantage primarily through a better product, better service, better price, or better distribution/marketing. Or if you are MacDonald's, all four. No wonder that they have created more millionaires than any other business in the world. Their strategy is unbeatable.

When it comes to most of your personal Goals, it's not a matter of how you are going to be better than the others, but rather how you are going to be better than yourself. But either way, you still need a winning strategy to succeed.

So, what does all of this mean to you in crafting a winning strategy? Well, for starters, it means that the slogan "just do it" is premature until you've worked out how you are going to "just do it." What is going to be the most effective way of "just doing it?"

I once wrote an article for a business magazine entitled *"Don't Just Do It, Sit There."* The premise was that people often complained about a shortage of time and other resources in business, and yet I could see tremendous wastage by organizations who had not taken the time to create a winning strategy. Worse, many businesses simply had no Conscious strategy and simply relied on the old Neanderthal approach of *"well it's not working so let's all do more of it."* In other words, their idea of strategy was no better developed than "work longer, work harder." They wanted to do more of what wasn't working, and they thought that would produce a different result. That's nuts, but it's also all too common. All the hard work in the world will get you worse than nowhere if you get your strategy wrong. Going faster in the wrong direction only gets you lost more efficiently.

GET YOURSELF A SUPERMODEL

When it comes to the achievement of personal Goals, one of the best ways that I know of to work out a winning strategy is to seek out what I call a Supermodel. And when I talk about a Supermodel, I don't mean the likes of Cindy Crawford or Naomi Campbell. I mean someone who has successfully achieved what you want to achieve or has successfully advised people on how to do the same.

I've long held the belief that one of the worst things that I can do is to learn from my own mistakes. I'd prefer to learn from the mistakes of others. Certainly, when I make a mistake, I want to remember what went wrong. But I'd rather avoid making the mistake in the first place. Mistakes are generally expensive and not always just in terms of money. Wasted time, wasted energy, loss of confidence, loss of motivation, and sometimes physical injury can result from valiant, but ill-advised efforts.

When I first bought a motorbike to race, I sought out a professional race trainer to act as my coach so that I could literally get up to speed quickly. Unfortunately, the promised training was continually postponed due to my coach's other commitments. That postponement cost me months of progress and two crashes that were the result of ignorance of standard racing practices. I had to spend over two thousand dollars in repairs to the bike, not to mention repairing a broken wrist. Ouch! People sometimes worry about the cost of a Supermodel. Not having one is a lot more expensive.

WHERE TO FIND YOUR SUPERMODEL

Believe it or not, Supermodels are everywhere. They appear and speak at seminars and workshops. They publish books and audio CDs/MP3s. They are on the internet and in the newspapers. You can see them on television and hear them on the radio.

Often these people have spent the thick end of a whole lifetime becoming an expert at their specialty, and if you ask them, many times they give you access to all that experience for nothing or for the price of the book they wrote.

Not everyone who appears in these forums is a Supermodel of course. You need to check your potential Supermodels out carefully. Believe it or not, just because someone has published a book or been on television does not qualify them as a Supermodel. Use your inbuilt "B.S. detector" (your intuition) to work out whether the person is just full of hot air or whether they really are the voice of successful experience. If you are proposing to pay your Supermodel, then you also have a right to ask the names of several of their clients you can call to check them out.

I was at a wealth development seminar once and the speaker recommended a book written by an expert in personal investment strategies. From memory, the author of the book had spent almost forty years as a professional investor in some 24 different countries around the world. He had amassed a personal fortune of over US$100 million and for $19.95 I could learn all that he knew. I couldn't wait for the break. I almost flew out of the auditorium and into the foyer where the book was on sale. I put down my credit card without so much as reading the front cover. During the break, someone came up to me and asked me, *"I see you bought that book. Do you think that it's worth it?"* "Let me see," I replied a little tongue in cheek, *"Four decades of experience as a professional investor who's traded in two dozen different countries and has accumulated over one hundred billion dollars for $19.95? Yes, I think it's worth it."*

Virtually every time I set a new Goal, I seek out a Supermodel. It doesn't matter whether it is a Health Goal, a Relationship Goal, a Money Goal, or a business Goal. I buy (and read!) the books, I listen to the audios, I talk to those in the know and I go to the seminars.

On two occasions now, I've even flown to another country to meet with a Supermodel to pick their brains. Both of these people were referred to me by colleagues whose opinions I highly respected. And both of the Supermodels had achieved exactly what I wanted to achieve. I still remember the phone conversation with one of them. After introducing myself and mentioning the name of the person who had referred me, I made my request *"Malcolm,"* I said, *"if I flew over to see you and bought you breakfast would you talk with me for half an hour?"* Malcolm's response was typical of what you'll experience: "Hell, if you're silly enough to fly all the way from New Zealand, I'll buy you breakfast!"

On one of these trips, I got my half an hour and not a minute more, but it was worth every cent and every second that I spent to get there and back. And then some. I gained valuable information that saved me years of unnecessary and expensive testing. On the other occasion, my Supermodel welcomed me into his home, and I spent most of a whole afternoon with him. He is a very generous man and to this day I keep in touch with him from time to time to let him know how I'm doing.

I want to make the distinction between a Supermodel and a Coach. The latter can be the former, but the former is not always the latter. In other words, you might hire a Coach, as in a personal Coach or Business Coach, who is also a Supermodel in that they've "been there and done that." The difference is that a Coach will meet with you regularly and will help you to stay on track. If you need that, then make sure that your Supermodel is prepared to Coach you as well. If, however, you don't need the regular meetings, then on many occasions a non-coaching Supermodel will be just fine.

Having mentioned that you can find Supermodels in books and in the media, there is another great source of Supermodel identification. This other way of finding a Supermodel is to think about the people you know who have done what you want to do. They can not only tell you how they did it but what they would do differently next time and who they got advice from along the way.

For example, when I wanted to compete in an Ironman Triathlon, I asked several people who had successfully completed the event who they used to put together their training program. All roads led me to Performance Lab in Auckland (www.performancelab.co.nz) and so I chose them. Find out who the Supermodels are, reference check them carefully, and then listen to their every word with great care.

What to Look for in a Supermodel

1. Look for their **success track record** at either achieving what you want to achieve yourself, or better still, someone who has successfully advised others on doing what you want to achieve. The reason that I prefer the latter characteristic is that the highest achievers don't always make the best teachers. Valentino Rossi is currently a six times world-champion motorbike racer at the highest level of competition in the world.

Would he make the best coach for me? Probably not. There is the obvious problem that Vale is unlikely to pop in and meet me at our local race track to give me some coaching for the "C and D" grade Club Championships.

There is another issue, though, which is that he is so developed in his riding ability that he would find it difficult to relate to my needs as a novice. It would be too easy for Valentino to assume that I know the basics well, when in fact I do not. I'm better off seeking out the likes of the excellent coaches at the Australian Superbike School (www.superbikeschool.com.au) who are not only successful racers themselves, but are also familiar with the coaching needs of amateurs such as myself.

Having said that, make very sure that when you find your Supermodel you are listening to the voice of experience. Remember, you don't want someone who simply knows the theory. *"The best earth is the earth that has gone through the worm."* There is no substitute for the experience of the Consciously competent.

2. The second characteristic that you want to have in your Supermodel is effective **communication skills.** You want someone who can not only establish rapport with you but who can also tell you what you need to know, not just what you want to hear. Someone who can face you up to reality. Someone who is not afraid to challenge your assumptions. Someone who will encourage you to speak your truth, your fears, frus-

trations, aspirations, and all. Also, someone who can make you think. And, of course, someone who can listen and understand. This means that you want a Coach who is not attached emotionally to the approval of you as a client (that's not normally a problem if you're not paying them of course!). While it's great when one of my clients thinks that I've done a solid job, but it's more important to me that I have delivered what the client needed rather than to simply gain their short-term approval.

If you are entering into a long-term mentoring or coaching relationship with your Supermodel, then you'll want to add this next characteristic as well.

3. A **congruent set of Core Values** is the next thing to look for. There needs to be a set of Shared Core Values so that each of you are in sync with the other. For example, it's unlikely that you would want to sustain a relationship with someone who violated Core Values such as honesty.

   But make sure that the Values you check out really are Core to you. I've seen too many people "burn" their Supermodel relationship simply because the Supermodel didn't Value timeliness as much or didn't Value "not swearing" to the same extent.

   Another example of where Shared Core Values are of less importance would be if I wanted to learn from someone who had a very specific area of expertise such as investment advice. If my Supermodel was a genius at investing, but was also overweight and unfit, I wouldn't care. Sure, they don't share my Values of "fit" and "lean," but who cares? That's not what I am there to learn. So unless your Core Values are being violated somehow, don't set yourself up to destroy a potentially beneficial Supermodel relationship by being overly judgmental or fussy.

Once you have found your Supermodel, then you are in a position to work out a winning strategy using their experience. Put together a simple plan based on their advice, but remember, too, that you always have the right of veto. Chances are you will exercise that right very rarely, but do listen to your gut feeling, your intuition, in making your final decisions when it comes to your strategy. Learn to listen with an open mind, but don't give away your power by following every recommendation blindly. Back yourself, and your follow your own judgment if you feel uncomfortable with your Supermodel's advice.

Chapter 27:

How to Achieve Your Goals.
Step 3: Take Affirmative Action

What we are talking about in setting and achieving Goals has to do with transforming your reality into something different from what you currently experience. If you want to change your house, your car, your job or business, if you want a better relationship or more Happiness, it all has to do with this process of transformation. So what is it that we are transforming?

We tend to think of energy in terms of petrol, gas, steam, electricity, and so on. But in fact, everything in the world is energy in one form or another. All matter, which means everything in the universe, contains energy. And we learned from Hiroshima how much energy could be released from splitting one microscopic particle of matter called an atom.

The seat you are sitting on consists of billions of atoms that contain extraordinary quantities of energy. Even your thoughts are a form of energy: an electro-chemical energy reaction zapping between a series of over 100 billion neurons. Money is a form of energy, in more ways than one, as are the building materials in your house and even the air in and around it. Everything is matter and all matter contains energy.

So back to my question. When we set and achieve Goals, what is it that we are transforming? Effectively, we are using energy to transform matter from one form to another.

Goal achievement is a "matter transformation" process. We take a form of matter, or multiple forms, and we transform them into something different. For example, if I become fit through jogging, I take mental energy in the form of ideas on how to train, I part with matter in the form of money, and I get myself a different form of matter called running shoes and sports clothes. I invest physical energy in training and thereby produce aerobic fitness. It's like a trading game. We trade multiple forms of matter and energy for a different form. We give ideas (a form of energy) in business and get money in return. We give energy to a relationship and feel love as a result. Any time we think or act we are expending energy and transforming matter. We are even transforming matter when we sleep. We go to bed, sleep for a while, and wake up refreshed. Our energy levels are replenished.

Achieving Goals is all about the transformation of matter via energy. So if that's the case, how important is the quality of the energy that you take into the trade? Make sure that you put quality energy in your body's fuel tank and quality energy into your mind's fuel tank. In regard to the latter, quality fuel comes primarily in the form of mental rest through leisure days and also in the form of quality music, books, and the like.

Because Goal achievement is all about the conversion of matter, it's appropriate to pay a visit to Galileo. The concept of "inertia" was perhaps Galileo's greatest contribution to physics. Inertia has to do with the fact that a body of matter will remain at rest until acted upon by an outside force.

In other words, it takes the application of energy (outside force) to get a body of matter to move. Interestingly though, once it's moving it takes the application of energy to stop it again. Most of us understand the first part of this statement easily enough. If we roll a ball over a wooden floor, we know we have to use a bit of energy to get the ball moving. But what about the second part: *"once it's moving it takes the application of energy to stop it again?"* We haven't applied any additional force to the ball and yet it stops moving, seemingly of its own accord. What we haven't taken into account of course is the concept of friction.

These observations are very helpful when it comes to our quest to transform matter from one form into another: i.e., achieving our Goals.

First of all, we understand that nothing will change in our life (matter) until we apply energy to the right area. Nothing changes until we make an effort.

Secondly, we understand that we need to continue to expend energy in the right area if we want to continue to make progress. Otherwise the "friction" of daily life will slow progress down and then bring to a halt the momentum that we created.

The reality is that you are already expending energy "24/7." As long as you are alive, you are expending energy. Energy *is* life. No energy equals no life. If you have any doubt about that statement, then the next time you are at a funeral take a peek in the casket. Have a look and see how much energy is in there. Not a lot.

So you are expending the energy anyway. The process of Consciously creating a life of choice through Goal-setting and achieving (transforming matter) is simply expending your energy in the right areas.

The bottom line is this: once you have formed your Goal, you need to Overcome inertia and take action. Additionally, once you have "started the ball rolling," you need to keep applying effort so that it continues to maintain momentum in the right direction.

So to Overcome inertia by creating energy, my rule is this: if at all practical, take significant and bold action on your Goal within twenty-four hours of having committed to it. Remember Goethe's admonition: *"What you can do, or dream you can do, begin it; boldness has genius, power and magic in it."*

And to combat the force of friction, my second rule is this: wherever possible, take some form of action on your Goal every day or every week, whichever is most appropriate. This will maintain momentum.

These two rules for overcoming inertia and maintaining momentum will keep you moving at a steady pace toward the Fulfillment of your dreams. You'll find that this process is mostly unexciting, as there are rarely any major breakthroughs or quantum leaps, only small but continual improvement. But it does work. The Japanese call the process of incremental but consistent improvement "kaizen" and with it they have created one of the world's most productive economies.

Consistent application of effort in the right direction over a sustained period of time is an unbeatable formula for success.

Chapter 28:

How to Achieve Your Goals.
Step 4: Align Your Inner World

Once someone has crafted the "perfect" Goal and has created a winning strategy, then the number one reason for failure is self-sabotage.

I don't mean that people Consciously decide to quit. That comes after the Subconscious decision to quit, which is what I mean when I refer to self-sabotage.

Self-sabotage can spring from any one of a myriad different reasons. Here are just the top two and without question they are the biggies. By my estimate, over 90% of self-sabotaging behavior has its source in these two issues.

1. Your Self-image (how you see yourself) is out of alignment with your Goals and you don't believe that you have what it takes to succeed.

2. Your Self-esteem (how much you value yourself) is low and you don't believe that you deserve to succeed.

My personal self-sabotage issue in the past was the first one. So I've developed a passion for proving myself, or more specifically my Subconscious, wrong. Every time I break through and achieve a Goal and every time I reach a certain level of mastery, I celebrate the victory and poke my tongue out, figuratively speaking, at my old Self-image. But enough of me, what about you?

You may be thinking that you don't have self-sabotage issues. I can assure you, though, that if you are occupying a human body, then these two saboteurs will feature to some extent in your life.

Bear in mind that these saboteurs live in your Subconscious and it's therefore possible that you are not even Consciously aware of them.

If you repeatedly fail to achieve your Goals simply through not applying yourself consistently, then chances are self-sabotage is involved. Here are some of the ways in which self-sabotage manifests itself:

- You procrastinate.
- You do things that damage relationships, even with the people you love.
- You stay in an abusive relationship.
- You gain weight that you don't want due to excessive eating or drinking.
- You lose weight that you need to keep due to dysfunctional eating patterns.
- You experience regular self-doubt.

- You seem to be addicted to struggle as evidenced by your life being a constant battle.
- You do things that jeopardize your career or business and financial life.
- You start projects and don't complete them.
- You regularly beat yourself up and belittle your own efforts.
- You regularly experience dis-empowering feelings of anger, resentment, and/or shame.
- You avoid starting or completing the important things on your to-do list.
- You avoid commitments.
- You are often dissatisfied with a self-generated result because it's not "perfect."
- You have to force yourself to stay committed to your Goals.

The chances are that you will identify with some of the above.

Self-sabotage is simply the program that your Subconscious mind runs when you give it certain sensory input. For example, if the input has to do with achieving weight loss and your Subconscious memory of achieving or failing at losing weight is a painful one, then it will do whatever it can to "protect" you from what it perceives to be the pain by trying to lose weight again. Or if you want to accumulate wealth, but you keep blowing your income on unnecessary or useless items that end up collecting dust or being given away, it's probably because you Subconsciously do not see yourself (Self-image) as someone who is wealthy.

I am sitting here typing this in a room that is air-conditioned. The air conditioner works in a similar way to the Subconscious, in that it has a thermostat that regulates its performance. Currently, I have the thermostat set at 22 degrees Celsius. If the temperature in the room drops below 20 degrees, then the thermostat kicks in and warm air is pumped into the room. If the temperate increases to over 24 degrees, then the thermostat does its job again and the air conditioner begins to pump cold air into the room. So the thermostat's job is to keep the performance of the air conditioner within a certain range.

Similarly, your Self-image and Self-esteem keep your performance within a pre-set range. For example, if you see yourself as a person who earns $100,000 income per year, then that's probably what you'll end up earning. If you find yourself on $80,000 per year, you will Subconsciously do whatever it takes to get back to $100,000. And if you over-shoot the mark and end up earning $120,000 and your Self-image is not adjusted, you will do something to sabotage that income and bring it back to where it "should" be.

Or, if you don't feel that you are capable or deserving of winning in sport against a certain competitor, and yet you find yourself ahead with only a few minutes to go, chances are you'll choke and "snatch defeat from the jaws of victory!" Afterward, you'll be shaking your head and wondering what happened. It's simple; your Subconscious thermostat kicked in and adjusted your performance to the level that it had been programmed to perform at.

The key to aligning your Inner World with your Goals is to reset the twin thermostats of Self-image and Self-esteem. A powerful key to resetting these thermostats is with positive "Self-talk."

You are continually having conversations with yourself. It's been estimated that up to 12 thoughts go zinging around your brain every single second that you are awake. That's 720 thoughts per minute and 43,200 per hour and 691,200 per day (if you have 16 waking hours). Even if this estimate has overshot the mark by 90%, that's still a massive 69,120 thoughts a day. And most of them we are not even aware of.

Taking control of your thoughts is vital. For example, if you want to raise kids with a healthy Self-image and positive Self-esteem, but you are constantly thinking about how much they screw up, then you'll manifest those thoughts in your words and actions, including your body language, and your kids will feel as about as loved and valued as a piece of dirt.

Also, if you want to be wealthy but your Self-Talk is always going on about nice new shiny things that you could spend your money on, then you are going to wind up with lots of devaluing toys and you'll also be very broke.

I have written a very comprehensive section on how to reprogram your thoughts so that your Inner World is aligned with success. It's all in Part Nine of this book, and I'd encourage you to read it thoroughly. If you do this, then you'll discover tremendously powerful tools for reprogramming your Inner World so that it is aligned with your Consciously formed Goals.

CHAPTER 29:

HOW TO ACHIEVE YOUR GOALS.
STEP 5: ALIGN TIME TO OUTCOMES

THERE IS A fundamental reason why people, if they have Goals, don't achieve them. It's really simple: they don't invest any time in achieving them. It seems so straightforward and so obvious and yet the issue of "not having enough time" plagues most people. How can we expect to hit our Goal if we fail to align our time with our desired Outcomes? It's like pointing the front wheels of your car to the left and wondering why you're not heading right.

Many years ago, I observed myself constantly saying, to myself and others, that *"I never have enough time."* I also then worked out that this was a totally dysfunctional belief in that I was never going to be able to get more time than I already had. The problem had nothing to do with a lack of time, but rather too much activity.

It was therefore understandable that verbalizing my belief of *"I never have enough time" r*esulted not in the creation of more time, but rather an increase in frustration levels, so I tried a different approach. I created and practiced the affirmation *"I have plenty of time."* I'd repeat this over and over whenever I had created a situation when I was squeezed for time. What I came to realize is that, in fact, I *did* have plenty of time; it's just that I kept over-committing it to activities that were not always my highest priorities.

The reason that I used to over-commit my time is that I did not schedule what I was going to do. Sure, I'd write it down on a particular day, along with a whole lot of other "things to do." But I never actually scheduled the task by blocking out a specific period of time to complete it. So I would end up with a schedule that had a list of calls to make, a list of things to do, and a list of phone calls. None of them were scheduled, as in *"I have blocked out this period of time to complete this task."* On top of that, I had meetings that were scheduled, but of course there was no mention anywhere about the e-mails that have evolved since the creation of the last generation of "Time Management" systems.

What this jumble of lists amounted to was that, on most days, I had sixteen hours of activity competing for ten hours of time. Consequently, I was forever carrying things over to the next day. And the next. And the next.

Interestingly, when I used the old system, I found myself to be very busy, but almost invariably on things that were "maintenance" activity or on things that others wanted me to do. Rarely did I have time set aside exclusively for proactively making progress towards my Goals.

Additionally, because I rarely completed the list of actions on any given day, I rarely felt fulfilled, and often felt pressured and stressed.

That's all changed. Now when I set a Goal and write down what I am going to do, that action gets allocated a specific period of time in my scheduler. Even if it is a five-minute phone call, it gets scheduled. Everything gets scheduled. Take note that this doesn't mean that I schedule all of my time, but rather that I schedule all of my Goal-related activity.

Wherever possible, I love to devote a whole day to one specific Outcome. It's clean and simple. For example, I can pretty much do that when I am training for Superbike racing and when I am earning money by running a workshop. In these cases, the whole day gets scheduled out for that one specific Outcome.

The reason that I like the "one day, one Outcome" approach is that it's very easy for me to see how I went in terms of making the day count. If I "wasted" the day, then my life goes backward. If I "spent" the day, then my life stays in the same place. But if I "invested" the day, then my life took a step forward.

However, on many days, this approach is not practical. On some days, there are multiple Outcomes that I am after and your life is probably the same. You may have meetings that others have called, clients who suddenly want to access you by e-mail, phone, or in person, or suppliers who do the same. Life is highly reactive at the best of times and demands on your time and energy are such that it can sometimes feel like you are the pinball in that giant pinball machine of life that I mentioned earlier. And other people are controlling the flippers.

So, if you want your life back, if you'd rather be a flipper than a pinball, if you want to feel that you are in charge again, then do what I do.

Every time you identify a Goal-connected action, schedule it. Go to your diary or software, and block out a specific period of time to complete the action. You already schedule meetings, which are commitments to other people, so why not schedule your commitments to yourself that appears in the form of Goal-related activity? Create an alignment between the Outcomes that you want and your time. Provided you are acting on the right things, and your Supermodel strategy should take care of that, then your success simply becomes the logical, and almost anti-climatic conclusion to the alignment of time to Outcomes.

As dull and simple as it may sound, scheduling your Goal-related action by allocating a specific period of time is one of the most effective things you can do to ensure the success of your life.

Be aware however that scheduling is like an art in that it needs to be practiced in order to get better at. Chances are that you will not allow enough time for most tasks when you first start to schedule everything. Pardon the pun but "give it time." It takes practice to get the scheduling thing happening accurately, but after a while you'll get the hang of it.

Scheduling is the missing link in the chain of Goal-achieving certainty. Always remember, as soon as you have identified a Goal-related action, schedule it.

CHAPTER 30:

How to Achieve Your Goals. Step 6: Build a Structure of Review and Accountability

ONCE YOU HAVE crafted the perfect Goal, created a winning strategy, taken affirmative action, and aligned your Inner world, the rest is largely a matter of persistence. And although persistence in itself is critically important, you need to create a structure of accountability and review, as this will add some steel to your resolve in persisting with your Goal.

There are several key components to the accountability and review structure that combine to make it a powerfully potent potion for persistence.

Recognizing and Valuing Progress

I recall that when I was very young, perhaps nine years old, being asleep and hearing a knock at the front door. For some reason, I took it upon myself to see who it was. I fumbled and stumbled, half asleep, out of bed along the hallway and to the front door. My parents were still up and awake, but I beat them to the door and opened the door to see my great Aunt, standing there with a warm smile of surprise on her face. *"Why you must be Tom!"* she exclaimed. *"Why look at how much you've grown! Last time I saw you, you were only knee high to a grasshopper."*

I guess that we've all had a similar experience as we were growing up. The Aunt or Uncle who hadn't seen us for a year or so and who comments on how much we had shot up. The thing is that I never noticed that I had grown and certainly my parents hadn't commented on it, probably for the same reason: my growth was slow and completely imperceptible to those who lived with me on a daily basis. In fact, none of us kids appreciated how much we had grown until we completed the regular and rather fun ritual of standing as erect as we possibly could and having Mum or Dad put a ruler on top of our head and mark our height in the door jamb. Then we could step out from under the ruler, turn around and see how much progress we really had made. And because I ended up at 186cm (six foot two and a half inches) I was used to making pretty regular progress. Funnily enough, when I saw how much I had grown, I was keen to grow even more! I'd finally found something that I was good at!

So what's the moral of the story as it applies our personal development and growth? Well there are a few and here they are:

1. We are often the last person to appreciate that we have changed.

2. Those who live and work with us have an image of who we are, and when we change, it takes a while for them to update that image.

3. Unless we measure our progress, we are unable to appreciate it.

4. Unless we appreciate our progress, we cannot be motivated by it.

5. We will rarely pause to reflect on our progress unless there is a structure for doing so.

The recognition and appreciation of progress is the chief distinction between those who feel fulfilled and those who, even though they are high achievers, walk through life feeling like a ghost looking for a home; they always feel that they are in a state of incompleteness. By definition, the act of appreciation has to do with "raising the value" of something. In this case, the "something" is your progress. In turn, this "raising of the value" of your progress has the parallel effect of raising your Self-Esteem. And that's got to be beneficial when it comes to making even more progress.

People who recognize and value their progress are putting fuel into their motivation tanks. Make a habit of being able to see and appreciate what you have done, regardless of how insignificant it may be.

For example, if you set a Goal that you were going to upgrade your computer network, did you at least pick up a brochure? If you set a Goal to get fit, did you at least browse the shelves of running shoes in your local store? If you were going to book a holiday with your son or daughter so that you could spend some quality time with them, did you at least invest some time reading to them at bedtime?

This is important. If you are like most of humanity, then you were programmed to notice what you didn't achieve, where you fell short or stumbled. If you got 80% in the math exam, your teacher or parents, well-meaning I am sure, offered a swift congratulations and then spent time looking at what you got wrong and why.

Also, when you didn't do what you agreed to do, it's possible that you got jumped on from a great height and told to do better next time. And probably on those occasions when you did what you were meant to do no one said anything. But the next time you screwed up again, you were back under the spotlight of scrutiny.

As a result, most of us were programmed to focus on our failures and to feel neutral about success. And this approach of seeing the glass as constantly being half-empty is counter-productive when it comes to creating people who possess a healthy Self-image and a high Self-esteem.

What I urge you to develop is a "Psychology of Success;" a mind that acknowledges how far you've already come and not just how far you have to go. It's critical to not only learn how to achieve at higher levels, but also to feel fulfilled in life. So I encourage you to create a habit of recognizing and appreciating every bit of progress that you make toward your Goal. It all counts in terms of motivating you to continue and helping you to feel good about yourself. Remember: it all counts, every little bit.

I recall training hard for the triathlon season many years ago in the same pool as then-World Champion Rick Wells. Needless to say, he was just a tad quicker than I was, but one morning after a workout, I found myself walking to the car park with our mutual Coach, Hilton Brown. I asked Rick how many hours a week he was training. *"About thirty,"* he replied. I was doing around 7–10 hours a week. *"Boy that's a lot,"* I said. With a twinkle in his eye and a bit of a smile on his face he shot back: *"It's not so bad if you're winning!"* That's the thing about winning. It's motivational. Early wins are the key. Start strong. Under-commit, but over-achieve.

Zachariah said it best in the Old Testament of the Bible when he encouraged us to *"despise not the day of small beginnings."* Lao Tsu added his voice by adroitly pointing out that *"the journey of a thousand miles starts with a single step."* Remember: *"Every action either creates the future you want, or destroys it. Nothing is neutral, everything counts."*

Review

We know that the mind is like a Goal-seeking missile. Once there is a Goal on the radar scope of your mind, you are going to track toward it at a regular pace. The issue then becomes keeping the Goal on the radar scope. For this reason, you need to make a habit of reading your Goals every weekday apart from holidays (give your mind a rest during your days off work so that you rejuvenate properly). Other things will compete for your attention and, if you let the Goal drop off the radar scope of your mind, then your life will revert to being like a giant game of pin the tail on the donkey, with a similarly low likelihood of hitting the mark.

Incidentally, I have a simple way of keeping my Number One Goal top-of-mind. I have my number one Goal inscribed onto a pendant and hang it around my neck and there it will stay until I have achieved the Goal. It's a terrific way of staying Conscious of my Goal.

So set yourself a specific place and time every week to recognize and appreciate your progress, as well as reviewing what you have not done, and also for planning the next week. This won't work unless you literally make an appointment with yourself in your scheduler or diary for a specific time each week.

Hour of Power

This is your most important meeting of every week. It's when you get to sit down and plan your life based around your Goals.

I call this review meeting with myself my "Hour of Power," and during it, I complete a number of steps that I have summarized for you below.

>**Step 1:** I read or write my first Goal slowly and carefully.

>**Step 2:** I read what I wrote that I was going to do that week toward that Goal.

>**Step 3:** I write down what I actually did that week for that Goal and I savor and appreciate my progress during this process.

>**Step 4:** I also mentally note, without any self-beating self-talk, what I wrote that I would do, but did not complete.

Step 5: I write down what I will do during the upcoming week for each Goal, which may include carrying over those actions that I did not complete the previous week.

You can complete this process using a simple piece of paper or an electronic tool such as a word processor or spreadsheet. I use a simple but specifically designed piece of software called my "Progress Appreciation and Planning Log," otherwise known as a "PAPL." You can download this powerful Goal-tracking software by visiting www.tompoland.com and going to the "Online Shop" and looking for the "Goal Creation and Achievement Planner" which incorporates the PAPL document.

The Hour of Power process is simple, subtle, and yet stunningly effective. The golden rule for this process is even simpler: *complete your Hour of Power every week, regardless of your results*, as though it is a religious obsession.

In other words, let nothing stand in the way of you completing your Hour of Power. And it doesn't matter whether you have had the most successful week of your life or the more dismal variety of a week; you still complete your Hour of Power. Where people fall down with this system is when they skip the Hour of Power because they didn't do anything toward their Goals. After a few weeks, their Goals drop off their mental radar scope and they revert to being the human pinball.

There is no more important piece of advice that I can give you in regard to achieving your Goals than this: *complete your Hour of Power every week, without fail*. The simple steps that you complete will ensure that your life stays on track for success.

And of course, as soon as you have made a note of a Goal-related action during your Hour of Power, the next thing to do is to immediately allocate a time in your scheduler to complete it. Always remember this vital extra step.

Accountability

This morning I completed a "Bikram" yoga class. I made a mutual commitment to a client that, if he attended one of these classes, then I would do the same prior to our next meeting. I needed to get up at 5:15 a.m. in order to be on time for the class. I have to tell you that it would have been very easy to procrastinate on this if it weren't for the fact that I am meeting my client tomorrow and I need to be able to tell him that I honored my commitment. Accountability holds each of us to a higher standard.

Another example of the effect of accountability would be if you set a Goal for fitness and wanted to get up a little earlier each morning to go for a walk or run. You'll increase your level of commitment, and therefore your likelihood of success, by arranging to meet a friend at the start of your exercise. When the alarm goes off and the inevitable thought of "giving it a miss" pops up, the next thing that you'll think about is your friend, forlornly waiting at the end of the street. So you'll get out of bed because you don't want to let them down.

Similarly, if you set up a regular meeting with a like-minded friend for each of you to review your progress toward your

Goals, then you'll increase your productivity. It'll give you a deadline to achieve the actions that you committed to and an added reason to complete your Hour of Power (i.e. steps 1 – 5) above in preparation for your meeting. Your meeting can be face-to-face or, if time is at a premium, you can e-mail your results to each other and then go through them on the phone.

The key is consistency, even if it is to the point that the process feels boring. Every week, without fail, your Hour of Power is your number one priority over every other event apart from that which is life-threatening. Look at it like this: if you don't have a structure of reviewing your Goals regularly, your ability to live life on your terms is threatened. In that sense, not having your Hour of Power does indeed threaten the success of your life.

Chapter 31:

How to Achieve Your Goals. Step 7: Practice 'Sensory Sensitivity' and 'Strategic Suppleness'

The only thing that you can be sure about in respect to your plans for achieving your Goal is that life will not follow the plan. I've never had any plan for any significant Goal go according to plan. We had all better get used to the reality that we cannot control life. It's like surfing. A top surfer understands that he or she cannot control the waves, so they don't waste any energy complaining about them or wishing that they were different. They simply become skilled enough to master the waves that they get.

Let's face it, most people don't plan. Unless it's for a holiday or what they want to have for dinner. So when they do plan, and life doesn't instantly transform itself by becoming the mirror image of what they wrote down, they give up. The nature of reality and our ability to see the future accurately is such that no plan is every going to go according to plan.

Ever. So get used to it. Plans are what we make when we want to give God a good belly laugh. That doesn't make the planning process valueless. On the contrary, it simply underlines the importance of getting better at it.

But the other lessons that our crystal ball-gazing deficiencies highlight are the need to be able to firstly detect when the plan is not working and, secondly, to be mentally flexible enough to adapt to the new circumstances. Easier read than done.

We really need to "get it:" life is not a movie script and it's not a book or a play where everything follows a predestined plot. It may be if you are God, but most of us aren't at that level of mastery just yet!

So when something doesn't go according to plan, simply treat it as part of a game. Surf the wave. Unpredictability and uncertainty are a natural and reasonable part of life and you would do well to mentally make them your friends. When the unexpected happens, indeed when something unwanted happens, learn to put a smile on your face and say, with conviction: "perfect!'

SENSORY SENSITIVITY

People often blind themselves to reality by choosing to believe what it is convenient for them to believe.

The Emperor couldn't see the obvious because he didn't want to see it. But everyone else could see that he was naked. If you invest significant time or money into a Goal, it's very easy for you to become emotionally attached to believing that your approach is working even when all those around you can see that you are flogging a dead horse.

I've seen people work themselves into bankruptcy and almost to death by continuing to push an approach that everyone else can see was futile. The admirable trait of persistence should never be confused with the stupidity of stubbornness or the blindness of obstinacy. Cutting your losses can be a wise investment decision.

The ability to detect trends is crucial for minimizing losses and diverting resources from places of low or no return to places of higher yields. If the tide is coming then even King Canute can't stop it so you're best to recognize reality and then respond to it in the most effective manner possible.

Many say that the definition of insanity is to *"continue to do the same thing and yet expect a different result."* For example, if you've been so successful at giving up smoking that you've quit seven times already (and taken it back up again) then try something different! Try nicotine patches, try acupuncture, try hypnosis, try reading Alan Carr's book on *Quit Smoking*. Swarm all over it. Show me a person whose still got a problem and I'll show you someone who hasn't yet tried everything.

Or if you've tried to lose weight and "it hasn't worked for you" (translated: "you haven't worked for it") then try a different system. Join a weight-loss organization or leverage your Goal using the twin strategies of "Reward and non-Reward" that I write about in Chapter 36.

The important thing is to be sensitive to what is working and what is not and to take affirmative action as soon as possible. I've worked with hundreds of successful business leaders and I've noted that the best of them are never complacent. In fact, I'd go so far as saying that they have a healthy level of paranoia about them when it comes to staying alert to anything or anyone that is starting to go off track.

A great example of Sensory Sensitivity from a commercial perspective is the story about the giant American retailer Walmart. Within fifteen minutes of the second plane hitting the twin towers of the American Trade Centre, Walmart's computer had picked up a significant increase in the sale of American paraphernalia. The same computer then automatically ordered every American flag and related patriotic paraphernalia from every supplier on its network. Within 24 hours, the only place you could buy an American flag in the USA was Walmart. Now that's Sensory Sensitivity.

Mental Flexibility

The capacity for Mental Flexibility is of paramount importance both in terms of enjoying the unplanned changes as well as getting on and focusing your energies on the next step.

Let me give you a couple of examples of Mental Flexibility and its opposite number - mental rigidity.

Today is Thursday. I had previously booked to go on a dirt bike tour today up the coast an hour or so north of where I live. I decided that I would work Monday, Tuesday, Wednesday and Friday but have today off. I spent last weekend and most of my evenings stripping down my dirt bike, cleaning it and servicing it in keen anticipation of the big day out on Thursday. Of course Monday, Tuesday, Wednesday, which I worked, were all dry and sunny, which is what you would expect when you live in a place called "The Sunshine Coast." This morning, being Thursday and "Tom's big day out," the heavens opened, and the forecast is for rain to continue all day and into the night. Friday, of course, is forecast to be sunny. Perfect! A few years ago I would have been crestfallen or at the very least disappointed. But after years of practice, I can honestly say that when it became clear that the trip was called off or canceled due to the weather, I felt fine. It was an opportunity. For what I didn't initially know. But then it became clear that I would write some more of this book, so here I am.

I'm not saying that I don't sometimes feel disappointed or annoyed. But when I do, I allow myself to experience that feeling, rather than suppress it, and then I get on with doing something that makes the most of the new circumstances. "Things not going according to plan" is what I call "situation normal." I believe that is the same for everyone on the planet. What separates the winners from the losers in life is not that the winners have plans that work out perfectly; it's their ability to respond to the unforeseen, to quit moaning about it, to quit blaming, and to get on and do something positive about it.

A few months ago, I stayed at a central city hotel. I arrived driving a large four-wheel drive towing an equally large trailer that carried my race bike. Unbeknown to me, the hotel's parking facility involved the use of space-saving car hoists that effectively stacked cars one above the other. The parking area was in a very confined space and I needed to take the trailer off first and manhandle that onto one of the hoists before maneuvering my vehicle, with what felt like a twenty-one-point turn, onto a separate hoist.

But I was delighted. My precious race bike was secure as no one was going to able to whip it off the trailer when it was 20 meters in the air.

At the same time that I was finishing up, an older couple who arrived after me were attempting to park their car in a similar manner. The wife was standing outside the car agitated and cursing none too quietly as she watched her husband maneuver their car onto a hoist. Her heightened degree of agitation was matched only by the redness in the face of her husband and the steam coming out of his ears. The wife then roundly abused the hoist operator and made a comment about how they would never have booked the hotel if they had known, and how were they expected to get their car out again on time and how … and so on and so forth. The episode of unbridled worry and anger continued rivaling some of the geysers found in my home country, but I'll spare you any more details of the unsavory expletives that ushered forth out of the mouths of this couple. Suffice to say they were not impressed with the hotel's solution to inner city parking problems!

I don't want you to think that I mentioned my somewhat calmer response to the same situation in order to impress you. Rather it's to impress *upon* you the contrasting experiences that I had versus the older couple when faced with the same situation. Their mental rigidity – *"this is not what I want"* — destroyed the quality of their experience, increased their stress levels exponentially, and probably ruined not only their whole evening but the rest of their stay at an otherwise fabulous hotel. I'd venture to suggest also that every time they went for a drive, or even thought of using their car, they would have experienced a repeat emotional performance. Thus, their lack of Mental Flexibility destroyed what would have otherwise been a terrific holiday. And that's a shame for them.

Every day you are faced with opportunities to grow your capacity for Mental Flexibility. Now you'll be even more aware of these "growth opportunities" and you'll have the ability to respond in an empowered way rather than be like the pair of victims I described above who allowed their Happiness to be hijacked by a hoist.

If, when things don't work out according to what you had in mind, you thump the table, complain about how unfair it is, blame someone or something else, and generally waste emotional and mental energy on being a victim, then you'll blind yourself to the gift that is in every "unwanted" circumstance. Look for the gift in your circumstances and then make the most of the situation using whatever resources you have at your command. Every unwanted experience offers us the chance to be more mentally flexible and therefore freer and happier. Practice makes perfect peace.

What I'm talking about here is not "positive thinking" in a kind of Pollyanna-style version of wishful thinking where we just grin and bear it. I'm a great believer in the concept of Reality Thinking which sees things as they really are as opposed to wishful thinking that sees things as I really want them to be. But I definitely buy into the concept of positive thinking when it comes to finding the gift in everything. After years of trying to convince myself that there is something useful in every experience, I have come to believe it as true. That's not to say that every experience is what I wanted or what I preferred to happen, but as long as it has happened, you can be sure that I will make the most of it.

STRATEGIC SUPPLENESS

Never give up on a Goal. That's the standard. I am a keen advocate of taking enough time to form the Goal and then taking even more time before committing to it. But once you have committed it's important to see it through so that you develop what I call the Psychology of Certainty. What I mean by this is that once you've consistently set and achieved a series of Goals, your mind will have great confidence around your likely success the next time you commit to a Goal. Continuing to build this mental muscle of confidence, called the Psychology of Certainty, is a key to increasing levels of greater success. Once you have developed this capacity for confidence, you will be able to set a Goal and "know" that it is as good as done. The only three questions that remain are how you will achieve it, how long it will take, and how much you will enjoy the journey.

It's important, though, not be confused about what you should and should not give up on. Never give up on a Goal, but the approach to achieving the Goal, or your strategy, is a different matter.

It's rare that your strategy will be a guaranteed hit with the universe. There may even be some doubt in your mind about its likely success. Interestingly, in interviewing and working with successful entrepreneurs for over a decade, I discovered that they rarely let an absence of certainty stop them from taking action. They don't have complete certainty all of the time, but they'll create what they believe is probably a winning strategy and then back themselves to make it work or to be flexible enough to change the strategy if it doesn't work.

So, once you have created what you believe to be a winning strategy, back yourself and go for it. But don't be so emotionally invested in it that you become like the Emperor prancing around in blind ignorance of his naked reality. Ignorance may be bliss, but when the harsh light of reality is shone on it, ignorance can quickly morph into *"oh crap."*

There is a terrific little story that Spencer Johnson created called "Who Moved My Cheese." The story was then made into a book written by Spencer Johnson and Kenneth H. Blanchard. The story is about two mice that were used to picking up their daily supply of cheese from a specific location in a maze. The cheese, of course, is a metaphor for what we want in life: our Goals. One day the cheese, which is always in the same location, is not there. This occurs again and then there is a parting of the mice ways. One mouse decides to take the risk of looking for the cheese elsewhere, and the other mouse keeps going back to the original location in the forlorn hope that someone has realized their error and is putting the cheese back where it "should" be.

The lessons from the story become quickly apparent. In my parlance they are as follows:

- ☐ Use Sensory Sensitivity and be aware when things have changed.
- ☐ Use Mental Flexibility and learn to enjoy the unexpected.

- Abandon "wishful thinking" and instead use "Reality Thinking" to move on when the unexpected happens. Use Strategic Suppleness to change your game plan if it stops working.
- Don't be emotionally attached to things staying the same.
- Don't be emotionally attached to the plan working out.
- Once you've changed your strategy and it starts working, get ready to change again.
- In summary: learn to love change.

Be committed to your Goal to the point that you never give up on it, but be committed to your strategy only as long as it's working.

Here's a summary of the seven-step Goal Achievement System (GAS) again:

1. Craft the "perfect" Goal.

2. Create a winning strategy.

3. Take affirmative action.

4. Align your Inner world.

5. Align time to Outcomes.

6. Build a structure of accountability and review.

7. Practice Sensory Sensitivity and Strategic Suppleness.

Now for a surprise. The seven-step GAS system actually has an eighth step. The reason I put eight steps into a seven-step system is not because I failed at math at high school (which I did), but rather because I wanted to highlight the most important step of the whole system, which of course is step number eight. Step 8 of the seven-step Goal Achievement System is this: recommit.

When you fail at following through with an action (which you will), or when you forget what it is you were trying to achieve (and at some point you will), or when you fudge the results and try and kid yourself that you gave it your best shot, there is only one thing left to do: recommit.

This is the best-kept secret of the world's elite achievers. It's not that they never fail or forget, it's simply that they never give up. They are habitual "re-committers."

PART EIGHT:

TOP TIPS FOR ACHIEVING YOUR GOALS

CHAPTER 32:

TOP TIPS FOR ACHIEVING YOUR HEALTH GOALS – WEIGHT GOALS

THE MOST IMPORTANT Goals are your Health Goals. There is not much point in having great relationships and all the money in the world if you are sitting in some hospital bed with tubes sticking out of every orifice. Health Goals may include weight Goals, fitness Goals, and other physical Goals, as well as Goals for mental, emotional, and spiritual well-being.

WEIGHT GOALS

A Goal to get your weight under control is one of your highest priorities. Note that there is nothing wrong about being overweight in itself. It's not right or wrong. It's just overweight. This is not an aesthetic judgment I am making here. It has nothing to do with my personal preferences. The issue with excess weight is that it carries with it the heavy cost of burning through additional energy. The energy that the excess weight robs you of could otherwise be channeled into proactively achieving your Goals. If you carry less weight around, you have a lot more energy to put into creating a life of choice. And the difference can be dramatic, not only to physical energy levels. I have seen people's mental energy levels transformed once they are down to their natural weight partly as a result of significantly boosting their Self-esteem and Self-confidence levels. So please understand I am not some Fat-Nazi who makes judgments about overweight people. My approach is simply and purely motivated by wanting people to enjoy the higher energy levels that come with a lean body.

Diets

Diets don't work because they are a temporary change in eating patterns. Diets do however get one thing right in that they make it very clear what you will, and will not eat. That clarity is a key ingredient in any successful change in eating patterns. The key, though, is not to go on a temporary diet, but rather to alter your lifestyle to a new way of eating. The difference is not just semantics; it's the time frame. A diet is temporary, a life-style change is indefinite.

One of the most successful weight-loss and weight-management systems in the world is Weight Watchers. Here's why:

- It's a simple and very clear system to follow.

- You don't need to buy any branded, pre-packaged foods.
- They have regular weekly meetings for accountability and progress review and peer support.
- They offer educational instruction.
- They have great role models.
- They charge only a small amount relative to others and offer terrific value.

Check them out on www.weightwatchers.com.

The most important thing to remember regarding Weight Watchers or any other similar system is that no matter how you've done during the previous week, you need to show up to the meeting and stay for the class session. If you will commit to that, and only that, your success is assured. It's then only a matter of time before you hit your weight Goal.

Changing what you eat is an exercise in will power. More specifically, it is only possible to change eating patterns by changing Subconscious thought patterns, and that's only possible by exercising your Conscious mind.

Most people over-eat and eat unhealthy food in an attempt to compensate for unhappiness or being too stressed. Over-eating or eating too much junk food is an exercise in temporarily escaping from reality.

Of course, we all need some certainty around pleasure in our lives and if work is stressing you out, money is always a hassle, and your relationships are a little strained, then food and drink is the most certain way you are going to feel a small slice of Happiness even if it is short-lived and ultimately counter-productive.

So, if you are going to change your eating or drinking habits, then expect a fair old revolt from the Subconscious. Warn your family that you may be cranky for a little while until you've reprogrammed your Subconscious!

You can also help by making sure that there is enough pleasure in other parts of your life while you are weaning yourself off the old food that you used to eat, or minimizing the alcohol that you drink. For example, you could book yourself a massage that you can look forward to, or promise yourself a treat at the end of the week if you stick to the plan.

A few more tips for weight loss:

- ✔ Focus on fat. Buy yourself a set of "Body Fat scales" and learn what you need to aim for in regard to your body fat levels. Body Fat scales will not only tell you what your weight is but will also tell you the percentage of that weight that is fat. The focus needs to be less on whether or not you are "overweight" and more on whether you are "over-fat."
- ✔ Don't keep food in the house if you don't want to eat it; remove temptation.
- ✔ Eat five times per day in smaller portions: breakfast, mid-morning, lunch, mid-afternoon, and dinner. Make all of these meals small.
- ✔ Eat no starchy, high-glycemic carbohydrates such as rice, potato of any kind, or pasta after 2 p.m., and only eat small quantities prior to this time.

- ✔ Make sure that fifty percent of the quantity of food that you eat on any one day is F.A.R. Food – that's "Fresh And Raw."
- ✔ Drink two liters of filtered water per day in regular but smaller quantities: e.g. 200ml at a time. You need to drink a lot more than this if you are working in hot climates.
- ✔ When you change your eating patterns, spend time to get very clear about what you will, and will not eat.

Here's a snapshot of my typical weekday diet:

- Pre-breakfast: filtered water.
- Breakfast: two free range eggs on wholegrain toast with a little olive oil (instead of butter). Or a protein shake with trim milk or soy milk.
- Mid-morning snack; two pieces of fruit, typically apples, oranges, peaches, or nectarines.
- Lunch: Salad with grilled chicken or grilled beef strips, light olive oil or similar, side of grainy bread.
- Mid-afternoon: Protein bar or fruit.
- Dinner: Stir fried vegetables or salad and either grilled chicken, fish, or beef, and plenty of it. No high glycemic carbs such as potato, pasta or rice.
- Post-dinner snack: small protein shake or small protein bar.

I will have a maximum of one cup of real coffee each day and other than that, I drink a decaf or a coffee substitute or herbal teas instead. I also have very little in the way of dairy products: little or no cheese, ice cream, cream, cream cheese, and I use soy or trim milk only. I also have very little in the way of high-sugar products such as sweets and cakes and so on. Alcohol is out as well because it is high in valueless calories, is an appetite stimulant, and is also the cause of less than optimal sleep patterns.

This is an energy-abundant system. I need high energy to use as fuel for achieving my Goals. If I eat junk food, sugar food, and fat food, it's like putting contaminated fuel in my race bike; it just won't go fast at all. Too many people cough and sputter their way through life.

No, I Am Not a Saint

The system that I've described above is reasonably strict. But I can assure you that I am no self-denial freak. I follow this system during the week except when I am on holiday when I will relax the rules. I do, however, have what I call a GFD or "Guilt Free Day" on which I do whatever I like. For me, a GFD might include French fries, a gourmet burger, and some beer. I'm a big advocate that there needs to be some light at the end of the tunnel, otherwise people won't stick to the system.

There is also a little twist on my GFDs that I'm sure you'll like. A GFD runs for 28 hours. This means that I can start my GFD around 6 p.m. on a Friday and have some wine, a burger, and fries and I can also do whatever I want to for the entire Saturday. Sunday, I go back on the system as I want my mind and body all fueled up with the "good stuff" ready for work on the Monday.

Use the GFD system to help you stay on track during the week.

Chapter 33:

How to Increase Your Energy Levels – The 2 Human Fuel Tanks

Physical Health has mostly to do with increasing energy levels, which is the raw material you need in order to achieve your Goals. Benjamin Franklin said that *"time was the stuff of which life is made."* With respect to the great man, I think that he may have only gotten it half-right. Certainly, if your time has run out, that means you are dead. But if you are out of energy, you may as well be dead because you are good for nothing. Want more life? Get more energy.

Think of yourself like a car. Just like a car, if you put low-quality fuel in, you won't get the same engine performance as if you put in high-quality fuel.

Your Physical Fuel Tank

As mentioned in the previous chapter, your physical fuel tank needs to contain fresh water, plenty of sleep, fresh and raw vegetables, and some fruit, protein, and other high-quality sources of physical fuel. If you don't get enough sleep, for example, your energy levels suffer in a similar way to being dehydrated, or if you were lacking any one of a hundred different vitamins and minerals such as iron for example.

That's all very well and most of us understand the consequences of filling up our fuel tank with too much of the wrong sort of fuel such as too much alcohol or fat. Performance drops and fatigue increases.

But what most people don't understand is that you actually have *two* different engines that have two different fuel tanks which require two different types of fuel in order for your whole being to feel rejuvenated with high levels of personal energy.

Your Mental Fuel Tank

Your mind requires a different type of fuel than the body. Remember that when I talk about your mental fuel tank, I am not referring to your brain. Your brain is the physical embodiment of your mind and as such, your brain is rejuvenated in the same ways as the rest of your physical body.

The mind however is different. Your mental fuel tanks will be charged by having a strong sense of purpose backed by powerful reasons and by appreciating and recognizing your progress. I have already touched on these things but there is one further vital ingredient to add to the fuel tanks of motivation. Without this last part of the formula, the rest of your energy plan will have minimal effect. In this day and age of global acceleration, this last vital ingredient is becoming scarcer and therefore even more precious and important as a master key to filling up the fuel tanks of the mind. It's this: rest time.

Many people have a strong sense of purpose and some have even developed the capacity for recognizing and valuing their progress.

But very few people understand that it's also vital to fill your mental fuel tank with time off. Free time. Leisure time. Time with no taxing mental issues. Whole days with no work whatsoever. At the ESP Programme, where I coach, we call these "ESP Leisure Days." A Leisure Day runs from midnight to midnight and contains no work. You don't go back into your office, you don't read the business section of the paper, and you don't do work around the house either.

All you do on a Leisure Day is rest the mind. If you are passionate about gardening, then by all means garden. If you love washing your car, then wash it. But if these activities sound like work to you, then do them on a different day or outsource them, but never do them on a Leisure Day.

In order to rejuvenate your mind and prevent burnout and become less than optimally productive, you need to have about 30 days out of every 90 days as Leisure Days. In every 90-day period, or 3 months, there are 13 weekends. So if you have every weekend free from all forms of work, and you have an additional 4 days off somewhere over that three-month period, you've got yourself 30 Leisure Days.

And always remember that, while I have been prescriptive in regard to the quantity of Leisure Days that you have and how to take them, you need to do the best that you can with the resources that you have. For example, if you have young children, it will be difficult for you to have a pure Leisure Day, so do the best you can by keeping your designated Leisure Days free from as much work as humanly possible.

Finally, If you want to really give your mental energy levels a boost, there is another "additive" that you can add to your Mental Fuel Tank. This extra additive is called Passion. By restructuring your life at work and at home to include less drudgery and more Passion, you will turbo-charge your levels of energy and achievement. Focus on Passion and the productivity will follow.

Chapter 34:

Top Tips for Achieving Your Health Goals – Fitness Goals

Another important Physical Health Goal is to achieve a reasonable level of all-around fitness.

A Goal for fitness should include three aspects : stamina (aerobic fitness), strength, and suppleness.

Note that this is a Goal separate from getting your weight under control. It's normally best to make the weight Goal a priority. If you want to start with exercise as well as a change to your lifestyle diet (as opposed to a quick fad diet), then don't make the exercise a Goal just yet. Leave it as an Intention. The difference between a Goal and an Intention is that the latter is not a commitment. So if you choose to commit to the weight Goal and to have "fitness" as an intention, don't be hard on yourself if you miss a training session or two. When you have achieved your weight Goal, then you can upgrade "fitness" from an Intention to a Goal and that's when you'll need to flex the iron will of your commitment muscle.

Here's a sample of my training routine. Remember that this routine is not designed for a specific event such as an Ironman, but rather it is purpose-built to be fit for life.

These inputs are reprinted here exactly as they appear on my Goal Planner.

- ✔ I have five workouts per week from Monday to Friday.
- ✔ I wake up at 6 am and I am out of bed prior to 6:15 a.m.
- ✔ I work out at 6:30 a.m.
- ✔ On Monday, I run for 45 minutes at a relaxed pace.
- ✔ On Tuesday, I do my weights workout as prescribed by my personal trainer.
- ✔ On Wednesday, I run for 30 minutes at a moderate pace.
- ✔ On Thursday, I do my weights workout as prescribed by my personal trainer.
- ✔ On Friday, I run for 20 minutes at a fast pace.
- ✔ On each day, I complete the stretches as prescribed by my personal trainer.

You can see that I like to have a personal trainer. Do yourself a big favor and hire one for yourself. You will truly experience a much better result as a consequence of this additional investment. Find the money and do it. Your health and your energy levels are vital keys to success in life and your investment in a personal trainer will be repaid many times over. The personal trainer strategy works so well because:

- You make an investment of money and are therefore likely to follow through.
- You have a regular time to show up.
- You make yourself accountable to someone else.
- You get to review and see your progress.
- You get educated in the most effective way to invest your time and effort in regard to your Goal of becoming fit.

Chapter 35:

Top Tips for Achieving Your Health Goals – Mental Goals

OTHER HEALTH GOALS include Goals that are related to Mental Health. These Goals would include anything to do with the arts, creativity, peace of mind, Happiness, meditation, or reprogramming destructive thought patterns such as jealousy or insecurities.

Mental Goals include anything from working out your specific Life Purpose to improving your relationship to God, whatever that term means to you. It could also be argued that any Goal that is related to helping others in a humanitarian or altruistic sense should be included here as they are an expression of love, which is universally agreed to be a spiritual quality. Alternatively, such Goals can go into the Relationships category.

Happiness and Freedom

Most of the time when we have an experience in our "Outer World" that we don't want, we mirror that with an "Inner

World" experience that we don't want. In other words, we feel emotions that we would prefer not to feel.

For example, this morning I tried to find an engineering shop that could repair the sub frame on my dirt bike, which had finally broken after one too many crashes. The date of writing this is the 29th of December and all of the engineering shops were shut down because they are taking the few days off between Christmas and New Year. I noticed that my mind began to feel frustrated. My "Outer World" was not how I would have it and so my "Inner World" began to protest.

You may have had similar experiences of feeling unwanted emotions when you wanted a fast trip but there was a hold up on the motorway, or the weather was wet and you wanted it dry, or you wanted to use an appliance but it broke down, or an unexpected bill turned up or whatever experience was different from what you wanted.

Similarly, I've also noticed that when people act in a way that I don't want, then I feel unwanted emotions as well. For example, I used to notice that my mind would feel impatient when someone didn't hear what I said, or it would feel annoyed when someone didn't do what they said they were going to do, such as turn up on time.

Every time I have one of these unwanted emotions, the spotlight of potential is shining on an opportunity to become a little more free of dysfunctional Subconscious conditioning and to increase Consciousness. There is always a gift in these experiences. I use what I call the Thought Transformation Technique that I outline in chapter 48 and work my way to Freedom.

RELATIONSHIPS ARE A KEY TO HAPPINESS

One of the most ironic phenomena that I have observed in myself during my early years in business is that when I became stressed at work, home was the place that I went to when I was tired of being nice to people. In other words, I would either not feel those unwanted emotions at work (for example when someone asked me to repeat myself) or I would suppress them. But when I got home, it was a different matter. I noticed that I found it easier to react with impatience or resentment with the ones I loved. At that stage, I hadn't learned the art of expressing what I was feeling so I gradually transformed into a large and frustrated two legged emotionally constipated ball of suppression.

The point is this though: my Life Partner relationship became the most effective way for me to observe Subconscious insecurities and thereby have the power to free myself from them.

Ironically, the woman I loved more than anyone else in the world was the person who triggered more unwanted emotions in me than anyone else. Every time that my Life Partner did something that activated a reaction and an unwanted emotion in me, she gave me a gift. The gift was the revealing of another Subconscious insecurity. Also bear in mind that my Life Partner is a most wonderful, kind, and compassionate person. So the problem was not with her actions; it was purely with my reactions. It's also worth mentioning that my reactions were not in response to behavior that violated agreed Core Values such as honesty or integrity. We're talking about relatively trivial things like being a little late or asking me to repeat myself. Also, I'm not talking about tidal waves of destructive emotional rage, just your everyday garden-variety flash of impatience or stress.

You've probably noticed that there are many other relationships that have a similar capacity to "rub you up the wrong way." There are several key points about this phenomenon that are worth pondering.

IT'S YOU WHO OWNS THE PROBLEM

Let's say that the personality of one of your customers really bugs you. Again, I'm not talking about a violation of your Values such as being constantly rude to you, but rather something like their style of behavior . For example, every time you hear them speak it grates on you. It just flat out annoys you. The symptom of the problem is an unwanted emotion such as dislike or resentment. Maybe they have a nasal whine when they talk. Who knows? Here's my point though: we would both agree that the cause of your problem is the customer. But the source of the problem (the cause of the cause if you like) is something inside you. This can be the only possible answer, as others might actually find the customer's whine humorous or even cute. So, the source of the annoyance is resident in you, not in the customer. They are just the "cause." Let me illustrate using my swimming pool as the example.

In my back yard I have a swimming pool which backs on to a large stand of rain forest. Sometimes the vacuum device, known as a "barracuda," gets blocked by berries and does not work. This means that the leaves which fall from the rain forest into the pool don't get sucked up by the vacuum and thus the pool looks untidy. This is not what I want, so I have a problem.

My swimming pool problem is the perfect way to illustrate an important model that will help you to understand the source of all of your problems.

Once you understand this model, you will have the key to unlocking unlimited personal growth opportunities.

The problem I have is an untidy-looking pool. I can take the leaves out from the bottom of the pool using a net, but this is only dealing with the *symptom* of the problem. I can unblock the "barracuda" vacuum device by removing the berries from it that cause the blockage, but that is only dealing with the *cause* of the problem. Or I can go to the *source* of the problem, which is the small branches of berries that grow on the palm trees that overhang the pool. Once I cut these bunches of berries off the palm trees, my problem disappears.

Often in life, we deal with *symptoms* of a problem and/or the problem's *causes*, but we fail to get to the *source* of the problem, which is invariably ourselves.

Let's now turn the spotlight back to the problem of you and your "difficult" customer who keeps activating unwanted emotions in you.

The *symptom* of your problem is that you feel an unwanted emotion. The *cause* of your problem is your customer's nasally whine.

The *source* of your problem is within you.

As mentioned previously, I know that the source of the problem is within you because your customer will not have the same effect on everyone else. He or she may have a similar effect on many people, but never on everyone. Let me further illustrate what I mean by this.

When a magnet is passed over a paperclip, the paperclip reacts. When the same magnet is passed over a sheet of paper, the paper remains inert, in other words, there is no reaction.

What can we observe from this simple experiment?

1. There is something in the paperclip that reacts to the magnet.

2. There is nothing in the paper that reacts to the magnet.

When we blame someone else for our unwanted emotions then we are like a paperclip blaming the magnet for being attracted to it. Of course there is something in the magnet that causes the reaction, just as there is something that the other person does that causes our unwanted emotion. But the source of the paperclip's reaction lies within its very own nature. The paper has a different nature so that, while the magnet remains the same as it was when it passed over the paperclip, it has no power over the paper.

Once you are free of unwanted Subconscious programming, no person and no situation will have the power to cause unwanted emotion to appear in your experience of life. That is true Freedom and is a foundation of true Happiness. Until then, every person and every experience that causes unwanted emotion in you is a gift that points to another area of your mind that you can be even freer in. The great twentieth century psychoanalyst Carl Jung referred to this experience of waking up to Freedom as "the birth of Consciousness."

But beware. I warn you now that it is easier to write about this or to read it than it is to practice it. You will want to instinctively blame another person for how you feel. You, or more specifically your Subconscious, will want to do anything other than accept responsibility for how you feel. Your Subconscious will reason that if you are not responsible, then it is not you who has to change. You are therefore protected from the perceived pain of personal change. Carl Jung also said that *"there is no birth of Consciousness without pain."*

Always remember that until you accept "respons-ability" for how you feel, you will be doomed to continue reacting. Responsible people are *able* to Consciously *respond* rather than simply Subconsciously react.

If all you can do is react (to act the same way again and again), then the same situations and people will continue to destroy the quality of your experience here on planet earth. Every time someone pulls their car in front of you, doesn't turn up on time, or forgets to say thank you, or whatever it is that causes you to react, you will have your Happiness destroyed and replaced with stress. How's that working for you so far?

I have a friend who has many rules around how other people "should" and "should not" act. For example, Kelvin (not his real name) gets so annoyed when someone who wants to sell him something leaves a message for Kelvin to call them back. He gets frustrated and stressed when people arrive late. He gets upset when people forget to say please and thank you. He dislikes people who ask him to call them on a mobile phone. And every time someone breaks one of his rules, which is about every 30 minutes, he destroys his own Happiness. I'm not suggesting that he needs to accept everyone else's behavior as being OK. Kelvin just needs to accept that it's not his job to make the world conform to his rules of right and wrong. Live and let live. Our Happiness is too important to make it conditional on other people living within our personal set of rules.

I have a radically different approach to unwanted experiences than most people. Many people find the concept that I am about to explain difficult to mentally process. You have had a lifetime of conditioning and programming that is contrary to what you are about to read, but if you keep an open mind, then it is the key to what I call "Three-Dimensional Happiness." Let me explain.

THE THREE DIMENSIONS OF HAPPINESS

One-Dimensional Happiness comes in the form of pleasure such as food, alcohol, shopping, sex, or any other form of externally stimulated pleasure. It's one-dimensional because it's short-lived and has no breadth or depth to it. And we all love it and so long as we don't use it as a substitute for real Happiness, we can continue to enjoy it is for what it is: a pleasurable short-term experience.

Two-Dimensional Happiness comes in the form of Happiness that relationships or significantly positive life changes such as winning Lotto can bring. You can witness Two-Dimensional Happiness at the airport arrivals lounge in any major city across the globe. In those places, people who care for each other are being reunited and of course "absence makes the heart grow fonder." But again, Two-Dimensional Happiness doesn't last and familiarity breeds complacency (hopefully not contempt in this case) and the feeling of Happiness fades. So there's depth to the feeling and breadth, but as mentioned, it's again all too short.

However, Three-Dimensional Happiness is not dependent on any external influence and results in what the great Hindu guru Paramahansa Yogananda (**www.yogananda-srf.org**) called *"an impregnable fortress of Happiness."* Three-Dimensional Happiness is pure Consciousness and in that place nothing disturbs our bliss. It's perhaps the ultimate personal Goal and it's one that may take me many more lifetimes to arrive at, but it's one that I am committed to achieving. You can read more about how to progress along the road towards Three-Dimensional Happiness in many of the chapters in Part Nine: The Soft Science of Success.

Finally, my top tip for achieving Happiness comes from Shantideva who was one of Buddha's direct disciples:

> *"Whatever joy there is in this world*
> *All comes from desiring others to be happy, And whatever suffering there is in this world, All comes from desiring myself to be happy."*

In other words, the source of Happiness is a motivation to be of service to others. No self equals no suffering.

Chapter 36:

How to Leverage the Likelihood of Personal Change

If you really want to effect a permanent change in your habits, you may want to leverage the likelihood of success by introducing the concept of "Reward and Non-Reward."

Let me explain how this works.

The Subconscious mind sometimes acts in a manner that is inconsistent with what we Consciously want because it is programmed genetically to protect us from any threat of pain and to move us toward pleasure. This is of course the prime reason why we still exist as a species. If we had not programmed concern for the avoidance of pain and death, we would never have survived the Stone Age. But let's bring this "pain and pleasure" programming into our age with an example of how it works.

Johnny is a case in point. Johnny is two years old and is curious as to what is on top of the kitchen bench. So when Mum pops out of the kitchen for a moment, he pulls up a chair next to the bench and clambers up to see what it is that she does up there. As he stands up, he can suddenly see what the big attraction is. There is a big bright round and glowing red plate on the bench. Adults call this a "stove element," but of course Johnny doesn't know what it is. And the way that Johnny finds out about his new world is to touch things. So he plants the palm of his hand onto the element and of course he then screams with pain. Mum comes running back into the kitchen and puts his hand under cool running water and generally nurses Johnny back to health and Happiness.

But now Johnny's Subconscious has processed the following data. *"Big, round, red objects give us massive pain."* It's locked and loaded in the Subconscious. It's now a Subconscious belief. Johnny of course eventually gets over his trauma and with the right treatment the scars on his hand have healed perfectly.

Five years later and Johnny is now seven years old and he's at the family picnic. Uncle Phil is out on the open grass playing around and suddenly turns to Johnny and throws him a Frisbee. The Frisbee is round of course, and it's also bright red. Johnny screams in terror and runs to his mother where he sobs uncontrollably. No one can understand what the problem is; after all, all the other kids are playing quite happily with the Frisbee.

What has happened is that Johnny's Subconscious has reacted thirty thousand times faster than he could Consciously think and retrieved from his memory banks the belief that *"Big, round, red objects give us massive pain."*

What have we learned from Johnny's experience? We have learned that there are some basic rules in regard to how our

Subconscious minds operate. A few of these are illustrated by Johnny's story and I'll also add some others.

1. The Subconscious is programmed to move us away from anything that we associate by memory with painful experiences, be they physically and/or emotionally painful.

2. In the absence of a threat of pain, the Subconscious will move us toward those experiences that it associates by memory with pleasure, be they physically and/or emotionally pleasurable.

3. The Subconscious will do more to avoid pain than it will to pursue pleasure.

4. The Subconscious will work to turn our most dominant thought into reality, regardless of whether our most dominant thought is fear-based (avoidance of pain) or desire-based (pursuit of pleasure).

5. The Subconscious has an immediate focus, in that it has a natural bias for short-term pleasure such as fatty food, over long-term pain such as a heart attack.

It is the function of the Conscious mind to learn how to Overcome this programming and to reprogram the associations so that the Subconscious is aligned with the Conscious mind. This is evident in that, for those people who know what they want and what they need to do to get it, the biggest obstacle then becomes actually doing it. For example, you Consciously want to lose weight but your Subconscious wants the pleasure and comfort of eating more chocolate. Or you Consciously want to be fit, lean, and energetic but the lure of a warm bed is just too enticing to the Subconscious that prefers pleasure over effort. So you fall victim to the Problem of Instant Gratification or "PIG" syndrome.

Increasing Consciousness is achieved in part when we develop the Capacity to Overcome, or to reprogram, any dysfunctional pain and pleasure activations, and thereby live Consciously at a far higher level: that of Purpose.

If you are focused on the Outcome, if you are motivated by powerful reasons, and if you are clear on the Input, then all that remains is for you to act in a manner that is consistent with your Conscious desires.

It's plain to see that it's difficult to do battle with the Subconscious. It normally wins the fight. But as I alluded to earlier, we can in fact reprogram it. Once you have Consciously thought and acted in a certain way (e.g. getting to bed earlier so that you can easily get up earlier to exercise), for twenty-one times, then, in most cases, you will have created a new mental pattern which results in consistent behavior otherwise known as a habit.

The tricky bit is getting those first twenty-one successes under the belt. And that's where the concept of "Reward and Non Reward" comes in.

Let's take exercising as an example. The strategy here is simple. If you are not already a habitual exerciser, then the chances are that your Subconscious associates exercise with pain. Believe it or not, I know of many people who felt the same way in their past, but who now associate *"not exercising"* with pain, and as a result, they find it harder not to exercise than they do to exercise.

So here's what you do to establish the new habit. Identify something that you regard as more painful than exercising. For example, I recall one of my clients, Sue, who decided that to give her Life Partner $500 from her own savings for him to spend on whatever he wanted would be more painful than an act of forcing herself to exercise. So Sue set herself a Goal of creating a new habit of exercising on twenty-one separate days. She set a date and told her Life Partner that, if she had not created the new habit by exercising on the specified mornings prior to that date, then she would give him $500. He was naturally delighted! But Sue hit her Goal with one morning to spare. The thought of having to give her Life Partner her hard-earned $500 was more painful than getting out of bed earlier every morning and briskly walking for thirty minutes around their neighborhood. Kudos to you Sue!

In addition to the Non Reward, Sue set herself a Reward. When she had successfully introduced the new habit of exercising, she would buy herself the diamond ring that she had her eye on for some time. So as well as creating a painful Non Reward that was greater than the pain of exercising, she also created a Reward that was more pleasurable than the thought of sleeping in every morning. Sue's strategy worked and today, some seven years later, Sue is still exercising regularly.

For myself, I recently had the pleasure of attending my son Larn's wedding in Scotland. I was on holiday for three weeks and enjoyed the hospitality of the Scots, the English, the Dutch, and the French over that time. As a result, I came back with a few kilos of excess baggage which hung around my midriff for more than a month after my return. Finally, I'd had enough. I set myself a Goal to lose the excess over the two months leading up to Christmas. I committed that I would not touch a drop of beer or wine (a personal passion of mine), or any other form of alcohol until I was down to my Goal weight. I also committed that, if I had not lost the weight within the specified time period, I would ride no motorbikes (another personal passion) over my vacation period. I was so motivated that I lost the weight within two weeks!

Do remember though that it is possible to make the Non Reward too big: e.g. "no sex for a year" — unless you are a monastic or a masochist you're never going to stick to that. The Non Reward just has to be a bit more painful than the pain of change.

Recently, a friend told me about a similar way that he and his Life Partner applied the principle Reward and Non Reward to personal change. Mike and his Life Partner, Jan, made a commitment to each other that whoever lost the most weight by Christmas had $20,000 to spend – either on a new motorbike (for him) or on the house (for her). They now have brand new floor coverings. Apparently, what motivated Jan even more than the opportunity to refurbish was the act of beating Mike! It doesn't matter too much where you draw your motivation from, so long as you draw it from somewhere.

I heard of another person, we'll call him Peter, who decided to give up smoking. Unfortunately, no sooner had he made his decision than his Life Partner left him for his best friend. Undeterred, Peter committed that every time that he so much as touched a cigarette, he would send one hundred dollars to his ex-best friend. The thought of sending cash to his former friend was so much more painful than the withdrawal from nicotine that Peter achieved his Goal of becoming a non-smoker.

So if you are serious about personal change, in particular weight loss or fitness Goals, then create a commitment to Reward and Non Reward. Remember that the key is to create a Non Reward that the Subconscious associates as being more painful than the required habit change, and a Reward that is more pleasurable than the option of not changing.

Chapter 37:

Top Tips for Relationship Goals – Values and Your Life Partner

Life Partner Relationship

I want to use the Life Partner relationship as an example of key principles that have the power to take any relationship, be it business or personal, to the next level of Freedom, fun, and Fulfillment.

Principle Number One: Opposites Attract

Often, although not always, opposite personalities are attracted to each other. Like different polarities of the same magnet, people come together more often when they are opposites, in a personality sense. It always causes me a quiet chuckle when someone declares their dislike of a person they just met who has an almost identical personality. Having said that, sometimes someone with a similar type of personality can make for a great friendship, but rarely does it make for a great Life Partner relationship.

A quiet person and a talkative person are often attracted to each other. Or a follower and a leader. This is by no means essential for a great relationship and I do know of a successful couple where their personality styles are similar. But they are the exception rather than the rule.

PRINCIPLE NUMBER TWO: COMMON VALUES ATTRACT

There are three different types of Values in every successful relationship on earth.

1. Shared Core Values

2. Individual Core Values

3. Minor Values (shared or Individual)

Shared Core Values

Let me explain what I mean by each word in this phrase.

By "Values" I mean those attitudes and beliefs that are important to you and your Life Partner. By Core I am referring to those Values that are so important to you that it becomes vital (life sustaining) to the relationship that behavior is aligned with these Values. And by "shared" I obviously mean that both people in the relationship feel the same way about this Value.

Examples of Shared Core Values include attitudes towards Fidelity, Love, Money, Parenting, Communication and others. Non-aligned behavior around these vital relationship Values results in placing the relationship under great strain and eventually dissolution, unless the alignment is corrected.

For example, most successful couples agree that Fidelity is a Shared Core Value, so much so that it forms a part of their marriage vows, and so it comes as no surprise to anyone when repeated violation of this Shared Core Value results in relationship termination.

As mentioned above, another example of a vital Shared Core Value is whether or not to have a Family. Most couples won't stay together if one wants to have children and the other doesn't. Similarly, if one person Values Thrift and Economy and the other just loves unplanned "retail therapy," then it's going to be difficult to create a harmonious and loving relationship.

All successful relationships have Shared Core Values. These are Values that both people in the relationship share and they form the basis for growing a strong and fulfilling future together.

If you and your Life Partner have no Shared Core Values, as demonstrated by the way that you each behave, then you have no basis for a long-term fulfilling relationship. For example, if you want Love to be a Shared Core Value, but despite repeated requests, your Life Partner treats you with disrespect, and his or her behavior is egocentric and self-serving, impatient, and abusive, then you're going to be looking for someone else real soon. And so you should. But do give them some feedback first and an opportunity to change.

Another example of not having Shared Core Values would be if you want your Shared Core Values to include Freedom, but your Life Partner is a control freak who gets jealous every time you speak to someone of the opposite gender.

You have a Values conflict between your desire for Freedom and your partner's Values of Control or Certainty. Checkmate. One of you will need to change his or her Values as demonstrated by behavior or the relationship has no chance of growing. Unless they strike up with a human doormat, the control freak is likely to destroy every relationship that they form until they realize that controlling a loved one is dysfunctional.

The bottom line is this: you each need to agree on your Shared Core Values and what that looks like in terms of demonstrated behavior . Additionally, you need to have some Shared Core Values in the form of personal interests such as sport, the arts, personal development, or whatever, in order to provide an opportunity for you to spend time together talking about and pursuing those common interests. The couples that play together stay together.

Individual Core Values

These are similar to Shared Core Values but as the term implies, these Core Values are not shared by each person in the relationship.

An Individual Core Value is a Value that is so much a part of who you are and what you stand for that it is inseparable from life itself. Just as the Shared Core Value is vital to the life of your relationship, if you had to live in a world that was devoid of any one of your Individual Core Values, you would probably prefer not to exist at all.

For example, an entrepreneur could value Independence so highly that he or she could never go and work for someone else. Their Life Partner might value Security highly and so would never start his own business. These two people could happily live together in a fulfilling relationship even though their Individual Core Value is not shared by the other person. Having Core Values that are not shared in a relationship is normal and in fact quite healthy as each person can enjoy and learn from the other person's Core Values.

A case in point

One of my Core Values is Adventure. I need Adventure in order to feel alive and fulfilled. I can still remember the day that I completed the "Great Unveiling Ceremony" for yet another madcap adventure scheme that I had "schemed up." I can't remember the specifics of the idea, but I do remember my poor Life Partner rolling her eyes heavenward in despair. Understandably so. My adventures have taken a fair bit of time and money over the years, not to mention the risk of losing the odd body part. While I empathized with her, I also explained to her that this is how it is in my world. *"It's like this honey,"* I said. *"Cats chase birds, dogs chase cats, and Tom has adventures."* Being free to have Adventures is who I am. I'd rather be dead, literally, than to have to endure a life of predictability. At this stage of my life, it's so much of a Core Value that I literally could not live without it.

While Individual Core Values do not need to be shared by the other person, they do need to be supported. The time and money that is expended pursuing Individual Core Values need to be agreed on in order for other Shared Core Values such as Money to not be violated. For example, I have an agreement with my Life Partner that my Adventures will not compromise our financial independence. So I stick to a budget and cut the Adventure cloth, to suit, so to speak. In principle, it is vital to the success of the relationship that these Individual Core Values, and their resultant behavior, are accepted and not resented by each person.

Minor Values – Shared and Individual

That leaves us with the third category of Values which are the Minor Values. Minor Values that are shared are easy. For example, you may both Value playing tennis, but you may not feel so passionate about it that you would kill yourself or end the relationship if you couldn't play again. I have met a few people who take their footy that seriously!

Individual Minor Values are by definition not Core to either you or your partner. In other words, your Minor Values may still be important to you, but if your Life Partner neither shares nor supports these Minor Values, the relationship can still flourish, albeit with the potential for a few niggles. Using the tennis example above again, if tennis was a Minor Value for you but not for your Partner, then the relationship can still be fulfilling and successful even though your Partner may not join you on the court.

By way of another example, let's say that Sam is a neat freak and Pam is not. Almost everything in Sam's space, being his office and his garage, is either labeled, in a box (which is also labeled), or in a file (also labeled). Sam has even labeled the door locks to make it easier to work out which way the deadlocks open and close. The recycle bin has labels telling people what can and cannot go in there. He hangs his clothes in his wardrobe in ascending order of use. At restaurants, Sam finds himself cleaning up even the smallest crumb that fell onto the table. He'll rearrange chairs if they are not straight and he likes clean simple lines in his living space. No clutter. Nothing useless.

Pam is not the same. Don't get me wrong, Pam likes things clean and tidy. It's just that, according to their children, Sam is bordering on being obsessively tidy. He can't understand why they think that way. But fortunately, tidiness is only a Minor Value for Sam. He can live in an untidy environment which is a useful adaptive quality when he has to live with kids, a dog, and two cats in the house. So wise man that he is, Sam decided some time ago that he could either have a tidy house or a loving home. He really does still prefer for everything to be in its place, but it no longer bugs him to the extent that it destroys the quality of his family relationships.

Minor Values can, however, be a source of great irritation in some relationships and it's a shame that this is the case, as it really needn't be. Provided the Minor Value is not violating any Core Values, the best approach is to "celebrate diversity." After all, acceptance of differences including Individual Core Values and Individual Minor Values is a large part of what Love is all about. It's easy to accept the parts of our Partner that are the same as us. That's not hard at all. We are really just saying that we like them because they are like us. The richness and rewards in any relationship comes more from what you *don't* have in common than it does from what you do have in common.

Celebrate diversity. If you're a neat freak like Sam and your Partner isn't, you can either put your energies into getting stressed trying to tilt at the windmill of changing your Partner's Values, or you can put your energy into nurturing the other person. Your choice. Your relationship. Trying to change the other person's Minor Values is a recipe for stress and relationship destruction. It's simply not worth the effort and risk. Change your Inner World to accept that people are different and you will take a giant step towards being Free from the effects of your Outer World.

TIME TOGETHER AND SHARED 'PASSION PASTIMES'

As intimated above, couples need to have enough in common to be able to spend time and energy engaged in pastimes that they both feel passionate about. Surprisingly though, most successful relationships often have some time apart either for business reasons or because, in addition to shared passion pastimes, they have their own individual ones. Some absence does make the heart grow fonder. Being together 24/7 easily leads to complacency and a little scarcity goes a long way toward increasing perceived value. It's all a question of balance. You can have too much time together and you can have too much time apart.

Chapter 38:

Top Tips for Relationship Goals – Identifying What Love Looks Like

I REGULARLY CONDUCT RETREATS for couples who want to enrich their relationship. (see www.tompoland.com under the "Events" tag) and it's always a delight to see the breakthroughs that couples make as we explore issues such as Values and Communication and also one of my client's favorite concepts of "What does love look like for you?'

What Does Love Look Like for You?

In a simple but groundbreaking book called the *Five Languages of Love*, Gary Chapman explores what has to happen in order for people to feel loved. The following is my spin on a great concept.

When I want more clarity around a concept I like to ask *"what does that look like to you?"* For example, if someone tells me they want more effort, I'll respond with *"what does that look like to you?"* If someone tells me that they are going to start exercising or change their diet, I'll ask them *"what does that look like to you?'*

I have found over the years that different concepts look different to different people and Love is no exception to this observation.

Piet Hien, the Dutch architect and poet, once wrote that *"Love is like a pineapple, sweet and undefinable."* His collection of "Grooks" as he called them are well worth the read. It's a bit like the US Supreme Court's ruling on whether an object was to be classified as art or pornography. They declared that pornography was difficult to define but "you know it when you see it." Again rather vague. Grooks and the US Supreme Court aside, Love is actually quite definable for most of us.

Keeping the tanks of Love full means that we need to know what sort of "Love Fuel" to put into the tank. I'll explain the concept of Love Fuel with the following analogy. On the left of the chart below is a list of engines or appliances and on the right are a list of fuel types. See if you can match them correctly. For example, a Car would be matched with "Petrol."

Tank Type	Fuel Type
■ Car	■ Kerosene
■ Camping Lantern	■ Electricity
■ Air conditioner	■ Water
■ Fireplace	■ Jet fuel
■ Steam Engine	■ Petrol
■ Jet Plane	■ Timber/Coal

Obviously, you aren't going to get a lot of joy out of a Jet plane by trying to make it go with some timber. And the car won't run so well if you put water in its fuel tank. So what's the morale of the story? It's this: what works perfectly well for one engine fails to ignite even a spark of interest in another.

There are five Fuels of Love, as I call them, and each of them will spark the passion of Love within someone, but none of them will fire up an interest with everyone.

The Five Fuels of Love are:

Fuel	Expression
■ Talk	■ Love expressed verbally
■ Task	■ Love expressed through acts of service
■ Time	■ Love expressed through togetherness
■ Touch	■ Love expressed through physical contact
■ Thought	■ Love expressed through personal gifts

What this means is that you (and your Life Partner) will feel loved when your Life Partner pours the right Love Fuel into your life. If your Love Fuel is Touch, your Partner can talk with you until they are blue in the face, but you won't feel loved until they give you the gift of physical contact. And if your Partner's Love Fuel is Task but you can't take your hands off them, they're going to feel more molested than loved.

I have a friend who, for the sake of anonymity, I will call Sally. She is a highly paid professional who is extremely good at what she does. Her Life Partner, Rod, may earn less than Sally, but he is simply fabulous with the kids and helping out around the house. He cooks, he cleans, and he does everything humanly possible to create an empowering and nurturing environment for Sally and their four kids. In fact, Sally reckons that there is a queue of women that would have Rod if something ever happened to her.

Sally comes home from business and wants to talk. That's her Love Fuel. Sally feels loved when Rod talks with her, when he listens and understands, offers his point of view and generally involves himself in conversation with Sally.

The trouble is that Rod's idea of a conversation is pretty much mono-syllabic grunting. Consequently Sally feels unloved. She knows on an intellectual level that Rod loves her, it's just that she never feels it.

Rod's Love Fuel on the other hand is Task. He feels loved when Sally goes out of her way to do something for him that she didn't have to do. Make him a drink, fix him a snack, or any other act of selfless service. But Sally is too tired from making a lot of money to do these things for Rod, she just wants to talk. She thinks that going to work and "bringing home the bacon" should be enough. So Rod feels as unloved as Sally.

Do you see what's happened in this relationship? Each Partner is giving their own preferred Love Fuel to the other person. Sally gives Talk (or tries to) and Rod is busting himself to get the kids lunches ready, breakfast on the table, running the kids around to sporting and music classes, cooking dinner, and getting Sally a drink, none of which makes Sally feel loved.

Having worked with many couples through our Life Partner Weekend workshops, I've made the following observations about Love Fuel:

1. Most people give the Love Fuel that they want to receive.

2. Most people end up with someone who has a different primary Love Fuel from themselves.

3. Your Life Partner will have the Love Fuel that you find the biggest effort to give.

4. Most people have a Primary Love Fuel which they crave the most, and also a Secondary Love Fuel which is also important for them to experience.

5. Often, both people in the relationship will have a secondary Love Fuel in common.

Talk with your Life Partner about this concept and try different Love Fuels until you each discover what works for the other person. Then make a point of behaving in a manner that is consistent with your Life Partner's Love Fuel. Many, many couples have found that a long dormant love interest has burst back into life, like flowers in the desert after rain, with the simple application of the right Love Fuel. As Jim Morrison of the Doors so aptly sung: *"Come on baby light my fire!"*

Whatever your Love Fuel, though, I will guarantee you this: the two concepts that are inseparable from Love are Acceptance and Giving. By Acceptance I do not mean that you need to be a doormat for behavior that is inconsistent with Shared Core Values, such as verbal or physical abuse or any other behavior that violates your Core Values. What I do mean, however, is the Acceptance, and even the celebration of, other Values that you may not have in common. One Partner can accept that the other may not value punctuality, or tidiness, or organization. The other Partner can accept that the first Partner is a stickler for detail, fussy, and sometimes a little impatient. Viva la difference!

Christ went out of his way to make a point of accepting people who were, in his day, generally regarded as the lowest of the low in society. He spoke of the parable of a good Samaritan, he dined with tax gatherers, and talked with prostitutes. It was the hypocritical, "superior than thou" Pharisees that he gave a hard time to. So don't imagine that for a moment that by being different from someone else that you are better. Stay humble and accept others for whom they choose to be, especially your Life Partner and children. When you give them permission to be different from you, you'll set them free to be who they were authentically born to be. And that is a priceless gift of Love.

Chapter 39:

Top Tips for Relationship Goals – Communicating Effectively

Communication – Part One: Giving Feedback

If there is one vital key, after the ability to Love, that is absolutely essential in creating a free, fun and fulfilling relationship it is the ability to communicate effectively. This chapter contains a few vital points on the subject.

Relationships that don't work well inevitably break down because one or more people in the relationship think that the relationship is about them. *Their* needs, *their* wants, *their* dreams. They are obsessed with "me." Love fixes that. Paramahansa Yogananda, the great twentieth century Indian Guru who wrote autobiography of a Yogi, encouraged his followers to *"Give everything and expect nothing."*

But even though one or more people in the relationship may forget to give to the other, the situation can be retrieved if each person is willing to communicate. However, what normally happens is that feedback is initially given, but the person receiving the feedback is so defensive or aggressive that next time the giver of the feedback ends up repressing what they are feeling, what they are thinking, and what they want. Smoldering resentment builds into frustration and eventually even anger and rejection. The following is what I call the "6 Rs of Relationship Destruction" and puts these patterns into an easily understandable model:

1. unReserved acceptance

2. Request (feedback)

3. Reaction (Subconscious)

4. Repression (feedback stops)

5. Resentment (frustrations grow)

6. Rejection (person leaves, finds someone else and starts again at "1 !")

I'd be the first to agree that the above represents a pretty grim view of Life Partner relationships. But hundreds of couples that I have worked with seem quick to recognize the same patterns in their otherwise loving and successful relationship.

But there is an answer and the answer is to learn how to communicate. Of all the great things I learned from my time in school, communication was not one of them. It was not directly taught, and it needed to be. It's a prerequisite for successful relationships and not just in a Life Partner context but with all people, everywhere. Hopefully, one day the people who write the curriculum for our education system will realize that life requires communication with other humans, of which there are quite a few of on the planet.

Some people aren't too sure however when to talk about how they feel with their Life Partner, or when it's okay to ask them to modify their behavior.

There are two types of Behavior Modification Requests or "BMRs" as I call them.

- **VALID BMRs.** A Valid BMR is where one person's behavior is inconsistent with a Shared Core Value. For example, most couples agree that Love is a Shared Core Value. Most couples also agree that Love involves investing regular amounts of quality time together. As a couple, you each need to work out and agree what "investing regular amounts of quality time together" looks like. You may decide that it's dinner together at least three nights per week and a whole day together each weekend, or whatever. If you or your Partner are spending so much time at work that you are not getting these "regular amounts of quality time together," then it's valid to make a Behavior Modification Request. Talk to your Partner about:

    A. What you feel

    B. Why you feel that way

    C. What you would like to be done about it.

    Remember not to attack your Partner and also to encourage them to keep an open mind to what you have to say. And vice versa. The last thing you want is for your communication to turn into two people verbally boxing each other. Better to be two explorers looking together for a solution; looking for a way to move forward. This requires the somewhat delicate mental surgical procedure of removing the ego.

- **OPTIONAL BMRs.** If something that your Partner does bugs you but it's not a violation of Shared or Individual Core Values, then you are best simply to learn to accept it. If it bugs you to the point that you really feel compelled to mention it to them, by all means communicate how you feel about it, why you feel that way, and what you would like to do about it. Maybe they squeeze the toothpaste from the wrong end of the tube or something heinous like that. Maybe they don't pick up their socks. You are entitled to make a BMR, but if it's about a difference in Minor Values (e.g. one likes to be tidy and the other doesn't give a toss about it) then your Partner is not obliged to change. Hence, it's an Optional BMR. My Life Partner has been an extraordinary teacher for me in this regard. She will fully and directly communicate with me on issues of importance, but tends to let the little things slide. She really is a terrific example of someone who can truly Love. She gives and she is accepting. Her approach to BMRs around issues of Minor Values is to simply tell me how she feels about my actions and to leave it at that. She doesn't nag or whine or moan.

So in summary, if something is annoying you in the relationship, you are allowed to communicate what you are feeling, why you are feeling like that, and what you would like to be done about it. Also remember that *you* "own" the feeling. You are the source of that feeling, not the other person. You need to deal with any unwanted emotions as an issue separate from your desire for them to change their behavior. In no way should you ask them to change who they are simply because you have a bunch of hang-ups that you haven't dealt with yet. Galling though it may be, unless there is a violation of Shared Core Values, it's not the other person who needs to change in order for you to be happy. If you have got this far in the book and you are still not sure who it is who needs to change in order for you to be happy, go to the bathroom and look in the mirror. There you will find the source of all your unhappiness ... and Happiness. It may be unpalatable, but at least it's something you can do something about.

Communication – Part Two: Receiving Feedback

In terms of communication, most people find receiving more challenging than giving. The latter is the harder part of the two aspects of feedback and it's normally where the process of communication breaks down. The Subconscious wants to protect us against the perceived pain of having to change, so we find ourselves becoming defensive and wanting to blame the other person. Here are the five levels of receiving verbal feedback. See how far down the list you usually make it when someone gives you some feedback.

1. Hearing

If you can't physically hear the other person, then you can't get to Level 2, listening. Most people get to this level but barely beyond. In 90% of situations, physically hearing the other person is not an issue.

2. Listening

You need to demonstrate that you are listening as opposed to doodling, reading the paper or playing a computer game. Giving the other person your attention is a sign of respect and demonstrates that you are interested in their "stuff." I estimate that only 30% of people get to this most basic level of communication. It's hardly surprising that communication breaks down so often.

3. Understanding

70% of communication issues are solved when a person feels understood. To demonstrate that you understand, you need to be able to replay to the other person, in your own words, what that person is feeling, what they are thinking and what they would like to do about it, if anything. And then you need to confirm with them that you understood them correctly. We call this process "replay and confirm." It sounds easy enough, but it takes a lot of practice to become good at it.

And remember too that there is a difference between understanding and agreeing. Effective communication does not obligate you to agree necessarily, but you do need to demonstrate understanding. I would say that less than ten percent of couples communicate effectively at this level. For the other 90%, the

Subconscious ego kicks in and the games and power plays begin.

4. Empathizing

This is the ability to identify with how the other person is feeling. It's letting them know that the way they feel is valid and reasonable. Practice using the phrase *"Sam, I can understand why you would feel like that, in fact I'd be feeling exactly the same way if I were in your situation."* Really try and put yourself in the other person's shoes and if it's at all possible, empathize with the way they are feeling. Again, empathizing is not the same as agreeing. It's just walking for a moment in their shoes.

5. Openness

This is the domain of the truly extraordinary couple. Most couples are like a pair of boxers when they communicate. Each person's Subconscious ego is trying to score points and verbally beat the other person into submission. The trouble is the other person is the umpire and isn't going to give one ounce of credit for any of the arguments put forward. When it comes down to the bottom line, all they really want is for the other person to agree with them. The problem is that the Subconscious mind associates being wrong with pain in the form of loss of love and will perform all manner of mental and verbal cartwheels in order to avoid such a "life-threatening" admission. We are so pathetic sometimes.

Instead of being a boxer, learn how to be an explorer. An explorer is always looking for a way forward. They are rarely emotionally attached to the way something "should be," they simply want to find out "what is." They are eager to learn and enjoy the adventure of discovery. They can live with uncertainty and they thrive on challenges. When you become an explorer in your communication, you'll want to discover the other person's territory and you won't be defensive about your own. There's only one person who can ever win a boxing match, but two people can both win through the process of exploration. Forget "lose-lose" and "win- lose" and focus on "win-win."

Most people let their "stuff" get in the way of receiving feedback. Our "pain and pleasure" programming and our emotional attachment to a pre- set Outcome prevent us from opening our mind and creating a true learning experience. Practice will, however, make perfect.

The reason that mastering communication is so important is that it is the key to solving relationship conflict. It doesn't matter if the conflict is around money, the kids, holidays, over-working, under-valuing, sharing the work-load, or the "in-laws." When you and your Partner can effectively communicate, you will have the Master Key to unlocking every single relationship issue that you will ever come across. Now that's worth putting "self " aside for a moment or two.

Finally, on the subject of communication, it really is central to the Fulfillment of Life Purpose. When we learn to get over our Subconscious "stuff," we increase our levels of Consciousness. When we develop the ability to listen, to understand, to be open, and to empathize, we expand our Capacity. And finally, when we learn to work together in creating win-win solutions, we make a Contribution to others the results of which may one day prove to be inestimable. More on that soon.

And remember that every principle and practice mentioned above works not just in your Life Partner relationship, but also in every other relationship in your life. Concepts such as Shared Core Values and Communication apply to relationships with kids, clients, colleagues, staff, suppliers, bosses, and pretty much every other human being in your world.

Communication truly is one of only a few Master Keys to living a fulfilling life.

Chapter 40:

Top Tips for Relationship Goals – The Value of a Life Partner Relationship

I am personally a great believer in the value of a Life Partner relationship, although I readily accept that there are those for whom such a concept is not the best way forward. Let me explain why, for most people, I am such a big fan of being in a committed relationship with someone you can walk through life with. Lots of reasons come to mind. Let's look at a few of them.

Firstly, the Life Partner relationship is one of the most effective ways that I know of to assist me in fulfilling my Life Purpose. My commitment with my Life Partner is to continually take our relationship to the next level of Love, Freedom, fun, and Fulfillment. It's a commitment to growing together and to be there to support each other and, when appropriate, to challenge each other.

You may recall from the first chapter that my Life Purpose model consists of three areas. Let me briefly recap each part of the model and with each part I'll also include how I think that my Life Partner relationship contributes towards it.

1. **Consciousness**

    The ability to increasingly live life Consciously as opposed to Subconsciously. Symptomatic of higher levels of Consciousness are an expansion of the ability to Love, an increase in Compassion for those who suffer, greater Peace of Mind, and the experience of three-dimensional Happiness. Not a bad plan!

    Firstly, my relationship with my Life Partner is my opportunity to perfect the Art of Loving and to learn to accept someone else, warts and all. My Goal is therefore to love 100% the aspects of my Life Partner that are different from me and to give unconditionally to her, regardless of her imperfections. And to do all of that amidst the daily nitty gritty of meals, dishes, kids, bills, clients, and so on.

    Also, every time I notice any unwanted emotion caused as a result of an interaction with her, I have an opportunity to free myself from that emotion using the Thought Transformation Technique in Chapter 48.

    As I learn to love (Give and Accept) more and learn to be freer, I am in fact shifting from the operating source of the Subconscious to that of the Conscious. In doing so, I am by very definition increasing my Consciousness. And nothing, in my experience, has given me more opportunities to increase my Consciousness than my Life Partner relationship. When it comes to increasing and expanding our Consciousness, my Life Partner is my greatest teacher and I hers. We also aim to be each other's greatest students, although I have observed that developing the humility to learn is proving to be more challenging for me than it has been for her. I suspect it's "a guy thing." More specifically, it's an ego thing.

2. Capacity

This has a lot to do with the expansion of my power to create the reality of my choice as opposed to living, like most people do, by chance. It's also about an increase in my capacity to cope with the mental demands that comes with greater choice. Furthermore, it's about developing greater internal abilities as well as external skills, be they business orientated or personal interests.

As noted in Chapter 1, there is an inevitable overlap between Consciousness and Capacity. Although different, an increase in one will strengthen the other.

Of course, life would be simpler without a Life Partner. Of that there is no doubt. My Life Partner and I have noticed an interesting phenomenon that occurs when I return from a week or more away on business. Although we invariably missed each other and are glad to be back together, we find that we annoy each other a lot easier than before I went away. This only lasts for a day or two, then we are back in sync.

The cause of our minor irritations is the fact that when I was away on business, I made all of my personal decisions such as what to eat, when to turn the light out, what to do in the evenings, and so on without reference to anyone else. I didn't have to be considerate at all. And of course, my Life Partner being "home alone" didn't need to defer to me or to consider me in any of her decisions. Simple, quick and easy. And lonely after a while.

The point is that living with another human being, and being considerate of their needs, expands our Capacity as we learn to cope with the additional complexity that a "live-in" relationship requires. And of course, that goes double, or quadruple, when you add children to the Life Partner equation. So many growth opportunities!

My Capacity to cope with additional mental pressure has expanded immeasurably since I had children. My Capacity to Love has increased as has my capacity for compassion. My inter-personal skills have expanded and so have my organizational abilities. Bear in mind that I still have a long way to go. Mega miles. But I have made significant progress.

All in all, I consider myself a more fully developed human because of my relationship with my Life Partner than I would ever have been had I continued on life's journey on my own.

The other point to note in this regard is that there have been times when both my Life Partner and I found it very challenging to remain in the relationship. At different times, we both thought that the other person needed to change significantly in order for us to remain together happily ever after. Without our commitment to each other, it would have been all too easy to walk out of the relationship and to escape into another one, taking our same old mental patterns with us. Our commitment to stay together has meant that we needed to find a better way of Loving each other. As a result, we have grown together and I am confident that while we are far from perfect, we are more Loving, more Free, and more Honest as a result of staying together.

3. Contribution

To make a difference. To alleviate suffering. To improve the quality of life that those around me experience. To help others get a better result.

I guess that this one is probably self-evident. I am learning to serve my Life Partner and make a difference in her life. I serve her not only when I make her a meal or take her a "cuppa," but also in the past when I vocalized my observation of "victim" thinking (rare these days) for example. Similarly, she makes a difference in my life and lightens my suffering when she acts as a mirror in helping me to see when I am running one of my old favorite patterns of "I am right," or impatience or denial or selfishness and so on. As we support each other, as we challenge each other and as we nurture each other, we improve the quality of each other's experience here on planet earth. Helping another person along the path of Freedom and Fulfillment is akin to throwing a stone into a clear and calm lake. The ripple effect on the lives of all the others, who come into contact with this person, is incalculable.

CHAPTER 41:

TOP TIPS FOR MONEY GOALS – USING WORK TO HELP YOU FULFILL YOUR LIFE PURPOSE

IT IS NOT true that Money is, as some people think, the root of all evil. The love of money is. It is true, however, that real wealth has little to do with what your investment portfolio looks like. Most people agree that wealth lies in the expansion and Fulfillment of our potential, in the development of our talents, and in the size of the Contribution we make to the world. "What does it profit a man if he gains the whole world but loses his soul?" Christ asks. Also, all the money in the world becomes quickly worthless when your health, physical, mental or emotional, fails. And the person who has no love in their life is truly the one living in poverty.

There are others who know more about wealth creation than I do. What I offer in this section are my thoughts and what has worked for me. I do recommend strongly though that you read what the experts have written. People like Martin Hawes and John Baker and their book *Get Rich, Stay Rich* (Allen and Unwin) will put you on the right track for financial independence. Buy the book, devour it, and then follow it to the letter of the law. Financial success will follow.

It also been said the rich person is not the person who has the most but rather the person who needs the least.

But before I launch into the important subject of creating income and wealth (two very different things by the way), I do want to take a stand against an idea that has gained considerable ground over the last few decades.

The idea is that we should attain financial independence so that we can dispense with the need to work. The argument assumes that work is not something that we should want to do; it is something that we are compelled to do by reason of needing to generate income to pay for food, shelter, transportation, education, and so on. Work, it is reasoned, is therefore a necessary evil, something that one should aspire to eliminate from life just as soon as humanly possible. It's a seductive argument that appeals to those who have not yet experienced a life without work. Many of the "Get Rich Schemes" including some (all though not all, by all means) multi-level marketing plans, pyramid selling schemes, property seminars, trading workshops, books and audio sets attempt to appeal to the gullible and greedy with the notion of a "work-free" future.

Of course it's prudent to have enough wealth accumulated to provide an income prior to one not being able to work due to failing health. And I for one do not want to rely on the government to determine at what level that income should be. So don't get me wrong. I am not against the idea of financial independence; in fact, I think that it's a great idea. What

I am against is the idea that we should desire such a state so as not to have to work.

Here's what would happen if there was no money on the face of the planet and you therefore did not have to go to work.

You would probably find a beach somewhere and lie in a hammock for about three months. Or perhaps you would play golf 24/7 or indulge yourself in whatever passion you wished to experience.

What all these things have in common is the "self" as the focus. Not a bad thing in itself for a period of time and actually quite productive as you rejuvenate mind, body, and soul.

But after you were fully rejuvenated you would start to feel like there was something missing. As a member of the human race, you are actually wired to feel fulfilled only when you make progress as a result of your efforts. Furthermore, you are wired in such a way to feel Happiest when you have been of service to someone or something else (animals included!). In addition to feeling unfulfilled and less than optimally Happy, you'd also feel a little lost. As humans, we are genetically programmed to need a sense of Purpose, a sense of Meaning, and unless you're a professional sportsperson, that sense of Meaning is not found in sufficient quantities on the golf course or at the beach.

Achieving financial independence has never been as possible for as many people in developed countries as it is today. For millennia now, the luxury of choosing whether or not to work was the domain of a privileged and protected few. For 99.99% of people on the planet, the best that they could hope for was survival and certainly not any form of abundance. So it's not surprising that the "work-free future" bandwagon has billions of hopeful customers clambering aboard. There's a buck to be made in selling to the greedy and gullible.

But here is how the concept of work contributes to the Fulfillment of your Purpose here on Earth. Work provides you with a vehicle to:

1. Increase Consciousness through overcoming Subconscious ego-centricity as you learn to serve others and as you learn to work with others.

2. Expand your Capacity as you develop your talents and develop new skills and abilities as you Overcome the various challenges inherent in succeeding at work.

3. Make a Contribution to others by creating products and services that are necessary for living, for alleviating suffering, or for improving the quality of their lifestyle.

Sound familiar? It is of course the Life Purpose model proposed earlier in this book: Consciousness, Capacity, and Contribution. And along with a Life Partner relationship, work is an extraordinarily effective vehicle for fulfilling your Life Purpose.

The New Testament of the Bible was first written in Greek. The Greek word that was translated as "sin" is "hamartia," which literally means "to miss the mark." I think that some church-goers have stood the concept of sin on its head. To me "sin" has little to do with pre-marital sex, swearing, rock and roll, homosexuality, or any of the other "sins" that people get so worked up about, and much more to do with the failure to utilize one's talents in fulfilling one's purpose here on planet earth. And fulfilling one's Purpose is done more effectively through work than by any other means.

No work = no purpose = no Fulfillment = missing the mark.

Money is, however, a valuable resource when it comes to fulfilling your Life Purpose, and an abundance of money is also pretty helpful when it comes to facilitating an enjoyable lifestyle, provided you know where to draw the line.

The following is not an exhaustive look at the Money issue, but I offer it to provide a few insights in developing both income and wealth.

Chapter 42:

Top Tips for Money Goals – Growing Your Income

Growing Your Income

Income is a measure of how people (employers and clients) perceive the value of your Contribution. Simple. And remember, it's their perception that counts and it's their Values that color that perception. If you are new to the workforce but have no specific qualifications, then you are amongst a large pool of others who are perceived by employers, rightly or wrongly, to have a Contribution that is of low value. Remember that scarcity increases perceived value, so if you are offering something that is the same as everyone else, then your Contribution will be perceived to be of low value and your income, if you can find employment, will be similarly low.

People with qualifications that are in demand will be able to derive more income from an employer than someone without qualifications simply because there are fewer people who made the effort to get the qualifications.

Similarly, people who are specialists in a field that is in demand will always earn more than a general practitioner. This is true in the medical industry as indeed it is in any industry.

It's worth noting, however, that some of the world's highest-paid people have very little in the way of paper-based qualifications. Bill Gates, of Microsoft, was a high school dropout and Richard Branson, of Virgin, was dyslexic and regarded by his teachers as stupid and lazy. Branson was regularly beaten for turning in poor-quality work. Success, as they say, is the best revenge. The moral of this little story is that you don't have to have tertiary qualifications in order to earn a lot of money. But you do have to provide a lot of Value, just as Gates and Branson continue to do.

Hard Work Is Not Enough

Last week I spent several days preparing our swimming pool so that it would be perfect for Christmas Day, which is traditionally hot and sunny here on the Sunshine Coast of Australia. I took a sample of the water and had it computer-analyzed and then faithfully added the recommended additives over several days. I then went away for two nights and when I returned, the pool, to my horror, was a very bright fluorescent green! No one wanted to go within ten meters of the pool without first being equipped with a lead-lined radioactive protective suit, let alone swim in it. What's the point of this story? The point is that it doesn't matter how hard you work, if you are not doing the right type of work you won't succeed. Clearly, despite my efforts, the chemicals that I put in the pool were not what it needed to produce the sparking clear water of my dreams.

Passion

The best advice I can give to those who are seeking to identify the sort of work they want to do is to create a marriage between passion and profit. In other words, don't just do something for the money. That misses the point of working almost entirely and time and again it has been shown to result in financial failure anyway. Working at something you don't enjoy but making money doing it is generally referred to as prostitution. There are a lot of hypocrites out there who look down their noses at the oldest profession but who then turn up to work simply for a paycheck. Personally, if I had to make a choice, I'd rather sell my body than my soul.

However, don't just do something because you love to do it. That's called being a missionary. My good friend Peter is a Christian missionary. Even though we have some differences when it comes to spiritual beliefs, I have massive respect for what he has sacrificed because he has had the courage of his convictions. The world needs more people like Peter and his wife, Jeannie. The world also needs more people like Mother Teresa of Calcutta who said her aim in life was to be with people when they died and to see a smile on their lips. This saint's passion in life was to make those last dying days as comfortable as possible for the forgotten ones who otherwise would have died alone and in pain in a gutter. So, I am generally in awe of anyone who sacrifices their life for their fellow humans – *"greater love has no man than he lay down his life for others."* But unless you feel especially called to such noble work, then I suggest that you find something that can make you a bucket load of money.

That's what I call a marriage between passion and profit. Wherever possible, don't choose to spend your time working at something that you don't have a passion for simply because it pays a few more dollars. You'd be selling your soul and being a traitor to your own destiny. And unless you want to be a professional missionary or volunteer, don't just do something because you enjoy it. Make that a part-time interest and put the bulk of your energies into making money while you serve mankind. That to me is the best of both worlds: passion and profit.

CHAPTER 43:

TOP TIPS FOR MONEY GOALS – WEALTH CREATION

ALMOST 70% OF financially independent people own a wealth-creating asset. That asset is called a business. So odds are that, if you are serious about financial independence, you will want to start your own business. But it therefore also goes without saying that there are still 30% of wealthy people who don't own their own business. And owning your own business is not for everyone, as it requires a Capacity to cope with risk and the associated stress that goes with that.

If you are going to start your own business, then find a role model who can guide you through the process. Similarly, if you are already in business on your own, then the best advice I can give you is not to learn from your own mistakes. Learn from someone else's mistakes by finding a proven method for building and growing your business such as the Entrepreneur's Success Programme (**www.espcoach.com**) so that you can take the guesswork out of success. Whether you choose ESP as your vehicle to help you grow your business or some other proven system, the most important thing is that you learn from professionals who can support you to create the business that you want in the most energy-, time-, and financially-efficient manner possible.

Whatever you do, don't fall into the trap that I see almost every day, of simply trading time for money. You want more money, so you work longer. Still not enough money? Put in even more hours and so on until you create a life of imbalance where you feel like a stranger to your Life Partner and kids. Cracks begin appearing not just in your relationships but also in your physical and emotional well-being. Not a good look.

Remember that business success is a science. There are eight areas to get right. Areas such as leadership, customer focus, information management and so on. Get those eight areas right and your success at growing a very valuable business, and becoming wealthy as a result, is assured. Think of it like trying to get into a safe. It's a lot easier if you know the combination as opposed to trying guesswork, or the old "just work harder and longer" approach.

There are so many great books out there on wealth creation that I don't want to take up a lot of space in this book about the subject, other than to offer a few general guidelines as follows.

DEFENSE IS MORE IMPORTANT THAN ATTACK

There is a lot of wisdom in working out how much income is enough. For most people, it's always just a little more. As financial commitments increase, especially with young families and equally new mortgages, the need to increase income increases. Parkinson's Law states that, for most people, expenses rise to meet or exceed their income. Many people now earn three of four times what they did when they first started working, but are still spending 100% (or more!) of what they earn. So learning how much is enough means that you decide how much you are going to put into your budget for living and then the rest can be invested.

It's one thing to earn income and it's another thing keeping it. A number of years ago, I was in a cash drought due in part to a recession and in part to my lack of cash management skills. So I developed the affirmation "Money flows to me like a river." I would say this affirmation over and over again after my morning meditation and again at night. With deep concentration, I stated my intention to stand in a river of cash. And indeed the money did begin to flow like a river. Unfortunately, it didn't stop when it got to me; just like the water in a river, it just kept flowing straight past me! In other words, I spent it as fast I earned it. So I developed the affirmation that I mentioned earlier which is "I am a magnet for money" and an improved result followed. You need to become as skilled at keeping the money as you are at earning it. Otherwise, you are like a sports team who are great on attack but lose their matches because they have lousy defense.

GET REAL CLEAR ON HOW MUCH MONEY IS ENOUGH

How much is enough for you to be financially independent? Consult a professional Financial Coach for this and ask them to help you work out how you are going to get there.

Once you know how much is enough, you'll then need to get a realistic strategy for accumulating the money. How are you going to build a wealth-creating asset? Start your own business; invest in property or shares or all three? Whatever you do, you will need a proven strategy to build your wealth-creating asset.

LEARN TO LOVE TO BUDGET

Acquire the necessary skills and keep a record of your income and expenses and compare them to your budget. It's one of the things that every successful business has in common and it works for individuals and families too. Managing Money is one of the few areas that I don't care if you have a Passion for it or not. Learn how to budget and how to stick to it. There is no alternative if you want long-term financial security.

DEVELOP GREAT DEFENSE STRATEGIES

Most people have acquired the skill of "how to spend money." If that applies to you, maybe it's time to learn the skill of "how to not spend money." The opportunity to spend your money will always exceed the available supply. When we moved from New Zealand to Australia, we had the "garage sale" of unwanted possessions. I was amazed at the number of useless pieces of junk that we had acquired over the years and even more surprised at people's willingness to hand over their hard-earned cash to take it off my hands. The Japanese have a word for it. They refer to the extra useless things we acquire as Chindogu. Twenty-two programmable features on your VCR, when all you really need are buttons that say Play, Stop, Pause, Rewind, and Record. A whole world of junk that people sell their souls for.

We shake our heads in wonder at indigenous populations around the world that sold vast tracts of land for a few trinkets such as beads or bangles. And yet how many people in developed countries mortgage their future simply so that they can possess the latest brand name "Shiny Thing." The new model has four seductive extra features (Chindogu) and for only a few extra dollars you can own the latest model Shiny Thing.

Eliminate Personal Debt

Your first priority will be to pay off high interest items such as hire purchase and credit card debt. Then attack your mortgage and pay that off. Then begin to develop an income producing portfolio that diversifies your risk; don't put all of your financial eggs in one basket. The key is to eliminate personal debt, which is very expensive when compared to business debt, the cost of which is tax deductible.

Invest in Financial Literacy, Financial Knowledge and Financial Competence

Financial Literacy is similar to normal literacy except instead of being able to read and write a language, I mean that you can read and write in the language of finance. Specifically you need to be able to read and understand:

- Financial Position Statements (Balance Sheet)
- Financial Performance Statements (Profit and Loss or Income Statements)
- Financial Prediction Statements (Cash Flow)
- Financial Parameter Statements (Budget)

You don't need to learn how to prepare these statements, a competent bookkeeper or accountant can do that for you. But you do need to learn how to read what each statement means in financial terms.

Financial Knowledge is about understanding what is happening in the marketplace. What are the trends and what works and what doesn't work in terms of successful financial strategies? For example, if you want to invest in property, then go to the property investment seminars. If you want to invest in the share market, then get clued up on that area and likewise for fixed term investments.

HIRE A FINANCIAL COACH

Just as a personal trainer can leverage your physical results, a great Financial Coach can do the same for your money. While I am an advocate of becoming Financially Literate, Financially Knowledgeable, and Financially Competent, I am also a great believer in creating a network of experts around you, each with their specialist areas. If you can't afford to hire a specialist, then find someone who would be willing to mentor you for free. Always remember, though, that while experts have a cost, often the cost of not having an expert is much higher. A few dollars invested with the right specialist in the short term will pay massive dividends longer term.

Make sure you reference any specialist carefully prior to contracting them. And make sure that you know exactly what the relationship is going to look like before you commit any money to it. How much will they charge and on what basis? Do they have a package that they offer, do they charge by the hour or do they charge based on results? What will they be doing for you and what do they expect you to do?

THE LAW OF GIVING AND RECEIVING

If you believe in the Law of Sowing and Reaping and you want to attract abundance into your life, then you would be wise to develop the habit of generosity. What goes around comes around, or as Ecclesiastes says *"Cast your bread on the waters; for you shall find it after many days."* I call this the Law of Giving and Receiving.

The Buddhist Law of Karma is similar. Karma actually has to do with the creation of "mental imprints." What Karma suggests is that when we act with the intention of wanting to help others, then we create a mental imprint in our mind that will attract positive results into our life.

Christ hints at this when he suggests that we should *"do unto others as you would have them do unto you."* There is an intimation there of the Law of Karma – you will reap what you sow.

What's the bottom line in terms of the Law of Giving and Receiving? Act in a way that you believe is in the best interests of others, and then you will find that events will unfold in your favor.

CREATE AN ENERGY THAT ATTRACTS MONEY

I know that it sounds obvious but people who spend money carelessly end up being broke. That's probably not news to you but I want to go a little further by adding that, in my experience, the flow of money into their lives seems to dry up as well.

You see, it's possible to have strong cash flow but to still be broke. The money goes out faster than it comes in. But that's different than what seems to eventually happen to people who are not wise stewards of the money that they earn. The first Outcome of being broke is a simple consequence of the Law of Cause and Effect: if you spend more than you earn, you will always be penniless.

The second effect of being unwise with expenditure is one that many people don't seem to be aware of. I call it the Law of Stewardship. Christ alluded to it when he said *"for to everyone who has will be given, and he will have abundance, but from him who doesn't have, even that which he has will be taken away."* Interestingly he made this statement immediately after he had told the parable of the talents. So what does it mean? What it means is that, if we are wise stewards of what we are given, then we are given even more. And the opposite is also true: if we waste what we are given, even the little that we have is taken away from us. Loose spenders eventually have their cash flow dry up, but people who are careful with their money tend to increase their cash flow.

This is not a religious law, it's a Universal Law and that means that just like the law of gravity, it doesn't matter whether or not you believe in it, it's still going to work.

According to Martin Hawes (**www.wealthcoaches.net**), the three biggest areas that people waste money on are:

1. **Houses** – investing too much into the personal home compared to wealth producing assets such as other property or shares.

2. **Hobbies** – going overboard and buying the best of everything but again, not investing enough into wealth creating assets.

3. **Holidays** – lots of expensive overseas trips.

Become a wise steward of your money and watch your cash flow increase.

Final Note

It strikes me as a paradox that on one hand we have the Law of Giving and Receiving that encourages us to be generous with our money, and on the other hand we have the Law of Stewardship that requires us to exercise discipline and control of our expenditure.

But the two balance each other beautifully and, if you practice both of these Universal Laws with persistence, then you'll get to watch and enjoy as you see your cash flow increase.

PART NINE:

THE SOFT SCIENCE OF GOAL ACHIEVEMENT

Chapter 44:

The Soft Science of Success - Introduction

In the last section, I outlined a step-by-step process for action that you can take in order to increase the speed, the certainty and the enjoyment of achieving your Goals. I called this the GAS system which stands for Goal Achievement System. "When in doubt, GAS it," as a Superbike coach would say.

Now I want to look at what goes on inside the head of a high-achiever and how you can use this information to develop your own thinking patterns to take your life to even higher levels. An awareness of what the nature of change looks like and the psychology of human change will lift your game immeasurably.

Once you have committed to a Goal, the only reason that you will not achieve it is if you give up on the process that I have outlined in the seven-step GAS System. Even a trained monkey will hit a Goal using this system — provided that it doesn't give up.

But some people do give up while others continue on. I have been fascinated by why some people, who appeared to be intelligent and dedicated fall by the wayside where others who were not as gifted sailed on to success.

There is no doubt that once you are clear on your Goal and have the knowledge of what needs to be done, the biggest challenge is simply doing it. Why is doing what we know we need and want to do, in order to get what we truly need and want, so damn hard? And why do some people persist despite an avalanche of adversity while others falter? How is it that some people seem to maintain such high levels of motivation? Is it possible to stay focused and still be relaxed? What does it take to stay committed to your Goals and to never give up until you've really nailed them?

What separates the winners from losers in life is not intelligence or any form of natural ability. It's not strength or stamina and it has little to do with the type of parents that you had or how much money you have.

What successful people have that others have not yet developed is a Capacity for aligning their thoughts with their desired Outcomes. It is the top 30 centimeters, and what goes on between the ears, that makes the difference between being the walking definition of success and dragging your sorry carcass from one defeat to the next.

The Soft Science of Success shows you how to develop your mental game so that success becomes simply a matter of time.

Chapter 45:

Reprogramming Your Mind for Success

Earlier **I wrote** about the need to align your Inner World of thoughts with your Goals. I mentioned that Self-talk can either hold us back or move us on depending on how it impacts on the twin thermostats of Self-image and Self-esteem. Let's refresh those thoughts a little.

Self-talk

Self-talk is a term that describes the thoughts that bounce around in the "mad monkey of the mind." As its name implies, Self-talk is a conversation that you conduct, except instead of having it with another person, you have it with yourself. Effective communication includes self-communication.

You see, there are two of you inside your body. This is of course something that we Gemini's have known for millennia! The strongest disagreements I've ever had have been with me. Yes, there are two of you. I mean, how can you ever say *"I was beside myself with worry"* unless there are two of you. Or

"I'm of two minds about this." Or ever want to do something like exercise and then find yourself doing exactly the opposite by "upsizing" yourself at a fast food outlet. If you have any doubt about the fact that there are two of you, just sit back sometime and listen to the conversation going on in your mind.

This conversation is what I call Self-talk. You need to understand that Self-talk is not a good thing and it's not a bad thing, it's just Self-talk.

But when the Self-talk degrades our Self-esteem or destroys a healthy Self-image or even damages the level of enjoyment within an experience, I call this "Destructive Self-talk." For many years now in my volunteer work, I've run workshops in prisons and I can tell you that the real Public Enemy #1 is as alive and well inside those prison walls as it is outside of them, and it's not an axe murderer or a bank robber; it's Destructive Self-talk.

Destructive Self-talk is one of the most insidious forms of Subconscious programming because most people are completely unaware of it, most of the time. Most people are not often aware of their own Self-talk because its origins are in the Subconscious mind, which by definition, we are not always Consciously aware of.

THE SELF-BEATERS CLUB

The largest club in the world is the "Self-Beaters" Club. Millions of people join the Self-beaters Club every day and billions renew every day. The price of entry is low, but the price of membership is very, very high. Entry is gained simply by degrading yourself within your own mind with Self-talk such as *"you stupid idiot,"* or any of the more colorful and more descriptive variations of that theme. You renew your membership every time you beat yourself up and the cost of renewal is damaging your Self-esteem and your Self-image.

Self-talk is going on inside your head constantly. And every thought is either taking you towards your Goal, by aligning your Self-esteem and Self-image, or it's taking you away from your Goals by creating a lack of alignment.

An Exercise In Awareness

The Buddhists have a technique for raising one's awareness of both positive and destructive Self-talk. A monk will carry with him a bag containing black pebbles and white pebbles. Every time the monk becomes aware of a destructive thought, he puts a black pebble into his left pocket and every time he is aware of a positive thought, he puts a white pebble into his right pocket. At the end of the day, he takes the stones out and counts them up. It is said that they have many more black pebbles than white ones at the end of a day.

If this is true of a Buddhist monk, it's probably even more likely to be true for you and me.

Remember, you create your world with your thoughts. If you have more destructive thoughts than positive thoughts, then it will be very difficult for you to make progress in any area of your life. Hence, there is a need to become more self-aware and self-honest about what we are thinking. We need to bring our thought patterns up to the light of Consciousness and examine each one. If the pattern is serving us, we can leave it alone. But if it is taking us further away from our Goals. then we need to reprogram the Subconscious with a more positive, or more creative, thought pattern.

If you program your Subconscious correctly, it will set your life headed for success like a train running on tracks.

GIGO

The Subconscious mind is very much like a computer. When I started my software company over two decades ago, personal computers had just made their entry on the world stage and ushered in a whole new dimension of opportunity. I have to say, however, that personal computers created a whole new way of getting frustrated as well!

Many is the time that I swore at the computer that I was programming because it wasn't doing what I wanted it to do. The frustratingly inescapable fact was, however, that it was doing exactly what I told it to do. We had a saying back then in the good old days of all-night caffeine and chocolate fueled programming sessions: "GIGO." This stands for "Garbage In, Garbage Out."

If I program the computer with garbage, then garbage is what it will give me back. And the Subconscious is no different. The Subconscious is simply not capable, literally, of making any decisions. It is only capable of doing what it is told.

The other day I observed my co-worker verbally abusing herself. *"Oh you silly cow"* she might mutter to herself or *"You idiot."* Interestingly, as this went on throughout the morning, she also began to hurt herself as she moved about the office. She would bump her foot on the desk or knock her elbow on a cupboard. The more she beat herself up verbally the more her Subconscious obeyed her programming and created situations where she beat herself up physically. Garbage in equals garbage out. Self-talk can be very destructive when it's negative, but equally constructive when it's positive.

A Lifetime of Programming

The programming that has taken place in your Subconscious mind occurred over many years and came from many different sources. Think of it like this. When you were born, your Subconscious mind was like a blank whiteboard and then lots of people began to write the programming for your Self-Esteem and Self-Image on that whiteboard. Here is a list of just a few of the people who helped to write the programming for your Self-Esteem and Self-Image:

- Your parents or guardians
- Your teachers
- Other authority figures such as politicians
- The television and radio
- The newspapers and magazines that you read
- Your friends at school
- Your colleagues at work

Additionally, you wrote some programming when you created experiences of pain and pleasure, both physical and emotional. And every time you associated a specific meaning with an event, you did some more programming. And when you treated other people the way that you did, right or wrong, good or bad, you wrote some more programming code.

Decades of programming has etched your Self-Esteem and Self-Image into your Subconscious. So how do you change it?

As mentioned above, the key is to bring to the light of Consciousness your beliefs about yourself and life in general. Beliefs are patterns of thought that you hold to be true. They are not one-off thoughts; they are thoughts that run over and over again in your mind, creating deep mental imprints that cause you to act in either a destructive or positive manner, in respect to achieving your Goals.

This is why it's possible for you to Consciously want something very badly but to have your Subconscious sabotage your efforts due to an unaligned belief, or thought pattern.

You can reprogram your Subconscious as you become aware of self- sabotaging behavior. The beauty about the process of reprogramming is that you don't have to spend hours, weeks and months with a counselor to uncover the cause of why you self-sabotage. Please note that I am not against counseling, as such. In fact I am a fan of counseling in certain situations and have referred a number of my clients over the years to an effective counselor. It's just that some people spend too much time on trying to find out why they self-sabotage, and not enough time actually addressing the issue and moving on.

Ours Is Not to Reason Why

What I have come to realize is that it is not necessary to identify the experiences that caused us to be programmed the way that we are. The past is the past. It's water under the bridge. There's no benefit to be gained by dredging up old muck from history. If you think that you had parents who were less than perfect, then welcome to the human race. If you are angry about what happened to you as a kid, then go thump a pillow and scream some. You'll probably feel better. Then build a bridge, and "get over it." You can either put your energy into being a victim and focusing on other people's imperfections, or you can invest some energy into fixing yourself and moving on. Not really a difficult decision is it?

Some people get confused when they quote from the Bible that *"the truth shall set you free"* (John 8:32). It doesn't say *"the reasons will set you free."* I believe that Christ is referring to what happens when we face the facts of who we are and where we are at. The denial of reality (the truth) keeps people imprisoned. You don't need to know why you are like you are. You simply need to know that you are like you are and more importantly, who you want to Be.

Just to motivate you even more to move on from the past, I want to remind you about the Law of Focus. Just like another universal law, the Law of Gravity, the Law of Focus works whether or not you happen to believe in it. What the Law of Focus states is that whatever you consistently focus your mind on, you will create more of. This is great if you focus your mind on what you want, but I'm sure that you can see the difficulty if your mind is focused on what you don't want, or what you didn't like about the past. You get more of the same Outer-World realities as well as more of the same Inner-World emotions.

Many people still feel that the past can be cleared by talking about it or re-experiencing it. While I agree that it is important to accept what happened as real and accept and experience how you feel about it, once that is done it's time to get on with your life and focus on what you are going to do in order to create a different and better future.

The great thing about reprogramming is that, while the old programming was often taking place without your Conscious awareness, you can easily reprogram the Subconscious with the beliefs that you want.

How to Reprogram Your Subconscious

There is a simple way to reprogram your Subconscious. The Subconscious is of course by its very nature, not Conscious. Because it is not Conscious, it does not make any distinctions between sensory input that is real and sensory input that is imagined. It simply has no capacity to care, and no capability to discern, which is which. To the Subconscious it's all just programming. And your ability to reprogram your Subconscious is only just a page or two away.

A significant aid to mental reprogramming was discovered by Johannes Shultz, a German doctor whose recovery rates for patients were some five times faster than that of other doctors" patients. What the good doctor discovered over one hundred years ago is what the Vedas talked about thousands of years previously. The best states for reprogramming the mind are very relaxed, meditative states. Shultz developed a process he called "auto-genic" conditioning, or "self-conditioning." What Shultz discovered and what others such as Maxwell Maltz have confirmed as true is that if a person relaxes their Conscious mind the Subconscious can be reprogrammed without difficulty.

Through techniques such as affirmations and visualizations, new thought patterns and beliefs can be etched deep into the psyche of any human being.

Different frequencies of brain waves have been identified by scientists to coincide with specific states of mind. The simple version of the scale looks as follows:

> **Beta level:** 14+ brain waves per second. This is your normal waking state.
>
> **Alpha level:** 8–13 brain waves per sec. This is a meditative or day-dreaming state.
>
> **Theta level:** 5–7 brain waves per sec. This is your state as you drift into or out of sleep.
>
> **Delta level:** ½ to 4 brain waves per second. This is your normal state when asleep.

The best level for reprogramming the Subconscious is Alpha. You can achieve this state by either meditating or by sitting in a comfortable chair and listening to slow-beat and relaxing classical music such as Mozart or a Johann Strauss waltz.

Once your mind is in a relaxed state, your brain waves will have slowed and the Subconscious is receptive to reprogramming.

Using Affirmations to Reprogram the Subconscious

An affirmation is a statement of the reality that you want to experience. If you have a Self-Esteem issue, then you might repeat, over and over again, with as much mental concentration as you can muster *"I am worthy"* or *"I'm OK"* or something similar. Affirmations should always be stated in the present tense and in the affirmative.

Let's practice with some wealth-creating affirmations.

'I don't want to be broke." Can you spot the deliberate mistake with this one? It's focusing on the opposite of what you want and the Subconscious is unfortunately unable to understand the reverse of an idea. If you use this affirmation, then all the Subconscious is going to hear is *"I want to stay broke"* and it will unerringly guide your Conscious thoughts and actions in an *"I want to stay broke"* manner.

'I want money." The problem with this one is that is focuses on the future and on lack. The word "want" actually means "I don't have it." "I want" and "I lack" essentially mean the same thing, so *"I want more money"* is a poor choice for an affirmation because it expresses the very opposite of what you want.

'I am going to be wealthy one day." Another dud! The Subconscious knows only about the present. It has no capacity to imagine the future. That is a function of the Conscious mind.

When it comes to affirmations, the Subconscious works on what it gets "here and now." So by repeating this affirmation, the Subconscious will ensure that it is true. And you will be in a perpetual state of *"going to be wealthy one day."* As far as your Subconscious is concerned, its role is to ensure that "being wealthy" will always stay in the future.

Two of the best ways, although not the only great ways by any means, of starting an affirmation are with the words "I am..." or "I give thanks for...'

For example: *"I give thanks for financial abundance in my life"* and *"I am a wise steward of money.'*

So create a relaxed mental state either through meditation or slow classical music and then repeatedly state your affirmation over and over again. Repetition and Immersion are the Mummy and Daddy of reprogramming the Subconscious. Your ability to relax and to repeat the affirmation with deep levels of concentration is the key and you'll get better at this with practice.

Don't expect miraculous changes overnight by using affirmations. It took your whole life to get programmed the way that you are now, and changes will not be noticeable within a few days. But they will occur with persistence. Once you find that you are automatically thinking and acting in alignment with your affirmation, then you can move on to a new affirmation.

A final tip for affirmations. It's best not to mix affirmations for one part of your life with others. For example, don't repeat affirmations in regard to a better relationship with affirmations about better health. Have a separate affirmation session if you want to reprogram more than one mental pattern.

AD-HOC AFFIRMATIONS WORK AS WELL

Finally, it's important to understand that you don't have to be in a super relaxed state in order to benefit from Affirmations. Certainly, it's easier to program your Subconscious faster when the Conscious mind is relaxed and in Alpha mode. However, that's real hard to achieve when, for example, you're on the tennis court or the race track or in the boardroom and you notice that your Self-talk is destructive. On many, many occasions, I have turned a losing performance around once I noticed my destructive Self-talk and then turned on the tap of Self-Esteem-building affirmations.

Last weekend is one example. I was out on my dirt bike with several more experienced riders. Lately, I've had a lot of crashes and injured myself as well as damaged the bike. As I rode, I noticed that I was being tentative and feeling tired. That was a recipe for disaster given the tough terrain we were traversing. Long, steep, and rocky hill climbs with jumps and loose stones on many corners. I noticed my thoughts starting to become negative and full of self-doubt. So I began repeating to myself *"I am strong and confident,"* over and over again with great conviction. Within five minutes I felt like my whole mental game as well as my physical energy levels had lifted. As a result, I went faster and enjoyed my day a whole lot more. Additionally, I didn't crash at all. Both my bones and the bike remained whole. Affirmations are a key to higher levels of performance as well as higher levels of enjoyment.

The bottom line is this: make it a part of your daily routine to observe your Self-talk and create a habit out of reprogramming your mind both with regular planned relaxation sessions as well as on-the-go ad hoc affirmations.

How to Use Visualization

In the context of this book, visualization is about imagining the Outcome that you want as clearly as possible. In other words, you create mental pictures in your mind of you having achieved your Goal. Similarly, you can attune your mind to completing the necessary Inputs required by imagining yourself completing them as well. Gold medal athletes use this technique before their performances, as do thousands of successful salespeople, theatrical performers, and business leaders.

Visualization can be referred to as being like creating a "future memory." It's like you create a movie in your mind and then wind on fast-forward to a point of time in the future and play back the success that you created. Just like you were remembering a success from yesterday. Only with visualizations, you're doing that in advance. So you get to create history in advance, hence "future memory." What do you want your future to look like? What will it look like as you go about achieving your Goal? And what will it look like when the Goal has metamorphosed from some dry ink on a piece of paper and into reality? That's what you are going to be visualizing, or imagining.

All of the principles that apply to reprogramming the Subconscious with affirmations also apply to visualization.

You need to get your mind into an "Alpha" state through some form of meditation (see www.tompoland.com for meditation CDs) or through listening to slow classical music. Waltzes, by the way, are great for this.

Then, once you sense that you are very relaxed, begin to picture yourself perfectly performing the necessary actions and then enjoying the perfect result. I recommend involving as many of your senses as possible by imagining not only what you would be seeing, but what you would be hearing, touching, physically feeling, smelling and if appropriate, tasting. And if possible, imagining what you would be feeling emotionally will take the effectiveness of the exercise to a whole new level, as the Subconscious is sensitized to feeling empowering emotions such as confidence, Happiness, success, or peace of mind.

Now here is one of my best tips. Nominate one Goal, and only one, as your Number One Goal. For this Goal, use affirmations and visualizations every day. Remember that affirmations and visualizations are most effective when your Conscious mind is relaxed and in an Alpha state. Achieve this state of mind through either meditation or by listening to classical music or any other relaxation technique.

Another powerful time to reprogram your Subconscious is during your waking moments. One technique that I recommend is to first write out your affirmation or visualization and then record them onto a digital voice recorder. Then invest in a CD or MP3 player that has an alarm feature. You can then wake to the calming sounds of Chopin, Mozart or Strauss, and while you are still half asleep, you can press the play button on your CD or MP3 player and focus on saying your affirmations along with the recording. This is a highly effective way to reprogram the Subconscious and beats the heck out of waking up to the news or advertisements on the radio every morning. By the way, if you share the bed with someone else, you might want to invest in a head set for when you play the affirmations. Your Loved One might not appreciate waking up to your strong and determined voice chanting *"I like myself! I like myself!"* booming out of your digital recorder.

Whichever method you choose, here's a reminder of my golden rule: practice your affirmations and visualizations for your Number One Goal every single work day. You can have the weekends off and you can have your holidays off. I believe that it's actually beneficial for the mind to have a rest from this process and having the weekends and holidays off will help you stick to the process by giving you a break.

The key point in respect to reprogramming the Subconscious or "changing your mind" is to use repetition and immersion. Frequently and Consciously choose to wash your mind in the new way of thinking and you will eventually begin to automatically think that way.

A Reprogramming Toolkit

To this end you can add other reprogramming methodologies to your toolkit. The complete list might look something like this:

1. Visualization

2. Affirmation

3. Verbalization (use language consistent with the new way that you want to think)

4. Actualization (acting in a manner that is aligned with the way you want to think)

5. Contemplation (thinking about the benefits of the new way of thinking and the consequences of the old dysfunctional way of thinking)

6. Observation (self-observation to note when you are and are not thinking in the new way)

7. Conversation (talking to others who think the way that you want to think)

Meditative Contemplation

Hinduism, Buddhism, Judaism, Islam, and Christianity have many, many Values in common, not the least of which is Love. Something else that they also share is a tradition of using Contemplation to reprogram the mind.

Indian Guru Paramahansa Yogananda tells us of a young Hindu disciple who went to his Guru to confess that he was sorely vexed by thoughts of sexual union with the opposite gender. The young man said that he found women irresistibly attractive, especially their curvaceous bodies.

In those days, the cemetery was on the outskirts of most villages and the graves were very simple affairs as dead bodies were simply left to rot in the open air.

The Guru instructed the young disciple to go to the cemetery and to sit near the body of an old decomposing woman and to contemplate "the end of all flesh." Having completed the exercise with diligence, the young disciple was no longer disturbed by persistent thoughts of fornication! Not surprising really.

Fortunately, I don't need to recommend anything quite as extreme to you. But what follows is a simple step-by-step question process that allows you to create a motivational shift in your thoughts away from old unwanted thought patterns and actions towards a new way or thinking and acting.

THE SEVEN STEP CONTEMPLATION SYSTEM

1. What is the thought pattern or behavior I want to change?

   _____

   _____

   _____

   _____

2. What is the payoff for keeping this thought pattern or behavior ? (there is always some dysfunctional payoff)

   _____

   _____

   _____

   _____

3. What is the price that I am paying for keeping this thought pattern or behavior? (include physical or "Outer World" consequences such as financial, relationship, and health consequences as well as emotional or "Inner World" consequences such as loss of Self-Esteem)

_____

_____

_____

_____

4. What new thought pattern or behavior would help me to create the Outcome that I really want?

_____

_____

_____

_____

5. What will be the payoff from this new thought pattern or behavior ? (Again, include physical or "Outer World" consequences such as financial, relationship, and health benefits as well as emotional or "Inner World" consequences such as greater Self-Esteem, security, peace of mind, etc.)

_____

_____

_____

_____

6. What new affirmation will I now create to reinforce this new thought pattern or behavior ? (summarize "4" above)

_____

_____

_____

_____

7. What new action will I now commit to in order to change my life?

_____

_____

_____

_____

REPROGRAMMING THROUGH THE POWER OF MENTAL FOCUS

Lastly, on the subject of reprogramming thoughts, guard carefully what you feed your mind. Whatever you focus on, with persistence, you will create as a thought pattern and that will then manifest in actions and you will get to experience the subsequent Outcome.

Let's say for example that Sam, a forty-year-old married man with three children is spending too much money on his hobby of snowboarding. It's gotten to the point where all his spare cash goes into this passion in one form or another. And then some. Despite the fact that he has an agreed budget with his Life Partner, he often blows it. He finds that he just can't seem to help himself. Consciously, he knows that he needs to cut back his spending and start investing for the future. But Subconsciously, he feels constantly seduced by the latest snowboard or associated paraphernalia.

How come? Well, every week Sam picks up a copy of the latest ski and snowboarding magazines. He subscribes to the local ones and reads them avidly most evenings. And once a week he goes to his local magazine shop and picks up the overseas mags which he reads on the weekends.

On Saturday, Sam gets the newspaper and just for fun he looks up any advertisements for snowboarding equipment. Then several times during the week at lunchtime or on the weekend, he'll visit one or more of the four snowboarding and skiing outlets in his city. He knows where they all are and, when he enters, he's greeted by his first name. Sam feels very much a part of the snowboarding community.

Sam has his next three holidays all mapped out. Each one is to a snow field overseas in an exotic location. If the budget is tight, he may go somewhere more local, but either way, he will spend most of his time on the snowboard.

He's a member of his local snowboarding club and attends the meetings and reads their newsletters with interest. He also surfs the web and downloads training notes, articles, weather reports and looks at snow field webcams around the world. Sam finds people who don't love snowboarding boring and so almost all of Sam's friends are snowboarders as well. This means that his social conversations are almost always about snowboarding.

Sam doesn't see himself as unbalanced though, just passionate. Others would say that he's crossed the line from passion into obsession.

Do you see Sam's problem? He wants to be financially independent and have a great Life Partner relationship, but his behavior is sabotaging his Goals.

If Sam added up the quantity of information that his mind consumes on snowboarding and compared it to how much he focused his mind on creating wealth, he would quickly realize why he behaves in the unbalanced and non-aligned manner that he does.

Thoughts are the most powerful force in the universe. Thoughts create our daily reality. Sam's behavior and his results in life will never change until he changes his mental diet.

If Sam really Values financial independence ahead of snowboarding, then he will begin to focus his mind on that subject more than on snowboarding. He'll cut back his snowboarding magazine subscriptions, have some holidays in the sun instead of the snow, go to the snow shops only when he really needs to, and operate within an agreed and balanced budget for snowboarding expenditure. He'll also subscribe to investment magazines and read them; he'll buy great books on how to become financially independent and he'll read them. He'll go to seminars on property and shares to increase his financial Capabilities.

The key for Sam is to change the focus of the mind so that it is aligned with his Values, Vision and Goals. The mental diet will produce an aligned set of actions. "Garbage In,

Garbage Out." The opposite is also true: "Quality In, Quality Out."

In short, if Sam changes the predominant focus of his mind from snowboarding to investing he will change his thought patterns, his actions, and ultimately his Outcomes.

Reprogramming the way that you think is really quite simple: *"With our thoughts we create our world."* What you focus on, you manifest. If you saturate your mind with concepts of compassion, love, patience, acceptance, and giving, then you'll create wonderfully fulfilling relationships. Books, as well as playing audio material in your car, are wonderful ways to reprogram the mind because they offer both repetition and immersion over an extended period of time.

And that's the key: repetition and immersion over an extended period of time. That's how thought patterns are changed. Where your mind goes, your life will follow.

Chapter 46:

How to Build Your Commitment and Persistence Muscles

Commitment

Here's my favorite quote on the subject of commitment from A.H. Murray:

> "Until one is Committed, there is hesitancy, the chance to draw back, always ineffectiveness. The moment one definitely commits oneself, then Providence moves too. All sorts of things occur to help one that would never otherwise have occurred. A whole stream of events issues from the decision, raising in one's favor all manner of unforeseen incidents and meetings and material assistance, which no man could have dreamed would have come his way."

Persistence

And while we're on the subject of favorite quotes here's another classic on the power of Persistence from ex-US president Calvin Coolidge (1872- 1933):

> "Nothing in the world can take the place of Persistence. Talent will not; nothing is more common than unsuccessful men with talent. Genius will not; unrewarded genius is almost a prov-

erb. Education will not; the world is full of educated derelicts. Persistence and determination alone are omnipotent. The slogan 'Press On' has solved and always will solve the problems of the human race."

I love those quotes. I really do. Commitment and Persistence rule! But how do you build a Capacity for Commitment and Persistence that's so strong that the moment you make a commitment to a Goal, you genuinely know that it's as good as achieved?

First of all, it's worthwhile to understand the Commitment and Persistence really go hand in hand. You won't persist unless you are committed, and you won't achieve what you are committed to unless you persist.

So think of Commitment and Persistence as being like two biceps on either arm of the same body. The bicep is the muscle on the top of your arm between your shoulder and your elbow. This is a great analogy because you build the twin muscles of Commitment and Persistence the same way that you use to build a massive "Arnie" type bicep – slowly.

The way to build a big bicep is by starting with a small bicep and then exercising it. But you don't just suddenly load up the bar bell with a mega-weight that only Arnold Schwarzenegger could lift. You start with something small. Something that your bicep can manage without injury or breakdown.

Similarly, if you want to build Commitment and Persistence, start with a Goal that requires only a little exercising of your mental muscles. Establish some success at that level and then build up from there. For someone who struggles to get out of bed by midday every morning, instead of Committing to get up a 5 a.m. and go running, they should set a Goal to get out of bed by 9 a.m. and work on locking that in for three weeks, or twenty one days, and then aim for 8 a.m. and so on until they hit their ultimate Goal of waking before their 5 a.m. alarm call.

Australian Graeme Alford is a great example of someone who turned his life around by starting with small commitments and building up to larger one. Graeme went from being a successful solicitor to a life of excessive drinking and gambling which led to armed robbery and a long-term jail sentence. In prison, shattered and destitute, he was forced to reassess his life, which he turned around. He is now seven stone lighter, has a happy family life, and is a tireless charity worker on the Board of Life Education. In addition, Graeme has created an extremely successful career as a motivational speaker. I recommend him highly.

The turnaround for Graeme came during his second and final stint in prison. Realizing that if his life was going to change then he needed to change, he set himself out a program for what he described as "Mental Toughness." He started by denying himself things that he liked, such as chocolate, or coffee, at first for a week at a time and then for longer periods. Then he went on to make Commitments to do things that he didn't want to do such as exercising. Again he started with small Commitments but built on his success to go on to make larger ones. He built his Commitment and Persistence muscles to the point that he went without white bread and potato for a year, red meat for five years, gave up cigarettes completely (he started by giving them up for three days), ran a marathon and has gone on to become one of Australia's most outstanding entrepreneurs and an inspiring guest speaker.

Graeme says that "Mental Toughness" is about creating *"the power to do what you have to do when you have to do it and not what you want to do when you want to do it."*

Building the Capacity for Commitment and Persistence hasn't changed since the dawn of time. We may have learned how to build biceps quicker by using steroids or other means of cheating, but we cannot shortcut building character. For all of modern science's medical, neurological, and technological breakthroughs, Persistence can only be built one step at a time.

I wrote about how to leverage your Commitment levels earlier when I discussed the principle of "Reward and Non Reward." The following story illustrates that principle perfectly.

OF VIKINGS AND VICTORY

When on one of their infamous raids, the Vikings were said to have had the habit of arriving at their targeted coastline and then burning their boats on the beach before they set off to attack the Village or town that they had come to plunder. In the mind of a Viking warrior, failure meant death. That's leverage.

It would seem, however, that if a group of Viking warriors were going on an especially dangerous and difficult raid, they were required to place into the boat with them an item that was more dear to them than their own life. The item was in the form of a small child, either a son or daughter or grandchild.

As usual, once the boats were beached, they were burned but on these occasions the children were gathered into a makeshift corral out of the weather and not too far from where the battle would be waged.

Each Viking warrior knew that if they lost the battle then not only would he lose his own life, but the life of his dear one would be forfeited as well — or worse, they would be abused by the victorious defenders, tortured, and taken into a lifetime of servitude and slavery.

During those battles, in the mind of a Viking warrior, there were only two possible Outcomes. One was victory and the other was …

… victory.

That's right: in the mind of a Viking warrior there was no other possible Outcome other than victory. And that's what I mean by Commitment. In my world, Commitment means *"no other possible Outcome."* It's steel-reinforced will power. I know, that no matter how tough the going gets, a strong will always finds a way. Commitment, Persistence, and Discipline are supreme acts of Consciousness.

Failure

Failure is what happens if you die and didn't hit your Goals. Everything else is feedback. The way I see it, I've never really come in last in a motorbike race yet; I just ran out of laps before the checkered flag dropped! I still get to have another crack at it next time.

So never confuse feedback for failure. Let's say that your world has crumbled down around you. You've lost your business or just been fired, your Life Partner and family have walked out on you, you're a drug addict, you're bankrupt and even your dog is so disgusted with the low state of affairs that he no longer wags his tail when he sees you. One question: are you dead? No? So it must be feedback. And feedback is the breakfast of champions. Feedback is like old-fashioned medicine. You can choke on it and spit it out or swallow hard and grow strong from it.

It's easy to tell the difference between failure and feedback. Just check your pulse. If you find one, then what you're experiencing is feedback. As long as you haven't given up, you haven't failed.

On Giving Up

Quitting is a decision. Some people talk about not being able to go on, but the reality is that no one ever quit anything until they decided to. No one forces us to surrender. No one throws in the towel for you or me, and if they ever did, I'd chuck it right back at them. Giving up is only something you have to do after you have gasped your last breath. Prior to that, quitting is optional. The person who falls over only loses if they choose not to stand back up again.

Chapter 47:

How to Stay Motivated

Where does the Capacity for Motivation come from? Many people get annoyed and frustrated when others say to them, "You should be more motivated" like it was some sort of news flash. Of course you "should be motivated," but how? "Well you've either got it or you haven't; it's an internal thing" they respond. Again, not very helpful.

Is motivation just something that some lucky few are born with or can we all benefit from increasing our Capacity for Motivation? The answer of course, is that there are specific steps that each of us can take to grow our Motivation muscle.

Motivation, Persistence, and Commitment are clearly tied in together. Extra-Ordinary achievements in life require an exceptional level of Motivation, Persistence, and Commitment. No sane person would argue with that.

What most people haven't quite figured out though is that one leads to another. Looking at it in reverse order, you won't Persist unless you are really Committed to your Outcome, and you won't make a Commitment or stay Committed unless you are Motivated to do so.

THE SEQUENCE

So this is what the sequence looks like:

1. Motivation

2. Commitment

3. Persistence

The more Motivated you are the more likely it is that you will Commit and stay Committed and therefore the more likely it is that you will Persist.

So it all starts with Motivation. If you can learn how to create and sustain high levels of Motivation, you'll be able to make and keep Commitments and you'll Persist in the face of obstacles.

CREATING AND MAINTAINING MOTIVATION

There are five keys to creating and maintaining high levels of Motivation. Think of each of these five aspects of Motivation as being like five separate ingredients for a powerful jet fuel. If any one of them is missing, then the chances are your Motivation levels will drop and as a result you'll notice a corresponding drop in your performance. If you are missing two of these elements, then your plane is going to start to nose dive and if you are missing three then you will never get your life off the ground.

A lot of these concepts have been discussed in other chapters, but I want to summarize them here in this chapter so that if you are struggling for Motivation it will be easier for you to work out what to do about it.

Here are the five essential ingredients for creating and staying motivated. If you ever feel like you are lacking in motivation, you can simply come to this checklist and use it as a diagnostic tool to see what you need to fix or repair.

1. Have a strong Purpose for living

Goals will provide you with this. Additionally, if you take the time to become clear on your Life Purpose, you'll get even more leverage in this area. My model of increasing Consciousness, Capacity, and Contribution is a solid start, but you'll want to spend some time working out what those labels mean to you. Use your Dream Day (refer Chapter 21) to flesh out your Life Purpose as well to look at your Vision statement (refer Chapter 12).

2. Keep your mental fuel tanks full

Make sure that you've read my comments on this vital area in Chapter 33 (How to increase your energy levels – the two human fuel tanks) but the issue is so important I want to touch on it briefly again here.

On many, many occasions, business leaders have approached me with the problem of lacking motivation. They complain that they don't seem to have the spark of enthusiasm that they used to have for their business and they're understandably worried about the consequences for their results.

More often than not, they are simply burned out. Motivation requires fuel and it's real hard to kick-start an engine into life when the petrol tank is empty. When I explain this to my clients, they sometimes say things like, *"But I shouldn't be, because ... others aren't/I just had a holiday/I'm only 35 years old...*" or whatever. The remedy for burnout is as simple as it is unavoidable: give your mind a rest. Find a beach or a mountain and get your mind off your work and your problems for a while. You may need two weeks or two months. When you feel like going back to work, you know that you have topped up the tanks. But before then, going back to business is simply counter-productive.

People say to me that they can't afford to take the time off. I tell them that they are just like me in that they already take plenty of time off. It's just that I have my time off at the beach and they have their time off in the office, being an unproductive pinball.

Most people think that holidays and time off come as a reward for a period of hard work. I think that they come before a period of high productivity, not after it.

If you are lacking in motivation and feel that you have lost your passion for something you used to love, then take a great relaxing and long holiday and rejuvenate your mind. It's an absolute non-negotiable prerequisite for sustaining high levels of performance. And remember: *"fatigue makes cowards of us all."*

3. Invest as much time as you can on activities that you have a Passion for

Assuming that you are rejuvenated, the next aspect of your motivation fuel mix to check is how much of your time you are investing in activities that you are passionate about. Some people stick at jobs they hate just to pay the rent.

Working at a job you don't like is important if it's the only way that you can meet your financial commitments, but for your own sake, get the hell out of it and into the heaven of a passion-filled role as soon as you can. It'll add jet fuel to your tanks of motivation. Additionally, if you find yourself swamped with activities that others have imposed on you, it's time to learn how to use the magic phrase *"thank you, but no."*

4. Making, recognizing and appreciating progress toward the Fulfillment of your Goals

Let's split this up a little. First of all, if you don't make any progress toward your goal, you will end up being demoralized and demotivated. Months or years of slog with no results is a recipe for quitting. If what you are doing is not working, there is no use in doing twice as much of it. Working harder and longer is often not the answer. You need to find a Supermodel (see Chapter 26) and find out how to work smarter.

If you are making progress but failing to really recognize and appreciate it, then you may end up feeling equally frustrated and unfulfilled as someone who simply isn't making any progress. The Hour of Power concept that I wrote about in Chapter 30 will soon fix this.

5. Stay Conscious of powerful reasons for wanting to achieve your Goals

The last key to motivating yourself is to identify reasons. As mentioned previously, it really doesn't matter too much where you draw your success motivation from, so long as you have some. You could be fueled by a desire to prove your high school teacher wrong or by bringing enlightenment to the world. Whatever spins your whizzer will do just fine.

THREE LEVELS OF MOTIVATION

There are at least three sources of reasons that can motivate you and they are pain, pleasure, and purpose. I covered each of these previously but here's a new twist on them.

Pain motivators

This is a pretty low-grade way to go through life. Sure, we're all motivated to stay safe, warm, and make sure that we have a belly full of food, but once our basic survival needs have been met, then pain only becomes a motivator when it gets annoying enough. An example of pain motivators would be the person who doesn't stop abusing alcohol until their liver is shot and it's life-threatening. Or the person who quits smoking once they are diagnosed with cancer. Or the person who develops the capacity for Loving only after his third wife has walked out on him and his kids won't talk to him anymore. You get the picture. Some people don't feel motivated to make commitments until they feel enough pain. This level has more to do with "self " than the next two levels.

Pleasure motivators

These include the better home, better car, more money in the bank and so on. This level has more to do with "things" than it has with people. Remember though, it really doesn't matter where one draws one's source of motivation from, so long as you have some fuel in that Goal- achievement tank. Regardless of the Goal or the source of motivation, when you set the Goal you create obstacles and as you Overcome those obstacles you increase Consciousness, Capacity and inevitably through a value-exchange process you end up making a Contribution to others.

Purpose motivators

This one has to do with others. To me, there is a deeper and more powerful source of motivation beyond the avoidance of pain (self) and the pursuit of pleasure (things), and it's where I want to operate from more and more. While I will use pain/pleasure motivators when I need to, I prefer to really hook into a source of power that's larger than me. Making a dent in the universe before I depart charges my Motivation batteries like nothing else. I want to be able to sit on that rocking chair, aged 95 or whatever, knowing that I was a great steward of my talents, that I made a solid Contribution to the success of others, and that my Capacities for Love, Freedom, Happiness, Compassion and a zillion other Values have expanded exponentially. All of my Goals relate back to my Life Purpose: Consciousness, Capacity, and Contribution.

Passion as a Motivator

As mentioned earlier, Passion is definitely an ingredient in the fuel of motivation. I align passion very closely with Purpose however, because I believe that the clues to our Purpose lie in our talents, which tend to be those things that we are Passionate about. Certainly though, as mentioned previously, if you can create an alignment between Outcomes that you are Passionate about and Inputs that you are Passionate about, your journey to success gets a whole lot more enjoyable. To me, life is too short to waste my energy on anything that I have no Passion for.

So in a nutshell, if you want to feel more motivated toward achieving a particular Goal, then mentally go through the three levels of motivation and make a list of reasons why you are considering committing to a particular Goal.

Start with pain-associated reasons and be sure to include both Inner World reasons (e.g. how rotten you will feel if you don't change) as well as Outer World reasons (e.g. the physical, material world cost of not changing).

Then move onto a list of pleasure-associated reasons. Again make sure the list contains both Inner World reasons (e.g. how great you will feel when you've hit your Goal) as well as Outer World reasons (e.g. the physical, material world benefits of hitting your Goal).

Then you can move on and do the same thing with purpose-sourced reasons. By the end of this process, you'll have a powerful arsenal of reasons for taking affirmative action.

Remember, reasons are the fuel in the furnace of motivation. Once you feel that you are sufficiently motivated, then you can make a commitment to your Goal.

A Salute to the Gurkhas

Finally, on the note of commitment and courage, let's take a leaf out of the famous and fearsome Gurkha soldier's book. The Gurkhas were Nepalese soldiers in an elite regiment and were trained by and served alongside the British in many wars. They proved to be courageous allies in the fight against the Japanese invaders during World War II. Legend has it that a Gurkha captain was approached by the British High Command for an especially dangerous mission behind enemy lines to rescue an important scientist from a Japanese prisoner of war camp.

The British officer explained the mission and said that because the mission was so dangerous it was on a "volunteer only" basis. The officer explained that the troops who volunteered would be dropped from a plane behind enemy lines at night and would need to complete the daring rescue against formidable and life-threatening odds and then find their own way back to safety through near-impenetrable jungles.

The Gurkha Captain agreed that it did indeed sound like a dangerous assignment and that he would have to ask each of his soldiers individually whether or not they would agree to the mission. The British officer and the Gurkha captain arranged to meet again later that same evening to talk about the troop's response.

When they met again, the Gurkha Captain explained that all of his men had eventually agreed to volunteer but on two conditions. Gurkha soldiers were renowned for never refusing a mission, so the British officer was surprised to hear that the soldiers' acceptance of the mission was based on certain conditions being agreed to.

'Firstly," the Gurkha captain said, *"the plane that we jump out of must fly at no higher than 50 feet above the ground and it must fly at a slow speed."* "Secondly," he stated, *"you must order the pilot to fly over soft and marshy land when we jump."*

'But" the British officer protested *"that would mean almost certain death for you and your men because if you jumped out of the plane at only 50 feet above the ground your parachutes would never have the chance to open!'*

'Oh, we'll have parachutes?" replied the Gurkha captain. "You didn't mention that in the mission brief. Well in that case there's no question. Of course we'll do it."

Now that's commitment.

Chapter 48:

'Getting Over it:' How to Handle Unwanted Emotions

Sometimes life throws us a curve ball. Most of the time it's us that stuffs up. However, regardless of who is at fault, there are moments when we are faced with a choice: be a victim and wallow in self-righteous pity whining about how unfair it all is, or build a bridge and get over it.

It's fine if you have already perfected the art of Three-Dimensional Happiness, but what if you are still stuck back in One-Dimensional Happiness and the road to the third dimension is lined with unwanted experiences that produce unwanted emotions such as self-pity, anger, resentment, or even jealousy?

This chapter is written so that you can be equipped with the mental technology to handle the unwanted emotions that come with unwanted experiences. How do you quickly "build the bridge" and get over it so that you can invest all of the emotional energy into finding a solution rather than wasting it by dwelling on what might have been or what should have been? Let's find out.

Unwanted emotions are a function of a stimulus and response mechanism that is triggered by any input from each one of your five senses. They are a reaction to an Input that occurs at a speed 30,000 times faster than you can Consciously think. That's quick, and chances are that unless you are a Guru, you will experience times when you are literally unable to prevent unwanted emotions from coming to the surface. But what you can do is to notice them and take action. This simple act of awareness brings you back to the Point of Power because then you can use my Thought Transformation Technique to reprogram your mind and move on to create a solution far faster than ever before.

THOUGHT TRANSFORMATION TECHNIQUE

First of all, it's important to understand the purpose of the Thought Transformation Technique. The first Outcome is to clear unwanted emotions so that your mind is free and to think of a solution to the problem that caused you to feel stressed or anxious or jealous or whatever the disturbing emotion is that you have experienced.

The second very important Outcome is to retrain the Subconscious so that, in the future when problems occur, they have decreasingly less power to produce disturbing emotions.

In summary, when you find your peace of mind affected by disturbing emotions, the Thought Transformation Technique can be used to:

1. Clear the unwanted emotion.

2. Re-train the mind so that the next time you have a similar experience, the resultant unwanted emotion is weaker.

Note that by persisting in practicing the Thought Transformation Technique, you will get your mind to the point where you will feel only calmness and peace of mind when experiencing situations that would have previously created stress. This is very cool.

The Thought Transformation Technique works as follows:

Step 1: Awareness

This is the Point of Power. You become aware that you are feeling a disturbing or unwanted emotion. That may seem obvious and yet many people so deeply experience the emotion that it can take a while between the reality of the emotion being created and the awareness. Use the phrase *"That's interesting, my mind is feeling [anxiety/uncertainty/whatever]."* By using this phrase, you separate your identity from the pattern of thinking. In other words, you remind yourself that this feeling is not who you are; it's just a chemical reaction that your Subconscious mind has produced. Swap the role of the victim for that of the observer.

Step 2: Acceptance

The secret of healing emotional wounds is to accept what you are feeling. Resistance or repression of unwanted thoughts or emotions only serves to further imprint the unwanted mental pattern even more firmly into the Subconscious. Use the following phrase to generate an acceptance of the unwanted emotion: *"Welcome my old friend [anxiety/*

uncertainty/ whatever]. Shut your eyes and breathe deeply as you repeat this statement of acceptance several times.

Step 3: Identification (of the Sponsoring Thought)

What you need to do now is to identify the "Sponsoring Thought" behind the emotion. Every disturbing emotion is created by a disturbing thought and I call this the Sponsoring Thought. Identifying the Sponsoring Thought is a very simple process. All you need to do is state the facts of the experience that triggered the unwanted emotion and then add *"and that's bad."*

Let me demonstrate further by giving you a set format for stating the sponsoring thought:

- "describe the event that triggered the disturbing emotion] and that's bad."

    For example:

    » "My Life Partner has left me and that's bad."

    » "The business deal has fallen through and that's bad."

    » "I've just received an unexpected tax bill and that's bad."

Step 4: Affirmation

Now it's time to clear the disturbing emotion and reprogram your Subconscious. Create an affirmation that is the exact opposite of the Sponsoring Thought that created the disturbing emotion (see above under "Identify'). Again, it's refreshingly simple to do this.

For example:

- » "My wife has left me and that's OK."
- » "'The business deal has fallen through and that's OK."
- » "I've just received an unexpected tax bill and that's OK."

You see the difference? All we have done is changed "… and that's bad" to "…and that's OK."

Take a deep breath and say the new affirmation out loud. Allow the disturbing emotions to rise up from the Subconscious in protest against this new way of thinking. Then take another breath and repeat the affirmation again. Repeat this process of synchronized affirmation and deep breathing 21 times. A very deep inhalation and a complete exhalation is important, as this is a key to shifting the disturbing emotions. Allow no pause between the in and out breaths and also remember to keep your breathing as relaxed as possible.

Remember that two important Outcomes are being achieved as you allow yourself to experience the disturbing emotions. Firstly, you are processing and clearing the unwanted emotions, and secondly you are gradually reprogramming your mind so that over time you will experience less stress and more mental calmness in the future.

You may need to repeat the Thought Transformation Technique a number of times prior to becoming free of the old Sponsoring Thought, but it will happen. Friends and clients have repeatedly told me how delighted they were at being able to reprogram their mind of decades-old thought patterns that had caused them to suffer intermittently in just a few short days or weeks.

You can repeat the Thought Transformation Technique anytime that the original Sponsoring Thought or it's associated unwanted emotion returns. Gradually you will reprogram your mind so that unwanted situations trigger no unwanted emotions. This is mental Freedom and it's powerful and beautiful beyond description.

Step 5: Action

Having cleared the disturbing emotions and begun the re-training of the mind, it may then be appropriate to take action. And a significant motivator for using the Thought Transformation Technique is to bring the mind back to a state of calmness and clarity so that you can choose the best possible action, if indeed action is appropriate.

Too many people take action without first processing the emotion. Not only does this result in suppressed emotion and its resultant diseases (dis-ease) but it also creates a mind that is clouded and in less than optimal state to make an effective decision.

So once you have cleared 90% of the disturbing emotion (a small level of emotion may linger for a while *"and that's OK !"*) and your mind is clearer, then it's time to work out what you are going to do about the situation that was the cause of the emotional activation. Make a list of possible actions, select the one that represents the most effective Outcome for the least effort (bang for bucks!), and if practical, complete the action immediately, or at the very least schedule a time to complete it at a time that is suitable.

A Note on Having Realistic Expectations

Don't expect to complete the retraining of your Subconscious mind in one session. It will take any number of sessions to completely reprogram your Subconscious so that the situation that activated your emotions loses its power over you. You will be free when you are free. No one knows how long that will take. But if you will diligently repeat the Thought Transformation Technique, then you will gradually become more and more free of disturbing emotions.

Are You Ready to 'Build A Bridge' and 'Get Over it ?'

Most of your opportunities to practice the Thought Transformation Technique on unwanted emotions will come from what I call minor or medium situations or things. Major situations mostly involve relationships or what feel like catastrophic life events, and it's important to note that there may be some occasions that you may actually want to feel disturbing emotions even though you now have a technique for transforming them back into Happiness. The Thought Transformation Technique is only for when you are ready to clear the unwanted emotions. In extreme situations such as the death of someone you were close to, or a major relationship break-up, it's healthy and appropriate to grieve and feel sad for a period of time. You will, however, get to the point where you recognize that it's time to move on, and that's when you should use the Thought Transformation Technique to shift your suffering back to Happiness.

What If I Can't Identify the Sponsoring Thought?

Sometimes it's possible to just feel "yuk" without being Conscious of what the Sponsoring Thought was. It's also possible to not be able to label the disturbing emotion.

In these situations, all you need to do is breathe your way through the experience so that emotion is released and then you can begin to move on. Once you are aware that you are feeling an unwanted emotion, simply accept that you are feeling like you are by shutting your eyes, imagining the feeling as a black ball of energy and saying *"welcome my old friend feeling yuk." Then breathe deeply for 21 times and with each breath repeat the phrase "I feel yuk and that's OK."* Be prepared to fully experience the emotion that is released by this process and in doing so you will gradually dissolve the feeling into oblivion.

Happiness Rules

While we are on the subject of Happiness, let me just say that I don't have any rules around my Happiness. Consequently, I don't describe an experience as bad, ever. Instead, I Consciously use the word "Perfect!" to reprogram "bad" out of my Subconscious vocabulary. For example, I started the Ironman bike ride and my heart rate monitor died: Perfect. My car needed $8,000 worth of work on it: Perfect. My client reneged and canceled the deal: Perfect. I came last in the race: Perfect. Crashed and broke my arm: Perfect.

I'll use the Thought Transformation Technique and then build a bridge and deal with reality. And each time I make the Conscious effort to see things as Perfect, even when they are the unwanted variety of Perfect, I take another step closer to the reality of Three-Dimensional Happiness, which is another term for pure Consciousness.

So if you have an unwanted experience that you had no control over, then use the word "Perfect" as discussed previously, with all of the authenticity that you can muster. I must admit to a few occasions when my "Perfect" got stuck in my throat and I almost choked, but I got it out eventually and then sat down, scratched my head and began to figure out exactly what it was that made this unwanted experience so "Perfect."

It's important to understand that reprogramming takes time. I call it the "Reducing Recovery" phenomena. Have you ever gotten so mad about something that it took you a day or two to get over it? Maybe it was an argument that you had with someone and much later you realized that you overreacted and so you apologized and then started the communication process again. I'd be fairly confident that we can all relate to that. It takes time to get over a big emotional blow-out. Smaller unwanted emotions also take time to get over. Let's say that you messed up at an interview for a new role or at a meeting with a new client and that you're feeling annoyed about it. You beat yourself up and you feel unhappy and regretful. *"Should have," "wish I'd"* and other equally useless phrases come into your mind. But you recall the Thought Transformation Technique and go through the routine and you recover from the emotional upset.

This is what your Recovery looks like in terms of a timeline:

Reducing Recovery Model

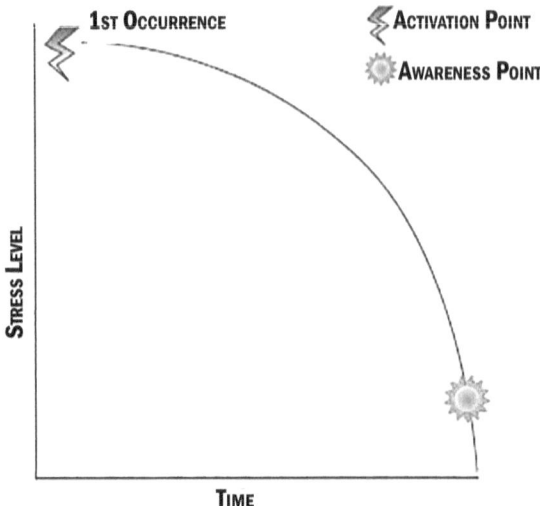

Notice that there was a long gap in time between the point of activation and the point of awareness. Up until the point of awareness, you were so *in* the activation that it's like you *were* the activation. When you reached the point of awareness, it's as if you separated from the activation and you were then at the Point of Power. It's at the point of Awareness that you then have the choice to use the Thought Transformation Technique to heal the source of the activation.

Then, having used the Thought Transformation Technique the first time, the next time you self-beat, three things change:

1. The activation levels are lower and that means the unwanted emotion is much weaker.

2. The awareness of the activation occurs sooner.

3. The recovery time is much shorter and that means that you'll "get over it" much quicker.

Reducing Recovery Model

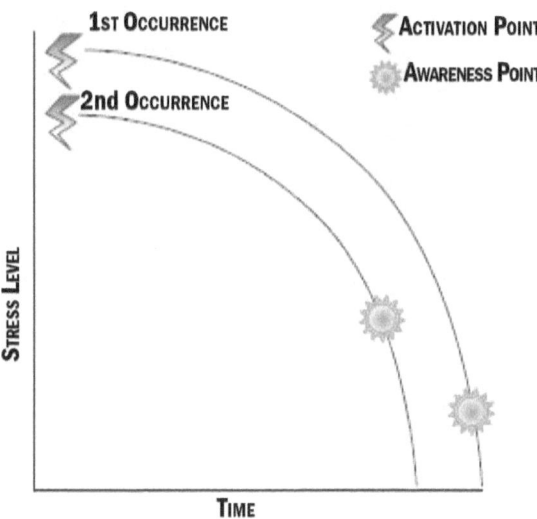

And each time you experience another activation in similar experiences, you use the Thought Transformation Technique and this is what happens:

Reducing Recovery Model

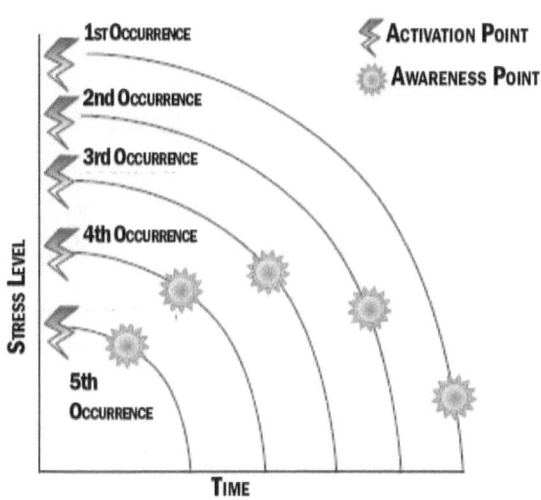

Again, each of the three key areas reduces in volume:

1. The activation levels are lower.

2. The awareness of the activation occurs sooner.

3. The recovery time is much shorter.

With practice, you'll get to the point, in some situations, that activation and awareness are almost simultaneous. This is increasing Consciousness and it's exciting and liberating. In other situations you'll get to the point where situations that used to activate you no longer do. That's called being free.

It's likely, however, that as long as you are in a human body, some things will still activate you. Even the Dalai Lama says that he still experiences *"a ripple on the surface of the water where others might feel an undersea earthquake,"* and he's apparently been practicing this stuff for several thousand years through numerous incarnations.

The beauty of this system, as opposed to the very unhealthy alternative of suppressing unwanted emotion or engaging in escapist activities such as alcohol abuse is that you get to truly heal any past emotional Subconscious scars and complete a reprogramming exercise simultaneously.

Remember too that I am not talking about trying to stop these unwanted emotions from surfacing. Far from it. Bring it on. The pathway to Freedom and increasing Consciousness is to feel them and deal with them.

There Is a Time and Place for Everything Under the Sun

On a final note, let me just add that there are situations when emotional attachments that cause what might otherwise be regarded as unwanted emotions should be fully encouraged and experienced.

Take for example an attachment to the well-being of others. There is no empathy or compassion without some element of attachment. Allow yourself to feel compassion for those who may be suffering and use empathy to help comfort them. But as mentioned previously, don't make your Happiness dependent on their recovery from suffering.

The second situation to which I will allow myself to become emotionally attached is in sport competitions of which I am a spectator. Have you ever turned on the television and started to watch a sports event between two teams that you have never heard of? Because you have no attachment to who is winning, there's no passion and no emotional rollercoaster rides as the lead changes hands. I'm a big Auckland Blues supporter in the Super Fourteen rugby competition and an even more committed supporter of the All Blacks, New Zealand's national rugby team. When my teams win, I feel jubilant and when they lose, I feel disappointed. But I get over it quickly and it's worth risking a little disappointment to experience the highs of victory.

When I compete myself, however, it's a very different story. The best performances always come when the athlete is focused on their performance in a relaxed and emotionally detached manner. So as best I can before the event, I detach myself emotionally from the Outcome and focus my mind purely on the performance. When I do that, the result mostly takes care of itself. Sure I feel great if I put in a great performance and I feel disappointed if I don't. But again, I get over it quickly and move on to correcting the performance next time.

Chapter 49:

Consciously What to Do When it all Goes Pear-shaped

Hitting a Problem

I sometimes talk with clients who are going through a particularly rough patch. It may be that everything has gone pear-shaped in their business, or that they have a challenge in one of their relationships. If they sound especially stressed and introverted (funny how often the two go together), then I remind them of who they are. They are someone who eats obstacles for breakfast. I remind them that they will get through this difficult period and that they will solve this problem. They always agree that this is true. *"That being the case,"* I explain *"there are only two issues left unresolved. The first issue is how long it will take you to solve the problem and the second issue is how much you will enjoy the experience."*

I want my clients to detach their emotional well-being from the resolution of their issue. I want to show them that having a problem is a sign of life and that Happiness and solving problems are not mutually exclusive. It is entirely possible to face a challenge, defeat it and to move through that whole experience while still being Happy and maintaining Peace of Mind.

STEP 1 ON THE ROAD TO RECOVERY: CHOOSE TO ENJOY THE JOURNEY

The key to changing your perception and enjoying the journey is as simple as choosing to quit being a prisoner to this problem and to start exercising the God given free will that we all have. A "prisoner" feels trapped and can't see a way out. It's the Subconscious not wanting to have to make an effort. A free person understands that, because they created the problem, they also have the power to create the solution. Accepting personal responsibility for having created the situation kick-starts empowerment.

By detaching emotionally from the problem, the mind becomes free to think of solutions. Destructive emotions such as fear, regret, or anxiety consume vital mental energy that can be more productively used in search of a solution.

I love it when a plan comes together. Like when I design something and it works perfectly first time, or when I take something to bits and put it back again perfectly first time. Or when I craft a winning strategy and it works from word go. But that's almost as rare as a Moa.

No doubt I'll get better at executing strategy, but in the meantime, I've learned to enjoy the journey towards the Goal. Taking the inevitable knocks and standing back up and dusting yourself off and getting back into the game despite the aches, the pains, the limp, the blood, the sweat, and yes, the occasional tear, all make the victory so much sweeter when you taste it. The sweet always tastes sweeter after you've just had some sour.

Have a read of Chapters 51-53 for more on how to really enjoy the journey.

STEP 2 ON THE ROAD TO RECOVERY: RECOMMIT

Despite the highest levels of motivation, the most powerful reasons, and terrific Reward and Non Reward strategies, you are human and you will fail, temporarily, at some point. It's a part of the human condition that none of us, apart from those who abide six feet under the earth's surface, are totally consistent. The world championship Wallabies Captain, the incomparable Jon Eales has this to say: *"Success in the middle looks like failure."*

So aside from my advice to become a Goal-aholic, here's the best advice I can give you in the whole book. Memorize and live this statement:

"When I fail, there is only one thing left to do: re-commit.

Let me write it again:

When I fail, there is only one thing left to do: re-commit.

And again:

When I fail there is only one thing left to do: re-commit.

Write this onto a piece of paper and put it onto your bathroom mirror. Put it onto your PC desktop, place it on the sun visor of your car. Tattoo it onto the inside of your eyelids if you need to, but drive it so deep into your Subconscious that it'll be the first thing you remember and the last thing you'll ever forget. I want you to be able to remember this phrase well after you've become old and senile and forgotten your own name:

When I fail, there is only one thing left to do: re-commit.

Teach that to your kids, your colleagues, your friends and even your dog. If there was only one Master Key to success, the ability to recommit would be it.

Chapter 50:

How to Find Solutions to Every Problem

Most people are obsessed with wanting to find answers. I am convinced that this is the wrong approach. Of course there is a place for us to learn from others, but the best teachers will precede the answers they give you with questions to stimulate your thinking. It's the difference between being given a fish and being shown how to cast your own line. Once you have mastered the skill of forming and asking the right questions, you'll discover a huge storehouse of knowledge that's currently hidden under the surface of your Subconscious mind. More on that soon.

Questions form a part of our Self-talk and therefore have an extraordinarily powerful effect on our Self-Esteem and Self-Image. As such, they have the power to move our life to the next level of success, but they also have the power, if phrased incorrectly, to take us down a few notches as well.

I class questions as either "Creative" or "Destructive." Here are my definitions.

DESTRUCTIVE QUESTIONS

Destructive questions either create an endless loop of disempowerment or create hopelessness because often they simply can't even be answered. In short, they destroy both the feelings and the future that you really want. Examples of destructive questions include:

- *"Why do I never know what to do?"*
- *"Why can I never get it right?"*
- *"Why am I such an idiot when it comes to relationships?"*
- *"Why do I never stop drinking when I know that I should?"*
- *"Why does this always happen to me?"*
- *"It's hopeless, what's the point?"*

You can see that destructive Questions tend to focus on the past and on failures. You can probably also see how such questions end up with the questioner feeling depressed and demotivated.

CREATIVE QUESTIONS

A Creative Question will not only lead you to the answer that you need, but it will also prepare the mind to take positive action by inducing feelings of empowerment and confidence. Creative questions lead you to both the feelings and the future that you want.

Examples of Creative questions include:

- *"How can I make this even better next time?" (having messed up!)*

- "What is the gift in this experience?" (when faced with an unwanted situation)
- "What would a confident person do right now?" (when starting to self- doubt)
- "How can I double our results and have even more time off?'
- "How can I double our profits and have even more fun doing it?'

Often when you come up with a Creative Question, the Subconscious will want to defend you from what it perceives to be the pain of potential change. So you'll either feel like you don't have the answer to the question, or you'll find yourself coming up with five or so reasons why the answer is not possible, too hard, or simply not realistic. Ignore that initial reaction and persist with the question. Getting beyond "my brain hurts" is simply a matter of persisting and the rewards can be startlingly worthwhile. Let me explain why.

You're going to need an open mind to what I am about to tell you since the implications are mind-boggling. I first began to experiment with questions around a decade ago and was regularly delighted with the results. Then I began to read more research on how the mind works. I read reports from scientific journals as well as ancient literature such as the Vedas which date back to 1500 BC. What I discovered was that our scientific community has a lot of catching up to do in terms of proving that which can be demonstrably experienced in real life. Twentieth century physicist Max Born once claimed that "science advances funeral by funeral." Intuition is a case in point. Millions have experienced that "gut feel" or the premonition, but as yet we can't prove scientifically that it's real. But that doesn't mean that we should wait until it's provable before we benefit from it.

What I discovered in my reading and in years of subsequent practice is that once you have formed a Creative Question and focus on it consistently you will access knowledge beyond your own experience and beyond the current limitations of time and space.

Let me explain by giving you an overview of the three minds.

Conscious Mind

This is the mind of one thought. It can be aware, it can rationalize, analyze, and choose to respond and make decisions. It's pretty useful at all of these things. But it really comes into its own when it's asked to come up with a question.

Subconscious Mind (or unconscious)

This mind will produce reactions (as opposed to responses) thirty thousand times faster than you can Consciously think. The Subconscious mind does a superb job of automating the running of our cardiovascular system, our circulatory system, our digestive system and the millions of functions that our body carries out every day as we go about the business of living, breathing and moving. The Subconscious is also a storehouse of information primarily designed to help us avoid pain and pursue pleasure. It is the best possible assistant and the world's most destructive boss. It is the mind of thought patterns, the mind of habitual thinking. Specifically it has stored every experience as detected by every one of your five senses for every second of your lifetime. People returning from a "near death" experience often say that *"my whole life flashed before my eyes"* as if the Subconscious was downloading all stored experiences. Every sound, sight, touch, taste, and smell is stored in the vast warehouse of the subconscious.

A great Creative Question will access this treasure trove of experience and will pop an answer up into your Conscious mind sometimes when you least expect it. You will have experienced times when you were trying to remember someone's name and having the answer pop into your mind when they were not even thinking about it, such as when you woke up in the morning or when you were taking a shower or going for a walk. Even though you were not Consciously thinking about the question, your Subconscious had continued to work on it and when it had found the answer, it sent it up to your Conscious mind.

But however powerful we believe the Subconscious to be, it's got nothing on the next mind.

SUPERCONSCIOUS MIND

My experience with the Superconscious Mind barely scratches the surface of what I believe to be its potential, but nevertheless even my few faltering steps into the realm of the Superconscious have yielded some very satisfying responses.

Carl Jung, the great Swiss psychiatrist and early colleague of Sigmund Freud, referred to the Superconscious Mind as the "Collective Unconscious." He claimed that the "Collective Unconscious" was *"characterized by being universal mental predispositions not grounded in experience. Like Plato's Forms (eidos), the archetypes do not originate in the world of the senses, but exist independently of that world and are known directly by the mind."*

What Carl Jung was expressing was his belief that there is what others term an "Intuitive Mind" that we all have access to. In this text, I'll use the terms Superconscious Mind and Intuitive Mind as meaning one and the same thing. However, it doesn't really matter which label we put on it as long we tap into its power.

Here's one theory on how the Superconscious works. The Conscious mind can hold only one thought at a time. The Subconscious Mind stores every sensory input ever processed during your life time. The theory goes on to explain that the Superconscious Mind however is not limited by time or space. The Superconscious Mind stores knowledge of experiences not limited by your own experiences but rather it encompasses the experiences of all human beings over all time: past, present, and future. This means of course that the Superconscious Mind also houses knowledge of experiences yet to come. A mind-boggling proposition.

Personally, my approach to the concept of the Superconscious Mind has always been that it is irrelevant as to whether or not I believe that the concept is true. I simply want to see if it works or not. It's like gravity – it's going to have an effect on me whether I believe in it or not.

I sometimes will tell the skeptics the following: *"Imagine for a moment that you had never tasted a piece of fruit or anything sweet for that matter. Now let me explain the concept of an orange to you. I can describe its color, its texture; I can list all of the vitamins and minerals that an orange contains and describe its flavor as well. However, you'll only know how real an orange is from the moment after you have peeled one, taken a slice, and placed it into your mouth. Now that you have experienced an orange, the previous theoretical knowledge of what an orange consists of is irrelevant."*

The Superconscious Mind is the same. It doesn't matter how much I read about it, the experience of it is what counts. Keep your mind open.

Gandhi once encouraged his followers to think of their mind as a house. In those days in India, most of the houses had wooden shutters instead of glass windows. He suggested that it would be best for one to keep the shutters of our minds wide open at all times so that the seed of an idea could drift in on the breeze. Once we have examined the idea, we can either choose to let it continue on through and out the other side of the house or allow it to settle and take root in our life. The most expensive thing a person can ever own is not a house, a car, or a boat, it is a closed mind.

I have created new business strategies using intuition, accurately predicted the direction of new business flows, gained valuable confirmation of whether to hire new employees, identified health issues, set win-win agreements with suppliers and distributors, and made countless other successful decisions based on information received from the Intuitive or Superconscious mind.

But a word of warning! Until you are well experienced and a Master of the Superconscious Mind, don't act only on what you think is intuitive guidance. While my belief is that information from the Superconscious Mind is always correct, our ability to tune into this mind is not always as reliable.

Becoming attuned to the Intuitive Mind is a whole book in itself, but let me just say that the practice of Meditation, of any type, is the best way that I know to fine-tune the receptivity of the Conscious Mind to the Superconscious.

A simple and effective meditation

Below is a simple meditation practice to get you started on this most valuable of practices. I have also produced an audio set that overviews the benefits of meditation as well as giving the listener three different guided meditations to practice – go to the online shop at www. tompoland.com for more details.

There are literally hundreds of different ways to meditate. Here is one that serves the purpose of relaxing the "mad monkey" of the Subconscious mind and allows you to practice exercising the muscle of your Conscious mind.

1. *Find a quiet place where you will not be disturbed for fifteen minutes or however long you have decided to meditate for. Even five minutes of quality meditation will be beneficial.*

2. *Sit either cross-legged on a large cushion or in a seat with your back straight. Whichever is most comfortable is fine. The most important thing here is to ensure that your back is straight.*

3. *Take a few deep breaths and exhale slowly. Allow your breath to find a natural rhythm of full, deep and yet relaxed breathing. If possible, always breathe through your nose.*

4. *Focus your awareness on the sensation of the breath passing in and out of the end of your nostrils. Give your attention to this sensation as fully as you are consciously able to.*

5. *When you become aware that your mind has wandered simply bring your focus back again to the breath passing in and out of the end of your nostrils. Patiently, peacefully and with persistence bring your mind back to this point of focus.*

6. *Continue this simple, but challenging, practice for the duration of your meditation session.*

THE QUESTION IN HAND

So let's tie these two concepts together. First of all, you come up with a great Creative Question. Something that lifts your emotions, and has the potential to do the same for your future.

Then you think about the question, type or write it out, and put it on your bathroom mirror, put it onto your screen saver or desktop (PC or otherwise), place a copy on the sun visor of your car and generally surround yourself with the question so that it stays "top of mind." You can write it out onto a yellow legal pad using a blue pen (color stimulates thought) and write out answers to it. You can brainstorm or mind map or use whatever techniques you want to in order to come up with answers.

Then leave it alone.

Then come back to the question and work on it some more. Then leave it alone.

Then come back to it. And so on until the answer hits you between the eyes. It may come as you are working Consciously on it or you may sit bolt upright in bed in the middle of the night with a Eureka! Or you may be out on a walk and the answer will pop up like a slice of toast right into your Consciousness.

This approach of Consciously thinking about the question and deliberately not thinking about it and giving the mind a rest yields the best answer in the most relaxed way possible. It's not dissimilar to growing a muscle in that the best way to get more strength into, say, a bicep is to put it under load and let it rest. Then you put the bicep under load again and give it a rest. If you load the bicep up every day, then not only will it not increase in strength as much, but you run the risk of it breaking down.

The same holds true with the Conscious Mind. Load it up every day without a break and eventually it will stop performing at optimum. But load it up and give it a break, and the Superconscious will perform wonders.

Top Tip

Remember to take time to get your question right. Don't get addicted to closure. A Creative Question has the power to deliver an answer that leads you to invest years of time and bucket loads of effort, so make sure that you get the question formed right before you start asking it.

And finally, always remember this: Intuition is more important than knowledge. Knowledge can tell you "what was" and "what is" but intuition has the power to tell you "what will be."

Chapter 51:

How to Really Enjoy the Journey
Part 1 – Develop 1st Class Goals

By now you will probably have realized that the only ultimate destination in this lifetime is death. There is no other ultimate arrival point, but rather just a series of journeys, in between stations or "pause points."

Imagine that you are on a flight to Hawaii where you are going for a vacation. You've been hanging out for this holiday for months, and now that you are on board the plane, you can't wait to get there. You just want to lie on those beautiful beaches and swim and read and thoroughly recharge your mental batteries.

All that stands between you and your Goal of rejuvenation is a long plane trip. But once that's over, you can really start to enjoy yourself. Until then, you'll just put up with the cramped seats and the lack of room to exercise.

Then the Captain comes on and says *"Ladies and Gentlemen, we have a problem but there is no cause for alarm so please stay calm while I explain our dilemma. Our electronic safety equipment has detected a critical fault in our landing gear and fuel tanks. The bottom line is that when we land the plane the faulty landing gear will ignite our fuel tanks and our plane and everyone in it will be incinerated."*

Don't get sidetracked with the improbability of the story, instead stay with it as I further explain!

Just as you think that you are all going to die a premature and fiery death, the Captain continues: *"So the bad news is that if we ever land this plane, we will all most assuredly die. However, the good news is that we can re-fuel midair, we can take on refreshments and other supplies, and over time we can train every passenger so that they can fly the plane. So this means that we can in fact continue to fly this plane until the last person on board dies, so that is what we will do."*

So there you are, sitting on this plane with the news that you can never land. How would it effect your attitude towards the journey? Would you decide, for example, that you may as well enjoy it since you're never getting off the plane? Probably. I mean, you may as well. Suddenly there is no destination, only a journey.

Life is similar. We tell ourselves that "one day when" I've achieved this Goal or that Goal, then I can relax and enjoy myself more. But have you noticed that once you achieve a Goal you set another one? There is no Fulfillment otherwise, so we continue to set and achieve Goals. Not a bad thing in itself, unless we continually postpone our enjoyment of the journey until that magical and mystical day in the future when we will finally "arrive." And of course we never do finally arrive because there is no destination, only a journey.

So just like the story of the doomed plane, it would pay us to change our approach to life and choose to enjoy the journey. This chapter shows you how.

Continuing with the airline theme, we can classify our Goals as either First Class or Second Class. Let's have a look at the difference between the two.

First Class Goal: Passion Outcome and Passion Inputs

What I mean by this is that you not only get excited about the Outcome (final result), but you also look forward to completing any Inputs (actions) that are required to achieve the result.

I mentioned before that one of my Goals was to race a Superbike. This was a First Class Goal because, not only was the Outcome Extra-Ordinary for someone like me, but I also enjoyed doing the practice days and the race meetings to train and prepare for the big day. It's "easy fun" in a scary sort of way.

Second Class Goal: Passion Outcomes and Unwanted Inputs

This is a Goal where you really want the Outcome, but you don't especially warm to the prospect of completing the associated Inputs. For example, you might really enjoy the thought of being fit, but you hate the idea of exercising. Or you want to be slim and toned, but you don't like the idea of swapping your nightly seven course meal for one dozen bean sprouts.

The key with Second Class Goals is to upgrade them to First Class by "Taking a P." By that I mean you either change the **P**rocess (Inputs) if that is possible, or if it's not possible, then you will change your **P**erception.

As an example of changing the process, if you want to be fit but don't like running, but you love in-line skating, then roller-blade your way to good health.

If it's a business Goal and you don't like the required Inputs, then see if you can delegate or outsource the Inputs so that you don't have to do them. For example, when I was seeking to expand my business internationally, I found a top CEO who bought into the business and handles all of the vitally important management issues that I lacked a passion for. Not only does he love management, but his style is ideally suited to the fast moving and flowing nature of our organization. My business partner does what he does and he does it very well, and I have upgraded by Goal for the ESP Programme from Second Class to First Class. And I do love travelling through life First Class.

Another example of upgrading from Second Class to First Class via a change of process is changing your vocation. Let's say that making a bucket load of money is important to you, but instead of making a living, you are "making a dying" because the job that you do seems to suck the life out of you. It's not a passion, it's drudgery. Change. You can do it. Yes, I know that there are practical considerations, not least of which will be that you have financial commitments to honor, but I also know that given time and commitment you will find a way. It's starts with a decision. Work out what capabilities you need, set a plan for developing them, and do it. It may take time, but you owe it to yourself to take the first step in the direction of your dreams.

Some Second Class Goals have Inputs that simply can't be delegated or outsourced, and this is in fact healthy because this is where we get to grow and expand our Capacities even more than normal. Physical and Mental health are great examples of this. Try as I might, I have not yet found any healthy and effective ways to lose unwanted fat other than reducing calorie input or increasing calorie output. Also, if you want Happiness and peace of mind, you can't effectively delegate this to drugs. That's a destructive and counter-productive strategy; the only effective answer is to change yourself internally.

Such Goals require you to commit to Inputs that you may find difficult to stick to and indeed there may be other Inputs that you would prefer to have out of your life, but it's simply not affordable for you to do so at this time. For example, your Goal may be a financial one and one of the appropriate Inputs is to keep track of your expenditures and ensure that you run a budget. You may not enjoy the process and you may not be able to afford to hire a bookkeeper to do the rather mundane task of logging in expenditure data.

Another example of Inputs that can't be outsourced is many of the actions that go with being a supportive father, mother, or Life Partner. Some have tried to outsource these actions, of course, but the relationship just isn't the same!

This brings me to our second "P," that of changing your Perception. For those Inputs where a change of Process is not practical, the alternative is to change your Perception of those Inputs. If you are going to do something, you may as well enjoy it.

The first step in changing your Perception is deciding that you are going to enjoy whatever it is that you are going to do to the max. The word "decide" is from the Latin "decidere" which means "to cut off." By making a decision to enjoy an Input, you are cutting off the possibility of not enjoying it. Try it on an activity that you routinely complete, but resent doing. You may be surprised how a change of Perception can transform a Second Class Goal into a First Class experience.

The next step in changing your perception about an Input is to stack up reasons why this Goal is important to you. When I was a young parent, I began to tire of being the family chauffeur on the weekends. Supporting the kids with their sports and other activities was an important Goal, though, so I decided to enjoy it.

Enjoying the experience of supporting my kids was made a whole lot easier when I sat down and made a list of all the reasons why the Input was important. I thought about how my parents had done this for me and how much their devotion had meant to me in later years. I thought about how I wanted my kids to feel the same way about me as a parent. I made a note also that I wanted to be a great role model for my kids in having a positive attitude about everything that I did. Furthermore, I wanted to maintain high levels of rapport with each of my kids so that when they had a problem, they would think of me as a friend and ask me for help when they needed it. Additionally, I reasoned that my Life Partner was doing her bit and it was only fair to be supportive of her by taking my share of the load as well. Finally, I decided that I just wanted to show my kids that I loved them by being there when they had their triumphs as well as their defeats. I wanted to share their emotions and be there to encourage and support them in the "ups" as well as the "downs."

Stacking up those reasons provided me with a shift in Perception to the point where I actually began to look forward to the opportunity of being "the family chauffeur."

Karma Yoga

An extension of the idea of changing one's perception comes to us from Hinduism in the form of "Karma Yoga." By the way, Karma Yoga has little to do with the traditional concept of Yoga – a series of asana, or stretches and postures.

Once people integrate the practice of Karma Yoga they find that their perception of otherwise mundane or unwanted tasks is transformed. Let me explain.

The aspect of Karma Yoga that is relevant here is the teaching that when a task is completed in a selfless manner, good Karma results and the opposite is true as well. If you practice Karma Yoga you will complete tasks in order to be of service to others without thought of return to yourself. In other words, Karma Yoga involves the concept of "selfless service."

To this end, a disciple who wishes to become a Karma Yogi will be taught to complete actions without thought of Reward. Putting it another way, the disciple will be trained to complete Inputs for the sole purpose of making a Contribution to others. A Karma Yogi needs no other Reward.

It's important to note that it doesn't matter whether you are a Christian, Buddhist, Jew, Hindu or atheist, you can still practice the change in perception that a Karma Yogic approach brings about. And while a conversion to Hinduism is not necessary, it's still beneficial to note that when any of us do something that is helpful to others, without thought of return, we tap into a source that transforms a previously unenjoyable Input into a satisfying and rewarding experience.

People comment that when they adopt the attitude of service that Karma Yoga espouses, tasks that they had previously considered mundane or unenjoyable such as looking after sick kids, doing the dishes, or helping someone clean up a mess, not only became enjoyable, but also increase their levels of personal Happiness. Karma Yoga rocks.

AUTOTELIC INPUTS

Another way to change your Perception comes from the opposite end of the geographical and philosophical spectrum in the form of Western psychiatrist Mihaly Csikszentmihaly. This is the man who gave us the concept called "Flow," which is where people become so engrossed in an activity that hours turn into minutes and they feel like they have merged with that activity and become one with it.

Csikszentmihaly went on to point out that it's possible for certain experiences to become what he called "autotelic." Here's what he says about this valuable concept.

"The word 'autotelic' is a word composed of two Greek roots: "auto" (self), and "telos" (Goal). An autotelic activity is one we do for its own sake because to experience is the main Goal."

A case in point follows.

Some time ago, I visited my father on his farm. After the initial "catch up" conversation, he said that he was going to do a little work on the barn and invited me to join him. We walked out of the house, climbed aboard the tractor, and headed off to the barn. We spent a couple of easy hours fixing the guttering and I noted that when we were working on the barn, my father really enjoyed the whole process. Even though there were some small challenges along the way, he didn't get stressed but instead treated the exercise as an enjoyable experience.

Later on back at the homestead, we settled in for a drink and I offered my observation that he seemed to have developed an ability to enjoy the little things in life like fixing the barn or taking the dogs for a stroll, or checking on water levels in the top paddock and so on. We talked about his new found ability to "enjoy the journey" rather than becoming stressed about the destination, or Outcome.

My father was fixing the barn for the experience of fixing the barn. It was as if the fact that the barn now has a fully functioning gutter system was simply a helpful by product of his autotelic experience.

BENEFITS OF THE KARMA YOGA AND AUTOTELIC APPROACH TO INPUTS

So, how do you apply these concepts to your situation? If you were to complete every action carefully and mindfully, as though it were the end result itself and as though it were a gift of service for others, then a number of things would transpire to transform your experience.

1. You would enjoy the experience a lot more.

2. You would improve the quality of your results.

3. You would make swifter progress.

4. You would dramatically increase peace of mind.

5. You would be happier.

That's not a bad list of benefits to start with and I'll go into each one of these benefits in more depth in the next chapter.

For now though I'll summarize by saying that I recommend you act with the intention of being of service to others at all times (Karma Yoga) and that you make more and more of your experiences flow by completing all actions as if they were an end in themselves. Your enjoyment of the journey will continually increase with these two transformational approaches to life.

CHAPTER 52:

HOW TO REALLY ENJOY THE JOURNEY PART 2 – PRACTICE MINDFULNESS

I WANT TO PICK up again on concepts that I introduced to you in the last chapter where I wrote about the benefits of the Karma Yoga and the Autotelic approach to completing actions.

Let's look at the benefits of again one at a time.

1. You would enjoy the experience a lot more

I regularly go for a run along Mooloolaba Beach in the mornings. Nine days out of ten, the sun is shining and the surf is up. The sand is golden and there are trees setting off the landscape with birds singing and all is well with the world. I go through a series of questions to make sure that I truly appreciate the experience of where I am. I call these questions the "Five Senses Check." It's kind of like a preflight check. I ask myself *"What am I seeing?"* And then I mentally answer myself. Often my experience of being in the moment goes to a whole new level as I notice the color of the sea, or birds overhead. The change is both subtle and significant. Sometimes I even see things that have always been there but that I had never noticed. I then ask myself *"What am I hearing."* Suddenly I can hear the surf or the seagulls which, again, were always there but I had somehow shut them out. I then ask *"What can I feel?"* and once more I become aware of previously unconscious experiences such as the texture of fabric on my skin or the ground beneath my feet. I repeat the same questions for *"What can I smell?"* and *"What can I taste?,"* normally with a less dramatic effect, but still a lift in Consciousness nevertheless.

The "Five Senses Check" is an exercise in what the Buddha would call "mindfulness." It enriches my experience and brings to life what would otherwise be a routine activity. And the same principle of increasing mindfulness via awareness of the senses can be applied to every activity on the face of the planet.

By way of contrast, I've observed myself and others literally on the same beautiful beach but figuratively a whole world away thinking about yesterday, tomorrow, or who knows what. Because of my lack of mindfulness at that time, I could just as easily be in a suburban street somewhere and I would be none the wiser.

But the point is this: if I completed my run in a state of stress simply wanting to get it over with so that I could reach my fitness Goal, I would not enjoy the experience nearly as much.

Here's a couple more examples, one from each end of life's experiences to further illustrate the point.

Just the other day, I was about to eat my breakfast. Two poached eggs on whole grain toast and a cup of Caro (coffee substitute). It's my habit to begin each day being very clear on what my number one Outcome is for the day. As I was about to eat my eggs, I noticed that my mind was full of the tasks that lay ahead. I said to myself *"For the next few minutes these eggs are my life and I choose to experience them fully."* And I did. I lived in that moment. If I hadn't taken a mindful approach to my breakfast, it would have been literally impossible for my mind to have enjoyed that moment; it would have been somewhere else. Sometimes it's like my mind sends itself on ahead of my body.

As an interesting observation, consider this. Like most days, I was keen to get started on my tasks that morning. When I pause to reflect, I think that I was keen to get started so that I could get finished. What about the bit in the middle? Have you also had this experience of wanting to get started so that you could get it over with? Or wanting to go fast so that you could slow down? Or creating a stressful mental condition so that you could relax when you were finally done? If aliens are watching and observing us, they must think that we are nuts sometimes. Slower, simpler, calmer, and clearer. It's hard to look out the window and enjoy the scenery when you're on a bullet train. Less is more. Slower is faster.

Here's the second example of Karma Yoga in action. Before I set off on the final successful ascent of Mt. Cook, I said to my guide *"Sam, I want to be present to every footstep of this climb. This is not simply about being able to say that I've knocked the bugger off; I want to enjoy what happens as much as possible."*

I Consciously chose to fully experience every avalanche, every crevasse, every calf-aching step, every feeling of fear, every bit of sweat as I climbed, and every sensation of chill when I stopped. I didn't just want to climb Mt. Cook, I wanted to experience Mt. Cook.

That's a big part of what Karma Yoga is about. It's adds a richness and quality to life that otherwise slips below the radar scope of your Consciousness.

2. You would improve the quality of your results

Take selling for example. If you want the sale, then by all means set that in your mind as the Outcome, but then focus entirely on your prospect and the sales process. If you have a prospect sitting in front of you, then our aim is to be of service to that person right here and right now. Practice being there for that person, being mindful of their needs and the best solution to help and support them in what they are trying to achieve. The ironical thing is that if you can add value to your prospect in a professional and timely manner, then the chances are that you will get the sale in any event, whereas if you go in with an egocentric and self-serving attitude, the prospect will smell it from a mile away and drop you like a hot brick.

Perhaps you work in a team of people and you are responsible for hitting certain business objectives. Obviously, I'd be the first to suggest that you need to be clear on both your Outcome and Inputs, but then I'd suggest you go about the tasks that will lead to the results you want as though the tasks themselves were all that mattered. This more mindful approach leads to a better-quality result. It's also the approach of many successful athletes and actors.

I know myself that there is a huge difference in the quality of my work when I am pushed for time and just want closure, versus taking a deep breath and focusing on completing the task itself to the best of my ability. Haste makes waste. Slower, simpler, calmer, clearer.

3. You would make swifter progress

A person who is committed to their Goals but detached emotionally from them will achieve their Goals faster than a person who is committed but is also emotionally attached. The reason is simple. The emotionally attached person wastes precious mental energy stressing when things don't go according to plan. Far better to invest that mental energy into moving forward than it is to squander it on feeling annoyed, angry, or insecure.

This morning, my printer decided that instead of printing in its normal twelve point font, that it would print GIANT letters of 48 points. Why? Darned if I know. Technology provides so many great growth opportunities!

Of course, at first my mind felt annoyed, then I became aware that my mind was annoyed and that meant I had made the shift to the point of power. Awareness gives choice. So I took a couple of deep breaths *('the printer is stuffed and that's Ok !")*, to clear the "annoyed" emotion and got on with the job of fixing it. Slower, simpler, calmer, clearer. I managed to move through the experience without the stress that I would have created a few years ago, and I also moved through it quicker as my mind was calm and clear, which in turn allowed me to think straight. I moved from being an angry victim to being a calm and empowered person. I'm not telling you this to impress you in regard to my emotional prowess but rather to impress on you that as you change your perception to obstacles, you will increase your productivity.

The reality is that obstacles and problems are a sign of life. The only people who do not have such challenges occupy a space approximately six feet below the surface of the earth. In fact, sometimes you can judge how successful a person is by the size of their problems. When you are successful it means that you succeeded in solving bigger problems than unsuccessful people. Success is being like a graduation diploma that qualifies you to create even larger and more difficult problems!

The obstacles we create are an indication of who we are and to what level we have developed. Every obstacle is a gift. Every obstacle contains a gem of learning, growth, and development. Every obstacle has within it the power to set us free. As we change our Inner World reality from victimhood to empowerment, we become a free person. Freedom comes through facing and overcoming a thousand self-created obstacles with the emotional evenness of a great guru. After all, that's how they got to be free. Every time you Overcome an obstacle with emotional equanimity, you not only transform your Outer World, but you also transform your Inner World. But remember, Freedom comes not through a single big decision, rather through a thousand small ones.

4. You would dramatically increase peace of mind

This is indeed a lofty Goal but a worthy one. Having a mind that continuously experiences Peace of Mind is a Goal that I may not achieve in this lifetime, but I've made significant progress towards it so far and I intend to continue.

I used to get stressed about everything. The kids messed up the lounge, the plumber didn't turn up, I was behind with my project, the client didn't sign, the traffic was too heavy (a queue of one was too long for me), it was raining — again, money was tight, I ate too much, the lawns needed mowing, the stereo stopped working, the car was dirty, and so on. You get the picture.

While I can assure you that while I am still far from perfect, I am however learning more and more to accept these things as being real, while at the same time continuing to take action to correct those situations that are within my power to influence. Increasingly I redirect the mental energy that I used to spend on being stressed into taking action while maintaining emotional equanimity (evenness). As a result I experience more Peace of Mind and less stress. That works for me and I'm very confident that it will work for you.

Chapter 53:

How to Really Enjoy the Journey
Part 3 - Stay Committed
but Not Emotionally Attached

At first glance, the philosophy of Karma Yoga and detaching your emotions from the Outcome may seem to contain some contradictions. To see what I mean, have a read of my top three rules for detaching emotions from Outcomes:

1. Be clear on your Outcome then focus on the Input.

2. Be committed to achieving your Outcome, but not emotionally attached (emotionally dependent) on it.

3. If you face an obstacle, accept it as being real while maintaining emotional calmness, and at the same time take action to Overcome the obstacle.

You can see the paradoxes in the above. We tend to think of being clear on Outcome and then focusing on the Inputs as being mutually exclusive. Likewise we think that our level of commitment is demonstrated by how badly we emotionally want something. And finally, we have the greatest of difficulty, in our culture at least, of accepting reality and taking action at the same time. We think that to be "accepting" means that we need to become passive and nothing could be further from the truth.

Let me explain how these seemingly mutually incompatible concepts can not only live side by side, but can also bring harmony into your mind.

1. Be clear on your Outcome, then focus on the Input

The analogy that I would use is swimming in open water during a race. I would start by swimming towards a buoy that may be

 500 meters or more in the distance. I would swim for fifty strokes and then lift my head up mid-stroke and see where the buoy was in order to ensure that I was still swimming in the right direction. Then head down again to concentrate on my technique. Another fifty strokes, then check the direction. The Outcome I wanted was to get to the buoy, but I focused 95% of my energy on the Input, not the Outcome.

As mentioned previously, having got clear on your Outcome, if you will then concentrate on perfecting the Input for the sake of the Input itself, you will learn to be "in the moment" you will enjoy the experience a lot more.

2. Be committed to achieving your Outcome but not emotionally attached (dependent) on it

There is a big difference between being committed and being attached. Being attached refers to being emotionally dependent on making progress towards and eventually achieving your Outcome. It's like saying, *"I'll be happy when the world changes to suit what I want and until then I'll be stressed."*

There are four ways that people move through any experience of Goal achievement. Let me start with the worst option and work up to the best one.

Level Four People: Uncommitted and attached. These are the people who really want the Outcome and their Happiness is dependent on achieving it, but they have not yet made the decision to really go full steam ahead for it. For example, they want to lose weight and are unhappy about not being slim, but continue to over-indulge. As a result, their Self-Esteem suffers and they feel "stuck." When you are being a Level Four person, you are in no-man's land. You get to experience the worst of both worlds. Not making any progress and being very unhappy about it. Some people can spend most of their entire life living in the mental wilderness of Level Four. Ugh!

Level Three People: Uncommitted and detached. These folk would prefer to have more money, a better relationship or to upgrade their car, but they can't ever get excited enough to actually do anything about it. Still, they will be content, if not happy, despite their casual and passive approach to their future. They will never feel fulfilled however, and this is a very different emotion from feeling happy. As mentioned, while they are not inclined to make an effort, they are comfortable about being mediocre. At least they are content, unlike the pour miserable souls stuck in the purgatory that is Level Four.

Level Two People: Committed and attached. It may come as a surprise to you that most successful people are committed and attached. They tend to achieve what they want to achieve eventually, but destroy the quality of the experience by getting stressed and unhappy when things don't go their way. A lot of high-achievers are Level Two people. Stressed and unhappy, but making progress. They have not yet leaned the heavenly art of emotional equanimity. They experience only fleeting moments of Fulfillment and Happiness as the world all to briefly transforms itself to their idea or perfection.

Level One People: Committed and detached. This is the highest level of performance as evidenced both in the Outer World that is detected through our senses, as well as the parallel universe of our Inner World or what we refer to as the mind. We would all do well to aspire to be a Level One person and, on the occasions that I live in this zone, all is well in my world.

Of course, it is possible to dip in and out of all four levels on any given day depending on what our frame of mind is like.

Earlier in our relationship, my Life Partner pointed out to me a growth opportunity. Oh how I used to hate them! She noticed that I became stressed about a lot of things and suggested that there was a better way to experience life than being so uptight about so many things. Looking back, I don't think that I was any tenser than anyone else and at the time

I thought that it was normal to have so many rules around what had to happen in order for me to be happy.

In what was then a rare moment of openly communicating about my emotions, I explained to her that I believed that having the energy of "force" around me and being a little stressed was inseparable from being a high-achiever and furthermore it was evidence that I cared about my results. I was concerned, I said, that if I lost my impatience that I might also lose the ability to achieve at high levels. She suggested that the two were not inextricably interwoven and that indeed it was possible to be at peace with the world and still get to the next level of results. And as is normally the case, time has proven her counsel to be of sage-like quality.

In the intervening years, I have slowly developed the muscle of emotional equanimity. I still enjoy and celebrate the victories every bit as much as ever, but I have definitely improved my ability to enjoy other aspects of the journey along the way.

A high-achieving lifestyle and peace of mind can indeed go hand in hand. Just ask Gandhi, Christ, or Buddha. They changed the world for generations that followed and did so with an enviable track record of peace of mind.

Let's look again at what I mean by "committed and detached."

As mentioned previously, when I talk about commitment, I like to think of it as meaning "there is no other possible Outcome." Having taken time to carefully contemplate both the new Goal as well as the cost of achieving it, I am a great fan of then making a commitment to achieving the Goal, regardless of the obstacles that I unexpectedly face along the way. An important distinction to bear in mind in the meantime is that the commitment is to the Outcome, not to the Input. As discussed earlier, you need to be committed to the Outcome but be flexible about the specific way that you are going to achieve it. If you have decided to get fit but repeatedly fail to get yourself out of bed to train, then change your strategy. Hire a one on one trainer or train with a friend.

Commitment is what the Mission Controller for Apollo Thirteen talked about when they had lost control of the spacecraft and he spoke to his team about how they must find a way to safely bring the astronauts back to earth: "failure is not an option," he declared.

On the other hand, being detached means that you are going to experience emotional well-being such as Happiness and peace of mind regardless of the results in your Outer World. This is what I mean by emotional equanimity or emotional evenness.

To extend the concept of detachment, think for a moment about all of the rules that you have around being happy. What has to happen in order for you to be happy? For most people the list would look something like this:

- I arrived at work on time.
- Boss is happy.
- No client complaints.
- My team are all doing what they are meant to do.
- Our competitors are resting up.
- The marketplace is getting bigger.

- Margins are growing.
- My car is clean.
- The weather is sunny and dry.
- I remembered everything.
- I am not overworked.
- My Life Partner is happy with my performance in all areas (man).
- My children are all content and behaving perfectly (woman).
- I won at golf/tennis/bridge/croquet (or whatever).
- I got the best tickets in the house.
- All of the technology and machinery in my life is functioning without a hitch.
- I did my exercise and I have no regrets in regard to what I ate and drank last night.
- My prospects all said "yes" to the sale and were really nice to me.
- The tradesperson showed up on time, fixed the problem quickly, left no mess and charged me a fair price.
- There are no leaves in the swimming pool.
- My credit cards are all paid off.
- I have all the money I need to pay all of my bills plus plenty left over.
- The kids have not made any messes.

So, if this list is representative of what your rules for Happiness look like, what are the chances of you being happy for anything more than a nanosecond?

My recommendation is that you train your mind to experience Happiness independent of what is happening in your Outer World. And that is what I mean by being detached.

Most people believe that *"if you can keep your head calm while all those around you are losing theirs you obviously don't know what's going on."* Ignorance may be bliss, but it's not the only reason that someone can stay calm amidst turmoil.

Detachment recognizes that your Inner World is not dependent on what is happening in your Outer World. Most people allow their Outer World to shape their Inner World. If something does not go according to their preferences in their Outer World, then their Inner World becomes affected in that they become stressed and unhappy.

Remember that just like everything else that's worthwhile, being detached takes practice. It's like learning to sing in harmony. But it's worth the practice in order to give up the discord that stress brings into your life.

I'll write more about staying committed but detached in the next chapter.

CHAPTER 54:

POSITIVE THINKING VERSUS REALITY THINKING

I'VE WRITTEN A fair bit in previous chapters about accepting unwanted emotions as real and dealing with them accordingly. Now I want to focus on your thinking as it relates to accepting the obstacle as being real and how to deal with that reality.

This chapter will help you to face an obstacle and accept that obstacle as being real and will therefore empower you to deal with facts rather than shadows.

Remember, acceptance is not the same as being passive. What we are after is the seemingly paradoxical state of accepting reality, then taking action to change it.

I am not a positive thinker. At least, not in the sense of what most people mean by the term. I prefer to think of myself as a "reality thinker." Sure, I am a great fan of backing myself and going for it and giving myself every chance of success. And yes, I like to make the most of what is in front of me and to see the gift in an obstacle and use Creative Self-talk and all that other good stuff. But that's all technology that

I apply to myself, not to situations that I have no influence over. Some people's idea of positive thinking is to ignore reality and to bury their head in the sand like the Ostrich and pretend that what is happening is not real.

Let me illustrate the point with what could have been a near-death experience. Two years prior to writing this, I found myself five hundred vertical meters below my Goal, the summit of Mt. Cook. I had trained on and off for a year summiting various smaller peaks around New Zealand and had invested thousands of dollars in equipment and training for this moment. It was around 6 a.m. and my guide Sam Bosshard and I had been climbing since 11:00 p.m. the night before. We had dodged the avalanches rumbling down the Linda Glacier and had also endured an hour of near freezing while we waited in vain for another member of our party to recover from a stomach condition. We had used our crampons and ice axes to cling to and traverse the dangerous "Linda Shelf," and we were ready to ascend the Summit Rocks and then to push on to Summit Ridge and to stand on top of the region's tallest mountain.

While we paused to rest and wait for dawn, it became apparent with the light slowly filtering through the Southern Alps towards us that all was not well with the world that surrounded us. Pink fingers of light crept through the mountain peaks towards us and eventually the sky and every mountain peak was bathed in a golden pink glow. *"Pink sky at night, shepherds delight. Pink sky in the morning, shepherds warning."* A storm was coming in from the south and the clouds were progressively becoming both thicker and lower.

As we sat there, below the Summit Rocks, on a ledge looking down on the peaks of the Southern Alps below us, I knew that Sam was weighing up whether or not to pull the plug on our final ascent. I was practicing positive thinking. *"We can do it! We'll be fine. The storm won't hit for a while yet. If we're quick, we'll be O.K. Sam. We've come too far to turn back now.'*

Sam Bosshard is a professional mountain guide and one of the very best in the business. He's still alive after two decades of professional climbing around the world because he is a reality thinker and not a wishful thinker.

Sam looked at me and simply said *"We're going back."* End of story. I tried to sell Sam on the idea of giving it a shot, but he was immovable. *"Look,"* he said, *"we could go up there and get caught and in all likelihood we'd die. Or we could go up there and get back off the mountain and get away with it. And you might get away with it nine times out of ten, but on the tenth time you'd be dead. If you take those sorts of risks, you will eventually wind up dead, it's as simple as that. This is not one of your marketing campaigns where if it bombs you lose a few grand. This is your life we're talking about. We're going back down."* End of story.

So down we went. We got off the mountain and into a hut in time before the storm hit and when it hit, it raged for three days, ending our chances of another crack at the summit for that year.

If we had taken the extra time to push on for the summit, we might even have made it back in time, if we hadn't run into any unforeseen obstacles, or if the storm hadn't come in any quicker. If. Maybe.

The point? If you employ the type of positive thinking that is really just wishful thinking which ignores reality, then reality will come back and bite you in the bum every time. Equally dangerous of course is negative thinking *"We're all going to die!."* But by practicing Reality Thinking, you learn to accept what is real and deal with it on the basis of "what is" rather than what you want it to be. Accept reality, warts and all, then build a bridge, and then "get over it."

Positive thinking is great for the things that you can control, such as our own actions and abilities; it really can lift your performance to a whole new level, and it is a terrific form of Self-talk. But positive thinking as it is applied to things that we cannot change turns into wishful thinking and a refusal to see reality, as it is can prove to be devastatingly counter-productive.

THE STOCKDALE PARADOX

Admiral Jim Stockdale was the highest-ranking United States military officer in the "Hanoi Hilton" prisoner-of-war camp during the height of the Vietnam War and was tortured over twenty times during his eight-year imprisonment from 1965 to 1973. Stockdale lived out the war without any prisoner's rights, no set release date, and no certainty as to whether he would even survive to see his family again.

When asked what sort of people didn't make it out of the hellish condition of the Vietnamese Prisoner of War Camp, Stockdale respond swiftly *"Oh, that's easy,"* he said. *"The optimists. They were the ones who said, 'We're going to be out by Christmas.' And Christmas would come, and Christmas would go. Then they'd say, 'We're going to be out by Easter.' And Easter would come, and Easter would go. And then Thanksgiving,* and then it would be Christmas again. And they died of a broken heart."

Stockdale went on to describe one of the greatest lessons that we can all learn in tough times. *"You must never confuse faith that you will prevail in the end – which you can never afford to lose – with the discipline to confront the most brutal facts of your current reality, whatever they might be."*

In summary:

1. Always keep the faith that you will succeed in the end despite the obstacles.

2. Confront the most brutal facts of your current reality, whatever they might be.

Chapter 55:

How to Deal With Survival Reactions

The acknowledged master of Superbike race training, Keith Code, talks about an interesting phenomena that occurs when a rider goes so fast into a corner that Subconscious fears begin to surface.

Code calls the manifestation of these fears "Survival Reactions," and suggests that they kick in once we have reached the limits of our Conscious ability.

It's like we each have only so much Consciousness to spend. When we practice something, for example racing a motorbike, we reduce the amount that we have to spend on a given corner. Let's say that we all have $10 of awareness, or Consciousness, to spend. A seasoned pro racer might use $1 of awareness on a corner that, as a learner, I spend $9.99 on.

However, once a rider goes into "Consciousness overdraft," the Subconscious takes over from the Conscious mind and he or she will begin to experience Survival Reactions.

In racing motorcycles, the following Survival Reactions are common among racers who have spent more than their $10 of Consciousness when going too hot into a corner:

1. Throttle off

2. Stiffen up and tighten grip on the bars

3. Fixed vision on where you don't want to go (and end up going there)

4. Freeze

5. Brake

Without wishing to go into all the reasons why, Survival Reactions actually create the very thing that the rider is trying to avoid: they de-stabilize the bike!

All of that is very interesting, but what, you may ask, has it to do with you and your Goals?

Just like learning to race a motorbike, any time that you take on a new Goal, you only have so much Consciousness to spend on it. Think of it as like having $10 of mental energy to spend.

For example, because I've exercised regularly now for 30 years, I might spend 10 cents a day of my mental energy when I exercise. Someone who is new to exercise may spend $9 of mental energy establishing the same habit. Creating a new habit spends a lot more of your Consciousness than maintaining an existing habit.

The cause of Survival Reactions in motorcycle racing is the overloading of the Conscious mind and just like racing a motorbike, when you overspend your $10 of Consciousness your Subconscious takes over and you begin to experience Survival Reactions which include:

1. Work longer
2. Work harder
3. Work faster
4. Work on short-term
5. Abandon planning
6. Delegate less
7. Become more reactive
8. Freeze and focus on what you don't want
9. Fluffing
10. Indecision
11. Eat more comfort food
12. Drink more alcohol
13. Ignore reality
14. Blame others
15. Exaggerate task size

16. Become more ego-centric

17. Lose sight of the big picture

18. Micro-manage

Essentially, what happens when your Subconscious takes over is that you go into flight or fight mode, and that's not always the most productive thing to do.

If you find yourself suffering from Survival Reactions, the answer is to do exactly the same as you would if you were on a Superbike: dial off the throttle a bit.

In other words, don't bite off more than you can chew. Learn to commit only to those Goals that you know that you have enough mental capacity to cope with. As mentioned in Chapter 30, it's true that stretching and challenging yourself is a great way to expand both your Consciousness and Capacity, but not to the point where you find yourself operating through Survival Reactions as a matter of routine. You need to create enough "space" in your life in the form of time and Consciousness so that you don't revert to the Subconscious to perform tasks that are more effectively performed by the Conscious mind.

It's interesting to me that I will put in a faster lap on the race track when I stay within the limits of my Conscious ability than when I try too hard and over commit myself by going into corners faster than I can mentally cope with. Under-commit and Over-achieve. Slower is faster. Less is more.

CHAPTER 56:

HOW TO PUSH THROUGH DISCOMFORT

I'M HURTING

WE ALL SUFFER from time to time. Suffering is mental (including emotional) discomfort as distinct from physical discomfort which we call pain. And remember, all suffering has its source within. There are times when we experience physical pain, and this may be unavoidable. But mental suffering is optional. At least, it becomes optional once you are aware of it and know how to apply the Thought Transformation Technique from Chapter 48.

Suffering is all self-sourced and self-created and therefore, with the right mind set and the right knowledge, it can be alleviated.

In point of fact, suffering is actually just an opinion. It's a judgment about what should be but isn't. And it's a judgment about what isn't but should be. Suffering is simply an inability for the mind to accept an unwanted reality as it is, here and now, without labeling it as bad. As soon as you accept that everything before you is perfect, the suffering ends and you are free to move forward. Your life will metamorphose from imprisoned caterpillar to magnificent butterfly.

PAIN

As mentioned, pain (physical) is different from suffering. If your Goal requires that you move through the "pain barrier," then the same rule applies as it does to your Capacity for anything else. That is to say, that the more you practice it, the better you'll get at it. You'll increase your tolerance for pain. You'll expand your Capacity to push on when others quit. It's a valuable Capacity to expand because as you expand your Capacity to endure physical pain, you'll also increase your mental stamina. There is always a cross-training effect whenever you develop any Capacity. The benefits from one strength will spill over and reinforce other abilities.

When in a situation where you need to endure in the face of emotional or even physical discomfort, you have two solid and reliable options. Let's check them out.

Always remember, however, that significant physical pain is a symptom that something is wrong, and if you persist you are likely to injure your body or your mind. Be aware that pushing beyond pain can create physical injury or breakdown. You have to know when to hold and know when to fold. Use your God-given common sense as well as your God-given intuition.

If you want to deal with discomfort, your two options are either "go into it" or "get out of it." Let me explain what I mean by those two terms.

'Going Into It'

By "going into it," I mean that you fully focus on what you are feeling and get your mind "inside it." The idea is to get so much inside the source of discomfort that you cease to notice it. It's a bit like not being able to see the wood for the trees. Amongst others, Zen Buddhists have mastered this technique so well that they can endure extraordinary levels of pain without so much as a ripple in their Consciousness. A fully trained Zen Master could sleep next to a train station with perfect peace of mind by going inside the noise. By accepting what you are feeling, by surrendering and not judging or resisting the discomfort, you cease to feel it. The more you let pain into your Consciousness, the less power it has over you. Like a Zen Koan (riddle), it's ironic that the more you let the discomfort into your Consciousness, the less Conscious you are of it. As with everything, practice is perfect. Our Buddhist brothers and other metaphysical advocates would suggest to us that there is a place that you and I can get to where pain has no hold over us. I'm open to that.

'Getting Out of It'

This technique is only for physical pain such as that experienced by endurance athletes. Depending on your Goal, you may need to endure some discomfort or even pain, and if it's not going to cause you any significant or permanent damage, then often the pain is manageable by "getting out of it."

As the name implies, "getting out of it" is exactly the opposite of "going into it." Endurance athletes are masters of "getting out of it." When the pain hits, they can transcend it by focusing on something else. Those with a highly developed ability in this Capacity will "get out of it" by shutting out the pain through focusing intently on their technique. Others "get out of it" by simply switching the focus of their mind to another subject. *"What am I going to be doing tomorrow?"* or *"What's for dinner?"* or *"I wonder if I left lights on at home."* Anything that distracts them from the pain and allows them to persist is fair game to use as a target and to mentally get out of the pain.

So the next time you experience some level of discomfort, practice one of both of these techniques and remember the practice will improve performance.

Chapter 57:

Understanding the True Nature of Personal Change

The failure to understand the nature of progress would have to be the number one reason why people become disheartened and give up in their quest for changing their reality. I want to spend a little time going over the nature of personal progress so that when you experience it, you'll recognize that what you are creating and experiencing is normal, and hopefully not revert to beating yourself up and then giving up.

Personal Change Means a Change of Thought Patterns

To understand the true nature of progress we need to firstly agree that what we are talking about is in fact not so much what needs to change in your Outer World, but rather what needs to change in your Inner World. No permanent or significant change will occur in your Outer World until you first change your Inner World. Let's examine this thought.

So you have some Goals now. Let's take one of those and call it an Outcome. What comes before an Outcome? Well in order to create the Outcome that you want, you will need to invest some energy and perform some Inputs. I know it sounds fairly elementary but it's a necessary starting place to illustrate a fundamentally important point. Let's look at our model so far:

The Creation Model

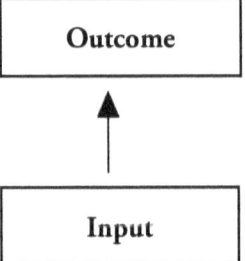

If we want to create a different Outcome, then you need some different Inputs. We understand that the definition of insanity is to keep performing the same Inputs and yet to expect a different Outcome. Nothing changes (Outcome), until something changes (Input).

When we begin working with a client at ESP Programme (**www.espcoach.com**), it's normal for us to start with what we call a Life Planning Day. It's a whole day devoted to nothing else other than getting very clear on what it is that a client wants to do with their life. Goal-setting is of course central to this process.

If I could hold a Life Planning Day for the world, all six billion of them at one time, then at the end of that day what we would discover is that in broad terms, everyone else in that rather large room would have the same Outcome in mind as you. The plan would look something like this:

Physical Health Goals

- More energy/better health/lose or gain some weight/get fitter

Mental/Emotional Health Goals

- More Happiness/less stress/more passion/more fun/more Freedom

Relationship Goals

- Deeper and more satisfying Life Partner relationship/spend more time with the kids/have more fun with my friends (and/or get some friends)

Money Goals

- Pay off debt/earn more money/develop passive income/better house/car/boat etc.

There will of course be some variations to the theme, but everyone on the planet is agreed that experiencing life at the next level in terms of health, relationships, and money is a part of their plan.

So here's my question: "If 99.9% of the people on the planet want the same things that you want, how is it that their Inputs are different from yours?" To rephrase the question: "What causes you to do the Inputs that you do versus the Inputs that the other 6 billion do?"

Yet another way of asking this question would be this: "If Input precedes an Outcome, what precedes the Input?'

The answer of course is the way that you Think.

So here's what our model looks like now that it's complete:

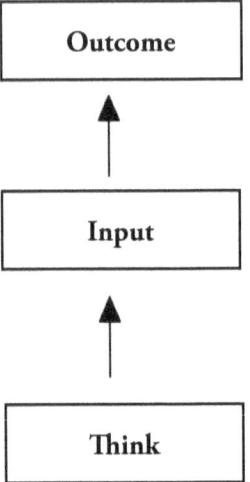

Buddha said *"We are what we think. All that we are arises with our thoughts. With our thoughts we make the world."* The Bible states *"What a man thinks, so he is."*

Think of it like this: Your life is like a 360-degree mirror that continuously reflects your thoughts. The quality of your Health, your Relationships, and your Money is a direct reflection of how you think.

You are what you think. Your "Being" is expressed in your thoughts, which is evidenced in what you do and manifests in what you have, or what you achieve. Be (think), Do (Input), Have (Outcome). We can simplify that model by saying that the way you behave is the key. Break the word down: Be-Have. Be, Have. Who you are is what you get, or more precisely (but forgive the grammar): "who you be is what you have."

The point is this: You will experience no permanent or significant change in your life until you change the way that you think.

Take the scenario of a Lottery winner. Let's call them Bob and Jane. These two live from paycheck to pay check with never quite enough money. Bob's idea of financial planning is to have an old shoe box they put their bills in. Jane gets her investment advice from the American talk shows and from her horoscopes. They spend their money on their lifestyle first, after all "we deserve it," and with what's left over they pay their bills. And with what's left over after that they invest for their retirement. Which is nothing.

So Bob and Jane (and God bless them because there's a little bit of Bob and Jane in all of us at some point in our lives), struggle financially simply because they spend more than they earn. Their level of thinking in regard to money is such that their Inputs have created an Outcome called "perpetually broke."

But one day Bob wakes up and on his way to the wholesaler stops off at the local Lotto shop and picks up a "Lucky dip." And indeed it does prove to be rather lucky because at 7:05 p.m. that night Bob and Jane become instant millionaires.

So, how do I reconcile Bob and Jane's change of economic circumstance given my previous statement: that *"nothing changes significantly or permanently in your Outer World until you change the way that you think."* Bob and Jane still have the same level of thinking in regard to money and yet they are millionaires. So how come?

The answer of course is simple. Give Bob and Jane five or perhaps ten years and revisit them. Unless they change their thinking patterns in regard to Money, guess how much of the million dollars they will have left. You know the answer and it's a nice round figure: 0. Zero, zip, nil, nada, nothing. Not much.

So Point 1 in understanding the nature of personal change is this:

> **Permanent and Significant Change in Your Life Requires a New Way of Thinking**

It was Einstein who said that you cannot solve a problem with the same level of thinking that created it.

Don't get me wrong, there is nothing wrong with the way that you think. Your thinking is not broken, and you don't need to fix it. In fact it's perfect. For your current level of Outcomes.

But if you want to experience life at the next level, you need a new way of thinking.

And please don't imagine that I am talking about anything particularly complicated or grand here. It's really simple stuff made difficult only by those who want you to pay them to unravel the complexity they packed into it. To paraphrase the Dutch poet Piet Hein, *"When all other roads to learning are barred, take something very simple, and make it very hard."*

Changing the way you think is simple, but it's not as equally easy. It's a messy process and it's messy simply because of who we are as human beings and how we are wired.

You can refer to the Thought Transformation Technique in Chapter 48 and my notes of Affirmation and Visualization in Chapter 45 on how to reprogram your thinking. How to change your thinking is not what I want to get across in this chapter; as mentioned, I've covered that previously.

The important point to get before moving on is so critical that I'll print it again: Permanent and significant change in your life requires a new way of thinking.

Herein lies the challenge. Let's say that you have procrastinated for years about exercising. If that's not the case, then think of something else that you've avoided doing that you really know you need to be doing in order to advance your life.

The only way that you are going to start, and continue exercising and experience the energy-enhancing benefits of being fit, is to reprogram your thoughts about exercise. You can refer to the notes on how to motivate yourself by creating powerful reasons from the section on changing your Perception in Chapter 54.

Contemplating the disadvantages (Pain) of not exercising and the benefits (Pleasure and Purpose) of exercising will also help in the reprogramming process.

This brings us to Point 2 of understanding the true nature of personal change:

> **Permanently changing the way that you think is never instant.**

This of course means that a change in the way that you act (Inputs) and your results (Outcomes) will be correspondingly gradual.

We would have it that change is quick and easy. That's what the 1-800 adverts want people to believe and people tend to believe what is convenient for them to believe. The problem with having an unrealistic expectation of the time frame for changing our patterns of thinking is that people get disheartened and give up. False hope breeds despair.

There are certainly occasional dramatic experiences that profoundly affect the way that we think. Intense emotional situations such as the death of a loved one, births, accidents, and so on can alter our patterns of thinking significantly. A point about these life-changing experiences: it's rare that the change of thinking we experience during these times is permanent; given time, the old patterns mostly creep back in and we find ourselves back where we started from unless we proactively and Consciously choose to lock in the new way of thinking.

People set Goals and decide on the most appropriate Inputs but don't fully understand that there needs to be a corresponding change in Subconscious patterns of thinking.

One of my favorite movies is "The Matrix." If you can get your head past the violence and look a little deeper, the movie has a tremendous "story beneath the story," which is all about waking up from unconscious living and really making choices. The hero, "Neo" and his side-kick, the fabulous "Trinity," can download instantaneously into their Subconscious mind pretty much any skill they want. Stuck on a roof top with no way off apart from an Apache Attack Helicopter? No problem, just download the army training manual into your brain and you're off! About to have a big fight and need to learn Kung Fu, Karate, Jiu-Jitsu, Judo and Tae Kwon-Do before morning tea? Before you can say "Beam me up Scotty," it's done. And we love that idea.

But that only works in Hollywood. Back here in the real world, learning, growing and developing, which are all different forms of change, takes time, persistence, and dedication.

So we can safely conclude that the nature of personal change is not that of a light switch. It's more like the tide coming in. It takes time and it is very, very difficult to hurry the process. Additionally, although progress is slow, it is steady and eventually the change will be complete.

Point 3 of understanding the true nature of personal change:

> **Permanently changing the way that you think is never linear**

Let's look at this in the form of a "getting from A to B" model. In the chart below "A" represents your situation when you start out to achieve your Goal. "B" represents where you want to end up, i.e. achieving your Goal. "A" might be unfit and "B" might be a marathon finisher. "A" might be a smoker and "B" might be a non-smoker. "A" might be broke and "B" might be financially independent. You get the idea.

A to B Model

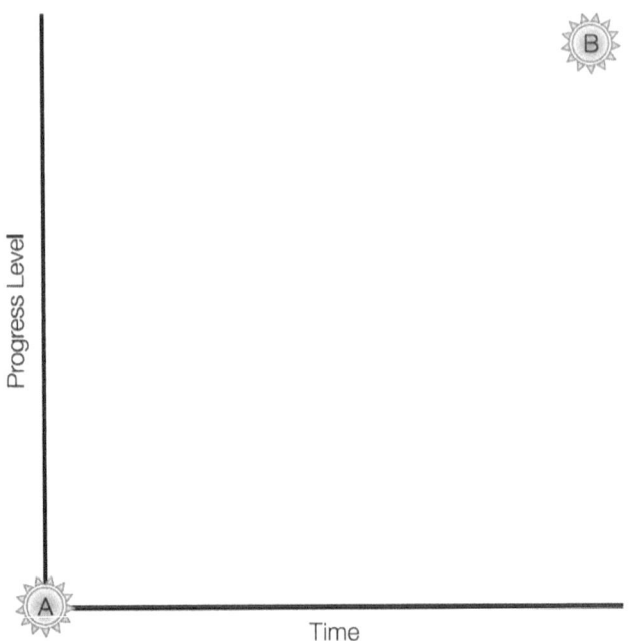

Most people have a Subconscious mind that associates change with pain (one of the best gifts you can give yourself is to reprogram that idea using the affirmation: *"I love change, I love change"*). So your Subconscious doesn't want you to leave the safety, security, and pleasure of the Comfort zone that is represented in "A."

However, let's say that your Subconscious senses that you are Consciously quite determined to shed the weight/get fit/create wealth/be a better parent or whatever "B" represents. Remember that your Subconscious, in its normal state loves certainty. In fact, the Subconscious would rather have "bad" news than no news as the latter represents uncertainty.

So, because humans believe what they find easy and comfortable to believe, the Subconscious creates its second-best scenario to "no change." It's called "linear change."

We then have a manufactured belief that our change process, both internally (thought patterns) and externally (inputs) will look like this:

A to B Model

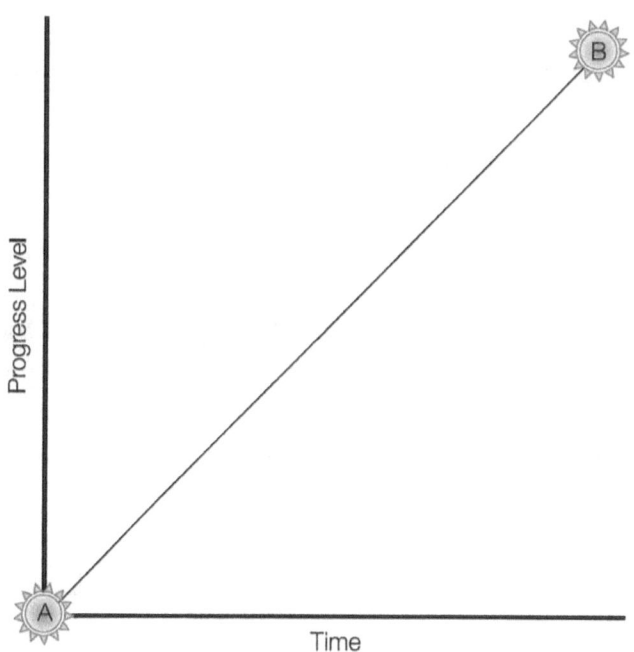

A straight line.

Let's say that you're a married man and A (present state) is unfit and B (Goal) is fit and the Inputs between A and B requires you to get out of bed 30 minutes earlier and go for a brisk walk.

You get out of bed on Monday morning and you metamorphose into a cape-wearing, Goal-achieving crusader. You back the car out of the drive and go to the park and you "just do it," 30 minutes of power walking, sweat bands, water bottle and all. Then back home again. Terrific. You feel pumped. So far so good.

Tuesday morning is the same. Nailed it. Great.

Wednesday morning, you're backing out of the driveway when you detect a small but definitely discernible thud under right rear wheel and you simultaneously hear a screeching "meow" type sound coming from the same wheel.

You think nothing of it and continue backing only to have a near identical noise, although at much reduced volume, coming from the front right wheel.

You then stop the car and get out to investigate and there lies in front of you a rather flatter version of an object that bears a remarkable resemblance to your Life Partner's cat. Which it is. And it's not dead … yet. "Perfect!," you say, feigning a weak smile.

And then what with the visit to the Vet and getting the gift basket for your Life Partner and being late into work, the walk just didn't happen. *"Never mind, tomorrow's another day"* you tell yourself.

But during the day, the bank manager phones and recalls your overdraft and that big account you landed last week calls to cancel and your biggest creditor falters and declares bankruptcy owing you tens of thousands of dollars. Another "Perfect!" day.

So you get home and deal with how you feel the way any mature adult would. You get legless.

The next morning you wake to find that you've slept through the alarm and you're now going to be late for your first appointment. "Perfect!" you say through gritted teeth. Bugger the exercise, it was silly idea anyway.

So now here's what your A to B model looks like.

A to B Model

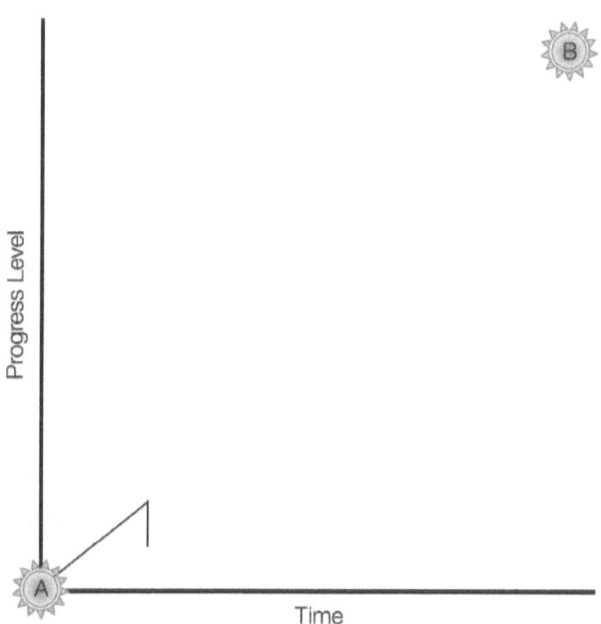

This is the moment that your destiny is decided. This is the point in time where the ordinary are separated from the Extra-ordinary. The ordinary will quit and put it on their list of things that they started but never finished. In doing so, they will continue to build a psychology of defeat. The winners will simply re-commit.

You see, the point is not that losers mess up and winners don't. We all mess up. None of us are 100% consistent. It's part of the human condition. Messing up is a sign that you inhabit a human body. Welcome to the human race.

The point is that winners get back on the horse after they fall off. They re-commit. No self-beating is required. A post mortem or blaming the cat is neither needed nor useful. Just re-commit. If you do this one simple thing, regardless of how you feel, regardless of how many times you messed up, your success is assured. It's really that simple.

Christ was asked by one of his disciples how many times one should forgive a neighbor who sins against him. *"Seven times?"* The great one answered *"Seven times seventy,"* meaning I believe, that there should be no end to our Capacity to forgive and forget. So why are we so slow to forgive ourselves?

The following chart represents what true successful change really looks like. And this applies equally to the process going on in your Subconscious as it does to the parallel world of outer reality.

A to B Model

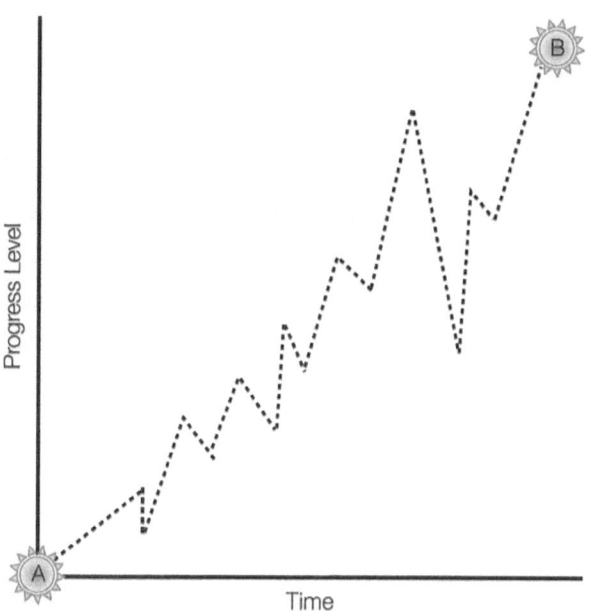

Real successful personal change, and the true nature of progress looks more like a share market graph than a straight line. When you quit after the first time that you mess up it's like you dumped a "blue chip" upwardly trending stock just because it lost a little ground. And just like stock, even if you go backward for a while, you don't lose anything until you quit.

In the last section, I wrote about how change is like turning on a light switch. The reality is it's more like the nature of the tide. I stumbled on this one morning when I was walking along Mooloolaba Beach. I was asking the question *"what is the nature of change really like?"* and allowing my mind to tap into the power of the Superconscious Mind. I had been looking for an answer to this question for some time and suddenly I noticed that it was literally right in front of me.

The tide was half out. Or was it half in? Have you ever walked on a beach and found it difficult to work out whether the tide is coming in or out? To the untrained eye, it's not easy. As it turned out, the tide was on its way in. What I observed was that one wave would sweep up the beach, further than the wave before it. But instead of the next wave going even further up the beach, it didn't even travel as far as the first wave. And for anyone who expected the waves to successively be stronger and longer, the next few waves were equally unimpressive.

Then after a few more waves, a set of larger waves came in and spread their foam further up the beach. And then of course the next set of waves was smaller again.

If you or I were God and we designed the whole "tide goes in and the tide goes out" thing, we'd have it that when the tide came in, each successive wave would run up the beach just that tiny bit more than its predecessor. Logical, orderly, and predictable. Just like Conscious thought. But of course there are a million different variables interacting in our daily universe and predictability is not a luxury upgrade option that comes with the package you bought when you decided to be a human. Remember that predictability only exists on this planet for those bored and stifled souls who never venture forth from their collective huddles within the safety of their stupefying Comfort Zones.

Change is normally messy, seemingly illogical, and rarely consistent. Once you can accept that this is the true nature of how you change internally, and how your external reality changes, you will be much more at peace with yourself, and with the world.

In summary, the paradox is this: On the one hand, we must resolutely do what we committed to do, and on the other hand, we must be quick to forgive ourselves when our inevitable human inconsistencies manifest themselves and be equally swift to re-commit.

I was once trying to explain this concept to a group of clients who were struggling with the paradox of commitment versus being gentle on themselves if they slipped up. *"So you mean it's kind of like a Catholic confessional?"* one of them asked. *"If you mess up, you fess up, get forgiven, and start again."*

It's hard to disagree with that analogy. The difference is that a confession is not required so much as a simple acknowledgment of the need to re-commit and also there is no penance under my system. But the core principle is the same: forgive and re-commit.

If you have started out with commitment and passion toward your Goal but find yourself avoiding those actions that you know you need to complete follow, this trouble shooting checklist and see if you can self-diagnose what you need to change in order to get back on track.

- *Am I passionate about the Outcome?*

    If not, then refresh your mind in regard to your list of reasons for wanting this Goal.

- *Am I passionate about the Inputs?*

    If not, then find new Inputs or drop the Goal.

- *Are my Mental Fuel Tanks full?*

    If not, then get an adequate number of Leisure Days (have a holiday) under your belt.

- *Have I taken on too much? Have Survival Reactions taken over?*

    Is my time squeezed due to too many Goals or too much clutter? If so, re-prioritize your Goals, put the less important ones on the shelf, and clean up any messes or clutter in your life.

These are the big ones. Failure to implement (FTI) is the problem. Often the source of the problem is a lack of motivation as opposed to a lack of discipline. If you have a problem with FTI, go back to Chapter 46 (How to build your commitment and persistence muscles) and Chapter 47 (How to stay motivated).

So always remember to allow for the fact that you reside in a human body and are therefore subject to the human conditions of imperfection and inconsistency. Personal change and achievement is normally messy and takes time and persistence. So on the one hand, be forgiving of yourself when your performance is less than consistent and on the other hand never, never, give up.

PART TEN:

THE EXTRA-ORDINARY PERSONAL GOAL

CHAPTER 58:

THE EXTRA-ORDINARY PERSONAL GOAL (EPG)

THE PURPOSE OF this chapter is to explain the concept that I call the Extra-Ordinary Personal Goal or "EPG" as I'll refer to it. Simply put, an EPG involves a Conscious decision to create an experience of success in your life that takes you well outside your Comfort Zone. By achieving such a Goal, your potential will expand and you will develop new Capacities where previously you had none.

EPG EXAMPLES

An EPG may involve climbing a mountain, sailing an ocean, having a book published, racing a car, or holding your own art exhibition. The type of EPG you choose will vary depending on a number of factors, the chief factor being what you are passionate about.

I started creating and achieving EPG type Goals over two decades ago, but it was more recently that I gave them a name and clearly defined what they looked like. As I shared the concept with my clients, I could see eyes begin to light up and hear hearts begin to beat a bit stronger as a small spark of personal passion ignited within each person. In short, my clients loved the idea.

More importantly, my clients started creating and achieving their own EPGs and as a result, they are giving their family, friends, and co-workers a mental "permission slip" to do the same. The ripple effect within the circles of each EPG achiever is incalculable.

Some of the EPGs that I can look back on now with real satisfaction include having completed two marathons and a "Half Ironman" triathlon.

Personally I never found half of anything very exciting, so I then went on to complete a full "Ironman" Triathlon.

I have also learned to kayak rugged white-water rivers, gone solo in mountainous bush regions in winter for days on end, volunteered for the army and completed overseas military exercises, completed bungy jumps and learned how to fall out of a plane and free fall solo from 12,000 feet to 5,000 feet before, with great relief, opening my parachute. In addition, I have completed the arduous and risky four day "Grand Traverse," or "GT" as it is known, of New Zealand's highest mountain, Mount Cook, and I have developed and taught Personal Development courses in a maximum security prison for four years in a row. And I have just completed my latest and most testing EGP of racing a Superbike. Since beginning to learn how to race motorbikes, I have raced in club, state (Queensland) and also in the national Australian Superbike Championships.

The Extra-ordinary Personal Goal (EPG)

Why I do these things will be revealed shortly.

But not all EPGs need to be of the "outdoor adventure" or "endurance event" variety. That just happens to be a passion of mine. Some of my clients are in the process of, or have completed, EPGs as diverse as a seven-day meditation retreat (three times!), having art work exhibited and critically acclaimed, setting up an international charity network, flying solo for amazing distances, and competing in an arduous multi-country car rally. This is the stuff of which an Extra-Ordinary life is made.

Why you would want to do such a thing will be beyond the comprehension of most "ordinary" people. But there will be those few brave souls who will "get it" almost immediately. If you're one of them, then something inside you will stir at the thought of experiencing the Extra-Ordinary. You'll be amongst a small band of achievers who want to make a dent in the world before they leave it. You won't be content with an ordinary life: "was born, went to school, got a job, got married, had kids, retired, died." That's not enough of an epitaph to satisfy the souls who feel the need to live life to the fullest extent and who dream of making their lives count as an inspiration to future generations.

Criteria for an Extra-Ordinary Personal Goal

So what makes an EPG different from any other Goal? Firstly, let's look at what an EPG has in common with a normal Goal. Both the EPG and a normal Goal focus your mind on achieving an Outcome. Both are very clear and specific in their descriptions and both are measurable in terms of the results.

What makes an EPG Goal different from a normal Goal is that an EPG is a Goal that meets the following four criteria:

1. An EPG will take you a long way outside your Comfort Zone.

2. An EPG is not motivated by any direct benefits to your career or business.

3. When you tell people about your EPG, they will either say *"Wow!"* or

4. *"You must be crazy."*

5. Your grandchildren will talk about your EPG at your funeral.

Let's have a closer look at the above criteria for an EPG.

1. An EPG will take you well outside your Comfort Zone

If Values such as Freedom, Fulfillment, adventure, and personal development are important to you, then you'll know that we only ever experience these when we sample life outside the Comfort Zone. Life outside the Comfort Zone is where we expand our Consciousness and increase our Capacities. In short, a life well-lived is a life lived outside your Comfort Zone.

2. An EPG is not motivated by any direct benefit to your career or business

I have found that many high-achievers channel almost all of their time and energy into their career or business. This creates a one-dimensional character that many others, including your Life Partner and friends, find a tad boring. Kids also find it hard to relate to a parent who they feel needs to "get a life" outside of work. A correctly chosen EPG not only brings more balance between business and personal development, but it also adds to the fabric of personal passion in a life that simply can't be created through business passion alone. In short, a well-chosen EPG will create a more well-rounded individual out of you.

3. When you tell people about your EPG, they will either say 'Wow!' or 'You must be crazy'

This of course is how you know that the Goal is above the ordinary aspirations of most people. When you tell people about your EPG, they will either be inspired or confused. I must admit to enjoying watching people's reactions; it's kind of fun. The ones who "get it" will be full of admiration for what you are doing. They may not understand fully why you are doing it, but they will warm to the spirit of adventure that you personify. Others who think that life is all about building a cozier Comfort Zone definitely won't get it. And that's OK.

There may also be a few people who feel threatened by what you want to achieve. They want to bring you down to their level; they personify the "tall poppy" syndrome. They'll tell others that you are nuts as this is their way of justifying why they should stay in their Comfort Zone. Fortunately, I have not met many of these small-minded souls.

Having said that, I do understand that an EPG adventure is not for everyone — it's for those who want to create what John Hodge called *"a life less ordinary."*

As Theodore Roosevelt said, *"It is not the critic who counts, not the man who points out how the strong man stumbled, or where the doer of deeds could have done better. The credit belongs to the man who is actually in the arena; whose face is marred by the dust and sweat and blood; who strives valiantly; who errs and comes short again and again ... who knows the great enthusiasms, the great devotions and spends himself in a worthy cause; who at the best knows in the end the triumph of high achievement, and who, at worst, if he fails, at least fails while daring greatly; so that his place shall never be with those cold and timid souls who know neither victory nor defeat."*

4. Your grandchildren will talk about it at your funeral

This one actually came to me at a funeral. My Life Partner, had an "Uncle Colin." I had met Colin a number of times over the years and came to know him as a likeable, quiet bachelor who appeared to me to be quite unremarkable in every respect. Until he died. Ironically, it was not until after Colin's death that I got to know him well. His funeral was well attended and in particular by a large number of grandchildren who quite courageously volunteered to share their experiences of their beloved uncle with the assembled friends and family. Colin's very active interest and support of his grandchildren was indeed heart-warming to hear, but the biggest surprise came when I learned that he was once one of New Zealand's foremost middle-distance runners. No mean feat in a country with a history of international middle-distance medal winners. Quiet "Uncle Colin" had won many regional and even national titles over many years and even competed in what was then known as the Empire Games, the forerunner to the Commonwealth Games.

The point of this story is that in addition to the time that he had spent with his grandchildren, what stuck in their minds was Colin's outstanding achievements. Not his ordinary ones. Who Colin had become was defined as much as anything else by his Extra-ordinary accomplishments. And that is the legacy that Colin left his grandchildren and the rest of us. What an inspiration. What a gift.

The experience of attending a funeral can be a little like turning 30, 40 or 50 years old. Like me, you may have found that such occasions can cause you to stop and think about what you are doing with your life. Will your life be ordinary, or will you create a legacy of inspiration and motivation that will be passed down for generations to come? The choice is yours of course, but if you choose the latter option, then read on because the EPG concept is your ticket to an Extra-Ordinary legacy.

CHAPTER 59:

TYPES OF EXTRA-ORDINARY PERSONAL GOALS

WHAT DO **B**ILL Gates, Richard Branson, and Steve Fossett all have in common apart from tens of millions in the bank? They have all plunged into the intoxicating world of EPGs and have become Extra-Ordinary human beings.

Along with his wife, Bill Gates has created the Bill and Melinda Gates Foundation and has targeted helping children through education programs as well as many health initiatives. One of the things I admire about Bill and Melinda Gates is that it would have been so easy just to throw money at Charities, but they have really thought about where the money could do the most good. They are passionately proactive in ensuring that the cash is converted into benefits that actually reach those for whom it was targeted. Bill and Melinda are Extra-Ordinary. I salute you both.

American billionaire Steve Fosset has swum the English Channel, climbed six out of seven of the world's highest mountains (he won't climb Everest because there is too much down time involved), and after six failed attempts, finally completed the first solo balloon circumnavigation of the globe.

Interestingly, when he was asked by a reporter what sort of pleasure he took from *"those extremely strenuous, cold and lonely trips,"* he replied, *"I'm not doing it for the pleasure. This is an endeavor. It's something that hasn't been done."* Fossett's passion for adventure has taken him all over the world. He has not always won, but testing his own strength and endurance is a way of life for this Extra-Ordinary being.

Richard Branson is a great example of someone who had no apparent "natural genius" qualities. In addition to his remarkable business success since 1985, he has been immersed in a number of EPGs. In 1986 his boat "Virgin Challenger II" crossed the Atlantic Ocean in the fastest ever recorded time. In 1987, Branson crossed the Atlantic Ocean in the "Virgin Atlantic Flyer," which was the first and largest hot air balloon to cross the ocean. Richard Branson is an inspiration to me and billions of others as a result of him choosing to be Extra-Ordinary.

It's too easy to look at these giants of the Extra-Ordinary and assume that they must be different, that they must have been born like that. Sure, we are all born with certain talents and a bias towards certain passion activities. But the point is that living a life that is Extra-Ordinary starts with a decision to be Extra-Ordinary. All of the Extra-Ordinary people in the history of the world at some point made a decision. They decided to back themselves, despite the knockers and the tall poppy cutters and the critics and the doomsayers and the doubters and the fearful and the timid, they chose to play the game of life full out.

While some Extra-Ordinary people show talent from an early age, in most cases the early childhood history of these remarkable people is in fact quite unremarkable. As mentioned before, Bill Gates chose to drop out of high school, Branson was considered a slow learner by his teachers, not helped by the fact that he was short-sighted and dyslexic.

It's also true, however, that all of these modern heroes have something that I don't have, and chances are you don't have it either. Access to trucks loads of money. But it's too easy to sit back and say *"it's all right for them, they're rich, so that lets me off the hook."* Just like us, Gates, Fossett and Branson had to start somewhere. The reality is that each of us can do the best that we can with the resources we've got.

Personally, I see the lack of recourse as adding some spice to the challenge. When Ernst Rutherford, the great New Zealand scientist, was handed the task of splitting the atom he gathered his team around him and declared *"Look, we don't have much money for this, so we are just going to have to think."* Lack of resource is simply another obstacle, and as we Overcome it, we get to grow. In this sense, lack of resource is a gift of far greater value than having plenty of money.

ORDINARY PEOPLE DOING THE EXTRA-ORDINARY

For every Extra-Ordinary person who makes the headlines, there are a thousand others who enjoy a more private victory. These heroes may only be known by family and a few friends, but they also understand that achieving the Extra-Ordinary is not actually about fame and public recognition that happens in the Outer World, it's about inner victories, or character development. The purpose of this chapter is to give you some ideas and insights into how seemingly ordinary people are achieving the Extra-Ordinary. This way, you can mentally dip your toe into the water or various EPG pools and see which one, if any, you want to plunge head-first into later on.

EPG Types

My EPGs tend to be adventure-orientated simply because adventure is one of my personal Core Values. But there are very many different types of EPG and here's just a few:

1. Artistic EPG

2. Adventure EPG

3. Educational EPG

4. Sport EPG

5. Spiritual EPG

6. Philanthropic EPG

7. Extreme EPG

8. Endurance EPG

In the next chapter I'll give you an insight into some of my EPG experiences.

Chapter 60:

My Personal EPG Examples

As mentioned previously, I've achieved many EPGs over the last two decades, but I'll just touch on several of them here to give you a quick peek inside an EPG.

EPG Example 1: New Zealand Ironman Triathlon

There were 1,200 entrants in the NZ Ironman triathlon to be held on 1st March 2003, which at the time was the largest field outside of the world championships based in Hawaii. The event was held in Taupo, a small town in the center of NZ's North Island. The whole town was packed for days before the event with athletes and their support crews. There wasn't a spare bed in town. The 2003 NZ Ironman was about to kick off.

But an Ironman event really starts at least a year before the race. A minimum of one year of training. Twelve months. Fifty-two weeks. Three hundred and sixty-five days. Early morning exits from a warm bed into what were often dark and cold winter days. Six-hour Sunday bike rides that went on while "normal" people enjoyed a sleep in, got up, wandered off and had brunch at the local café and then went to the movies. Meantime, I would still be out there grinding away on the bike. Three hours of running hills and then off to work for a full day of appointments. Often tired, always fit, and never enough time.

The Ironman race itself starts with a 3.8 kilometer swim which, in order to have a successful event, you need to finish feeling like you have barely begun.

You then transition and start a 180 kilometer bike ride. Trust me, that is a long way, especially when you have to bike into a head wind for half of it.

But both the swim and the bike are just a warm up for the main event. Ironman is really a running race and it all starts to get serious when, after some seven or eight hours of swimming and biking, you lace up your running shoes and begin a full marathon: 42.2 of the most physically grueling kilometers in my life.

You may never understand the Ironman event unless you experience it. If you don't "get" why people do this race, then do yourself a favor and be a spectator or volunteer at one. If you know someone who is competing, then that is even better. Arrive before the start and stay until after midnight. Seriously. You will be inspired. You may not actually use that inspiration to compete in an Ironman event, but I assure you that you could channel it into any number of projects or Goals. And if they are old enough, take your kids. The Ironman race is a spiritual experience.

The Ironman expanded my Capacity for endurance and persistence like no other experience. Ironman also taught me that no matter how big a Goal seems, if you get the right

Supermodel and break the Goal down into small bite-size pieces, it is truly Extra-Ordinary what a person can achieve.

In the case of Ironman, my supermodel came in the form of the world-renowned Performance Lab in Auckland NZ, led by my good friend and exercise physiology guru Jon Ackland (www.performancelab.co.nz).

EPG EXAMPLE 2: THE GRAND TRAVERSE OF MT. COOK

A dangerous place

Although Mt. Cook is "only" 3,754 meters high (12,316 feet), it's the bit at the top that counts. Mt. Cook ranks as one very serious climb that not only demands high levels of physical fitness, but also presents a very significant health hazard. Every year, climbers are killed on Mt. Cook. Every year, someone gets wiped out by an avalanche, swallowed up by a crevasse, or killed by gear failure or through misadventure or ignorance or any number of other reasons. More people have been killed attempting to summit Mt. Cook, than have died attempting to summit Mt. Everest.

Ignorance is bliss

Prior to setting the Goal to climb Mt. Cook, I had done no mountaineering whatsoever. None. It is entirely possible that, if I had known the full extent of the dangers involved, I may not have set the Goal in the first place. So I'm glad that I didn't know then what I know now.

My climbing buddy, Geoff Wilson, and I had a year to prepare. Like me, Geoff was a mountaineering virgin. We did the recommended courses, bought the best gear, and hired the best guides. And then it was game on.

As mentioned previously, we failed first up. A storm robbed us of our first summit experience after a year of training and preparation. As also mentioned previously, I was some 500 vertical meters below the summit when we had to turn back. Disappointed. But as my friend, Doug Hanna, said to me on my return, *"That's great Tom, you get to plan and prepare and anticipate it for another whole year. Remember that the Inputs are just as much fun as the Outcome."* There are times when it's difficult to swallow my own philosophies played back to me! But of course Geoff and I re-committed and had another crack a year later in the next climbing season.

Hazards

Between the training and the two expeditions, we experienced the lot. I fell down several crevasses and we dodged many avalanches. We had all night climbing sessions when we scaled solid ice walls over a hundred meters high, and traversed Summit Ridge for four hours where one wrong move would have meant almost certain death.

It was scary and cold and magnificent and endless and very hard work, all at the same time. And yes, we finally knocked the bugger off. Not only did we summit Mt. Cook, we completed the much-prized Grand Traverse of all three of Mt. Cook's summits.

So, what did I gain from the Grand Traverse of Mt. Cook? Certainly my Capacity for endurance, persistence, patience, and perseverance were all expanded. Mostly though, I expanded my Capacity for courage as I continued to climb despite my fear of falling. For someone who doesn't like heights or cold temperatures, I think that I did OK.

EPG Example 3: Volunteer Work in Prison

I am a believer that we should do something with our talents with no thought of direct personal gain. Giving money to a worthwhile cause is a part of that philosophy and so is giving an even more valuable commodity: time.

Several years ago I approached a maximum-security prison with an offer to teach their "guests" the basics of Goal Achievement and personal development. They readily accepted and since then I've completed some fourteen programs within the walls of correctional facilities, across two countries.

I've found the work both demanding and rewarding. In one facility, the internal offending rate dropped by over 90% for the group of prisoners who were in my class. I've had prisoners tell me that they learned and put into place new alternatives to violence and crime. Others have rediscovered their love for their children and used that love as a motivator to stay clear of trouble on the outside.

I'm proud of the results that some of my "clients" have achieved, and I salute them from my heart for their persistence in what is a most difficult environment. If you think you find it hard to stay positive about progress, try living behind prison walls with a bunch of murderers, rapists, arsonists and pedophiles for 7 or 8 years!

What have I learned from my "life on the inside?" I've learned of course that none of them "did it !" But I've also developed a Capacity for compassion for those who were born on "the wrong side of the tracks." I've dealt with plenty of guys who were abandoned by their mother, in and out of foster homes and orphanages, brought up by drug-addicted role models who stole for a living and lived lives of violence and crime. And while I believe that, if they did the crime they need to do the time, I also ask myself if my life would have turned out so well if I had been born to similar parents as theirs. Some people were dealt a tough hand in life.

I've also learned that the power of personal responsibility is virtually miraculous when it comes to transforming a life of crime into a life of choice. Additionally, I like to think that my Prison EPG has made me a little humbler and a little slower to judge my fellow man.

EPG Example 4: Superbike Madness

Prior to completing my last EPG, which was the NZ Ironman, I began thinking about the next one. I decided that I would learn how to race a Superbike.

There were a couple of reasons for choosing this EPG. The first was that prior to setting this Goal, the last motorbike that I rode was a Honda CB125 as a student over a quarter of a century earlier. Going from that rather sedate experience to racing a Superbike appealed to my twisted sense of humor.

I also chose the Superbike EPG because riding motorbikes was a long dormant passion of mine and racing motorbikes

My Personal EPG Examples

is fun in a kind of white knuckle "scare-yourself-to-death" sort of way.

So I commenced training and racing on less powerful bikes while learning the art of road racing motorcycles. Start small and build from there was the plan.

My first race meeting consisted of four races and I came last in three of them by a long way. In fact, in one race, I was so far behind that the Flag Marshall thought I was the winner, and gave me the checkered flag! Lots of people clapped and for a brief moment I felt like a cross between a world champion and a very happy impostor.

Still, my Goal was not to be better than the other guys, it's was to be better than me. It's to be the best that I can be with the resources that I've got in the time that I gave myself.

After two years of preparation and several broken bones, my date with Superbike racing destiny finally arrived. Given my relative lack of experience, I was pleased with the result which I refer to as "finished in the middle third." Translated this means 12th out of 18!

What I learned from racing motorbikes has a lot more to do with understanding who I am and how I tick than it has to do with any riding techniques. I learned about how my Subconscious works and how I can override it's pain-avoiding "survival reactions" through practicing Conscious choice. And that in turn has serious benefits for the rest of my life.

As my race buddy, Brent Lenehan, once remarked, *"You learn more about yourself on one fast lap on a motorbike than you do in five years or ordinary living."*

Chapter 61:

Choosing an EPG

The reasons for achieving an EPG are simple. If an "ordinary" Goal has the power to expand your Consciousness, increase your Capacity, and enlarge your ability to Contribute to the world, then an Extra-Ordinary Goal does all of these things in an even more Extra-Ordinary way.

Balance Is Key

A word of caution though before you rush off to conquer the world. Of paramount importance is that you are able to maintain a sense of balance in your life while achieving your EPG. For example, don't take on an Ironman or other endurance events unless you have your life sorted to the point where you are confident that it won't negatively impact on your career or relationships.

When I did the training for Ironman, I had a General Manager in my business who allowed me to get in around 10 a.m. most mornings and take the days off that I needed in order to complete the lead up events and also to recover from extra-long training sessions. Also, my kids were old enough to be semi-independent of me, which meant that they didn't suffer as a result of the long training hours. It's no use having your grandchildren talk about your EPG at your funeral if your children don't show up! This could be a very real scenario if you choose an EPG that is so time-consuming that it destroys your ability to spend some quality time with your family.

It's a great idea to talk over your EPG with effected stakeholders such as your Life Partner and kids. Resistance is normal, so it may pay to polish up a bit on your negotiation skills but certainly don't try to oversell or twist their arms. It'll come back to haunt you with truckloads of resentment manifesting in the relationship later on. Find an EPG that excites you and that your Life Partner can live with. There is no doubt, however, that it helps that I have a very supportive and understanding Life Partner.

Follow Your Passion

In line with my earlier recommendations, I strongly recommend that you choose an EPG where you will enjoy the Inputs as much as possible. I have to say that I enjoyed going to the race track and practicing on my motorbike a lot more than I enjoyed my 6-hour training rides on my bicycle when I was preparing for the Ironman event. Despite the fact that racing a motorbike is still hard work physically and incredibly mentally demanding, it's more fun than cranking the "pushy pedals."

GET YOURSELF A SUPERMODEL

This is even more important with an EPG simply because it's likely that your EPG will demand the commitment of an Extra-Ordinary amount of resource, most notably time, money, and energy, than other Goals. So you want to make extra sure that you have the most effective and efficient strategy to ensure that all of your hard work is taking you in the right direction.

I won't wish you good luck. That's for people who need excuses. Instead I'll sign off with my favorite last words:

Be more.

**Tom Poland,
Maleny, Sunshine Coast, Queensland, Australia
Saturday the 24th December 2005**

About the Author

Tom Poland is living his Extraordinary Life. He's the father of four children and seven grandchildren (and counting). He's a multiple best-selling author with clients in almost every time zone around the world, and he's personally launched, grown, and sold multiple businesses including leading teams of more than 100 and revenue in excess of 20 million. In addition to his years of prison volunteer work, he's climbed death-defying mountains, raced superbikes, completed Ironman and ultra-marathon events, and a ten-day silent meditation retreat. Tom practices Zen and describes himself as voluntarily married and lives on golden sands next to the blue sea and white waves of beautiful Castaways Beach in Queensland, Australia.

Experience the *Your Extraordinary Life* companion course at **www.TheGas.Community**

www.ingramcontent.com/pod-product-compliance
Lightning Source LLC
Chambersburg PA
CBHW030103010526
44116CB00005B/75